Lazy-Ass Gardening

D1599674

Robert Kourik

Metamorphic Press

Metamorphic Press
634 Scotland Drive, Santa Rosa, CA 95409
www.robertkourik.com

Library of Congress Control Number: 2018911785

ISBN: 978-0-9615848-7-0

Distributed in North America by:
Chelsea Green Publishing
85 N. Main St., Suite 120
White River Jct., VT 05001
Orders: 800-639-4099, Phone: 802-295-6300, Fax: 802-295-6444
www.chelseagreen.com

Front cover illustration concept by Amie Hill, alterations by Patti Buttitta & Lori Almeida

10 9 8 7 6 5 4 3 2 1

On the bottom of both covers: The nasturium is easy to grow and has three edible parts on one plant: edible leaves, flowers, and young seed pods. Life is simpler when you grow three-in-one edibles. For more, see pages 38, 39.

Printed in the United States of America on paper made from 100% renewable mixed-sources paper. Cruelty-free, not tested on animals. Vegan paper. Recyclable. Totally groovy.

Dedicated to:

Paula Blaydes has stood by my side through the good and
bad times. A wonderful woman who makes me laugh. Paula
encouraged me during the writing of this book and so much more.
The special woman in my life.

❦ Acknowledgments ❧

Amie Hill (Sebastopol, CA) has been my steadfast editor over the years (decades!). She has added wit, style, and correct grammar to this book and many others. I lost my writer's "voice" at times while writing this book; my writing got way too serious and not entertaining. Amie helped me find "Bob's" voice. And she even "Bobified" it in places. I'm no longer discomBobulated.

Robert Kourik (Santa Rosa, CA) did all of the layout, based on the template provided by Patti Buttita. Any mistakes or odd layouts are my responsibility and not a reflection of the excellent work of Patti Buttita.

Wendy Krupnick (Santa Rosa, CA) provided much-appreciated moral support and technical advice.

Marty Roberts (Sebastopol, CA): thanks for helping me organize, build, and manage my website. (www.robertkourik.com)

Betsy Timm and Don Ketman (Santa Rosa, CA) have been dear and supportive friends over the years (decades!).

Patti Buttitta (Santa Rosa, CA) provided the gorgeous and striking design of the front and back covers.

Michael Weaver of Chelsea Green (White River Junction, VT) gave me much advice about ISBN numbers and guided me through the process of getting into the Chelsea Green catalog and onto Amazon.

Bob Higham, (Santa Rosa, CA), my walking buddy, has provided a kind ear to all my self-publishing ramblings—and much more.

Jamie Jobb (Martinez, CA) has been a shrubbery buddy since 1974. Besides turning me on to Monty Python, he's been a great source of information and frivolity. We also commiserate about writing and publishing.

Deb Martin (Allentown, PA) is a very professional proofreader and editor. If you find an error, it's due to me missing her notations.

Barbara Fick (formerly from Oregon State University) was gracious enough to provide much of the text for the section: "A Fickle Way to No-Till."

Anne Hocking (San Anselmo, CA) has been my intellectual-property lawyer for decades. She actually treats me more like a pro-bono client.

Ellen Sherron (Sebastopol, CA) has provided the indexes for five of my books. (She adopted my approach to drip irrigation after indexing the book, and loves the results in her garden.)

Frederique Lavoipierre (Sebastopol, CA) has helped me with good buggy advice for years. Her understanding of syrphid flies in particular has been very helpful.

Jesse Ketman (Santa Rosa, CA) provided excellent insight into the book's appeal to younger adults.

Karl Frauhammer, (McNaugton & Gunn, (Saline, MI) is my helpful rep for the printing company I've used for three books since 1993. He helps me keep my printing in the USA.

Kelsi Anderson, (Freestone, CA) is a kind millennial-aged person who reviewed the manuscript.

Linda Parker (Sebastopol, CA) has worked

diligently with me over the last four decades. She drew insects for me in 1986, does my bookkeeping, and is a good friend. My accounts are balanced and audit-proof because of her.

Margo Baldwin (White River Junction, VT) helped me become a client of Chelsea Green Publishing. She assisted in bringing my edible landscaping book (*Designing and Maintaining Your Edible Landscape—Naturally*) into distribution by Chelsea Green.

Myra Bates-Portwood (Sebastopol, CA) was the inspiration for doing this book. Over five years ago we were chatting over tea and crumpets and she suggested I write a book for lazy-butt gardeners. The rest is history.

Rue Furch (Sebastopol, CA) really believes in my work and is a good friend. She is very good at spreading the word to her large network of gardeners, farmers, politicians, and "regular" people.

Toby Hemenway (of permaculture fame, formerly of Sebastopol, CA) and I had a lunch every month for over two years. We talked shop and discussed publishing. Unfortunately he passed on in 2016 from pancreatic cancer. I certainly miss him.

Ros Creasy (Los Altos, CA) has been a kindred soul and friend since 1978. Her work as an edible landscaper has inspired me since that time.

Genevieve Schmidt (Eureka, CA) provided great insight into the hori-hori and other gardening tools.

Tom LeBlanc and Dustin DeMattieo (of Daily Acts in Petaluma, CA) also kindly reviewed the manuscript from a millennial point of view.

Edward R. "Ned" Hearn, Esq. (San Jose, CA)

helped me untangle the law behind computer domain sites. Thanks.

Sebastian Bertsch (Petaluma, CA) and I get together to talk shop. He is a very astute proponent of Permaculture, and translated blocks of German text for my book *Understanding Roots*. He also contributed very helpful feedback for this book's appeal to the millennial generation, and provided technical horticultural insights as well.

Kate Burroughs (Sebastopol, CA) offered comments and corrections on the insect text.

Darwen and Vally Hennings, (Arlington, WA) Thanks for the use of the gorgeous vegetable illustrations.

Ben Levitt (Hardwick, VT) rendered the fantasic drawings for much of the Practical Pruning & Shaping chapter.

Lori Alemedia (Santa Rosa, CA) provided all the detailed and gorgeous drawings for the tools chapter and much more. A wonderful addition to the "crew."

Craig Latker (San Francisco, CA) allowed me to use his amazing insect drawings on pages 146-147.

I hope I didn't miss anyone. If so, I apologize.

A Note on the Cover Price: it a lot more expensive to print this book in the USA than to farm it out to China. As a demonstration of moral fiber and support for the USA, I print in Michigan, even though it costs me almost $1.00 more per copy.

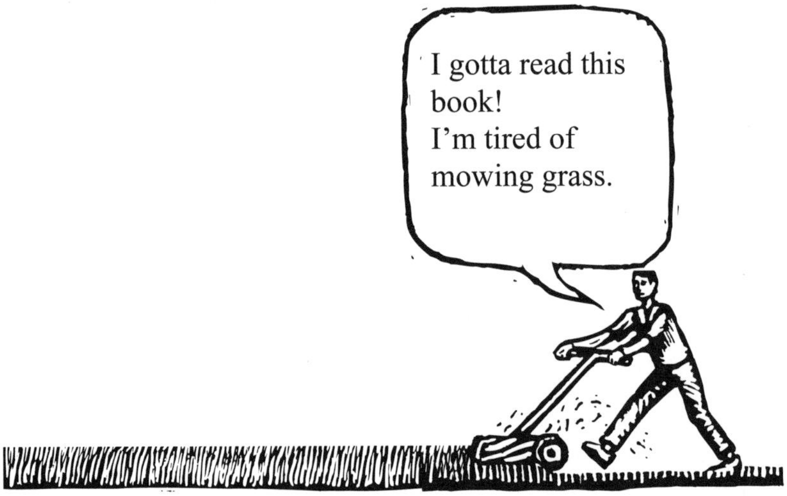
I gotta read this book!
I'm tired of mowing grass.

℘ Table of Contents ℘

Lazy-Ass Gardening

Maximize your soil; Minimize your toil

The Official Introduction

Gardening is the most popular outdoor recreation in America, but (surprise!) the work involved isn't everyone's idea of bliss. Although "lazy-ass gardener" seems like a contradiction in terms, perhaps some of us are just a bit slower-paced and more laid-back than others; or, consider this: we just might be more efficient. (The opposite is the compulsive, frenetic gardener with a picture-perfect garden that nobody visits because they feel they're just getting in the way of this turbulent cultivator.)

So, congratulations; you got off your butt and bought this book. (Better still, you typed your way to my website and bought it from me instead of the Big "A".) Now sink back into your favorite chair, grab a beverage (perhaps, like me, a gin & tonic.), and meander lazily through its pages in search of inspiration and information for your gardening needs.

Careless versus Less Care

Some gardeners are just careless—sloppy and inefficient. Others are inspired, plan carefully, and pay attention to detail—and manage to cultivate their gardens with much less effort than the disorderly types.

A good first step for any potential gardener is to figure out, realistically, how much garden he or she can or wants to handle, especially given all of life's other demands. A good garden moves in pace with the gardener; a poorly designed garden becomes all work and little pleasure. The difference between the garden-as-burden and the garden-as-delight is what I call "inspired laziness."

Inspired Laziness

Ease into laid-back gardening. You're about to learn how to relax into the rhythm of tranquil cultivation, reducing your effort by using your brain.

Inspired laziness is simply the intentional saving of time and effort with good planning that masquerades as laziness. It doesn't mean being slothful or a do-nothing, but instead conserving energy with foresight, preparation, and clever techniques. Brain muscle first, body muscle second. The point is: be laid-back—the inspired way.

Start With Media Withdrawal

You can't learn to garden from TV or fancy gardening magazines, which usually portray the best of the best, with plenty of skilled gardeners just off-camera and ready to pounce on any wayward fallen leaf, spent blossom, or leggy stem. Realistically, you probably don't have the time, money or skill to match very many of these gardens. TV gardening shows generally offer inspiration and settings that are beyond the reach of the typical gardener (you'd be better off bingeing on *Game of Thrones*).

Like the TV shows, most gardening magazines—off- or online (and especially the garden articles in most women's magazines)—are glamorized wishful thinking, bearing about the same resemblance to real-life gardening as Vogue does to real feminine beauty; appearance is everything. Every little leaf is primped into place before each photo shoot; they may even tie tomatoes to plants to make them look so much more prolific. Real people with real gardens don't Photoshop™ them.

A select few outlets (including some YouTube how-tos) do feature real people who aren't the Justin Timberlake or Elon Musk of gardening. In such presentations, the attention is on the lessons, not on the real-life backgrounds.

ENJOY YOUR LANDSCAPE; IF IT'S JUST DRUDGERY, YOU'RE DOING SOMETHING WRONG.

These videos, however, can only convey techniques, and are no substitute for getting to know your garden or landscape from the soles of your feet up.

Neighborhood Notes

To find realistic inspiration, start walking (or, if necessary in a country setting, driving) around your neighborhood. Take long, casual rambles through its streets or lanes, on the lookout for:

SEEK OUT THE WISDOM OF YOUR NEIGHBORS; SOMEONE ELSE MIGHT JUST KNOW MORE THAN YOU DO.

- Different styles of gardens.
- Interesting and healthy varieties of turf, trees, and flowers.
- Simple and thorough methods of irrigation.
- Helpful garden techniques, such as mulching, bed borders, and pest-control devices.
- Garden tools, lawn mowers and other garden machines that appear to be sturdy, long-lasting and effective.
- Attractive structures, such as walks, patios, arbors, trellises, and masonry.
- Art or sculpture that suits your fancy.

Bob sez: *Back in the '70s, although I couldn't deer-fence my entire rented property, I did build a very small fenced area next to the western side of the house. Since I'd noticed that a neighbor was able to grow tasty grapefruits (unlikely in this planting zone) by taking advantage of a western exposure, I planted a dwarf 'Meyer' lemon tree, which did just fine.(I learned years later that deer don't eat citrus. Oh well, chalk it up to newer wisdom.)*

lots of notes. Here's an example of "neighbor gardening": In the 1970s, I moved into a rental in a deer-infested area and didn't want to pay for a large fence. From observing and talking to the neighbors, I learned a lot about what plants to use for a deer-resistant garden.

Your neighbors are by far your best gardening "experts," because they've had to live with what they grow. Talk to them. Ask how many hours they spend maintaining their yard, garden, or landscape each day, week, or month. Ask them if you can photograph components of their gardens that interest or fascinate you (this is a great ice-breaker). Ask them over for lemonade, a margarita, or (if appropriate) a toke and lounge around talking gardening. Take notes. Yep, take

TIME & MONEY SPENT EARLY MEANS TIME & MONEY SAVED LATER.

The Paradox of the Lazy Garden

Here's a paradox for you: since gardens obviously don't plant or cultivate themselves, in order to become a lazy gardener, you have to step up at first and do the planning and work necessary to let you relax and enjoy in the future.

This, of course will vary according to your situation: You may have inherited an existing garden that you can adapt to lazy methods, or you may want to remove a lawn and start from absolute scratch. You may be new to an area or have lived there for years. You may be a novice gardener, or someone who's just unhappy with your existing garden. You may have a deck or window box that's just calling out for container plants. You may have moved to a house with boring landscaping, inherited a place in the country, or taken over Grandpa's farm. Inspired laziness can be adapted to any or all of these situations.

PLAN IN ADVANCE: MAKE YOUR MISTAKES ON PAPER, NOT IN YOUR LANDSCAPE.

dahlias? Lush herbaceous borders? Ornamental trees? Cannabis? Do you want to go entirely organic? Do you want a lot of room to relax and play and invite your friends over for picnics? Is there plenty of room for the kids to play while the Baby Boomers discuss all their ailments?

Getting Started

You may have the impulse to tear into your brand-new project immediately. Unfortunately, (unless you're a veteran horticulturist), gardening solely by inspiration or guesswork usually leads to a faltering or failed garden or landscape. A big part of inspired laziness is to study your property for some time, even up to a year, in order to know it intimately before planting—like surveying the roll and pitch of a putting green before you take your shot.

During your period of assessment, you don't have to be idle: for one thing, you can experiment with temporary patches of annual flowers and vegetables to get a feel for placement, for sunlight exposure, and for your soil. Any soil improvement done for the annuals will help anything else that is planted in the same spot later on. You can prune, cut back and/or shape any plants that have been neglected or are growing out of control.

Just don't yield to the temptation for permanence until you've done some homework to lay down the foundations for inspired laziness:

Here are some activities that are necessary for starting to create any garden with a lazy-ass factor:

1. **Figure out what your garden is for.** Do you want to concentrate on food crops? Prize

2. **Find out what planting zone you're in.** Farmers, gardeners, and publishers of almanacs have long since divided the US into handy zones that indicate where various farm/garden/landscape crops will thrive. This will save you the headache of trying to nurture a Zone 11 plant in Zone 4. Learn from your neighbors or online sites which plants are native to your area, and thus maybe easiest to grow and maintain.

3. **Find out what kind of soil you have.** Obviously, different plants need different soils. If your soil feels reasonably similar in most places around the yard, take soil samples from several places around the yard and mix them together

 Bob sez: *A quick dig on my property revealed that I had a relatively shallow dark, fertile soil—only 18" to 24" deep, so I could plan my planting accordingly to take advantage of these conditions.*

to be tested. (Ask your Cooperative Extension people for the best place to send the sample.) Don't just say, "Looks poor over there; I'll throw some fertilizer around." Learn exactly what you need or don't need.

In bigger yards or gardens, dig lots of test pits to find out what types of soil you have and how deep or shallow they are. (YIKES, the first hint of physical labor. Don't wimp out.) Learn the benefits of various types of fertilizers, so you can make enlightened choices.

4. **Figure out your water sources.** One thing that will definitely determine the kind of gardening you do is the availability of water. Where does your water come from and how? Google your local rainfall statistics; do you live in an area with near-constant rains or periodic droughts? Also consider the financial angle; some gardeners are lucky enough to irrigate from a well. But if you're hooked up to a municipal water system, every drop will cost you.

Your kitchen tap may be fine for window boxes or small container gardens, but for larger areas, you'll need to locate any hose-bibs, underground pipes or irrigation systems that are already in place—or, if you're dealing with virgin territory, figure out where and how you need to install them. (A hose-bib is a spigot on a pole or board high enough to allow for attaching hoses and fill-

Bob sez: *In my location, I was blessed with an average 58" of rain each year, primarily in the winter months. This helped my garden thrive in the spring, but my soil was just as dry as anybody else's nearby come July or August.*

ing containers,) The very best lazy-ass option for watering is drip irrigation (See P. 90), which is a little labor-intensive at first, but will pay off in the future with better crops and a lot less work.

Also watch for drainage problems. (Water up to your knees in the basement is a good indicator.)

5. **Get weather-wise.** Become familiar with weather patterns in your area. For instance, in a larger landscape, watch which way storms come from and what their effect is on trees and shrubs. (Some trees may be too close to the house for safety's sake.) Observe where and how snow and

PLAN FOR THE UNEXPECTED: NATURE WILL BE, IN ALL PROBABILITY, UNPREDICTABLE.

ice build up (if applicable). What does winter do to plants in your area? Observe patterns of sun and shade over time. Container gardeners are lucky here, because they can buy or construct rolling plant stands that allow them to move plants around a deck or patio to maximize the light.

6. **ID your pests.** Check out any existing plants for pest or disease problems. (If a plant looks funky, ask an experienced neighborhood gardener to check it out, or go online to Google the symptoms.) If you're dealing with an established garden or landscape, note which plants have higher levels of bad insects and disease. (See P. 136-148 for hints on pest control and how to attract beneficial insects.)

I was also blessed to be living far into the woods, with no other fruit trees growing nearby. Thus, I had none of the dreaded codling moths attacking my apples; this saved me countless hours of effort.

Deer were my biggest pest, in both definitions of the adjective. (If you have a Bambi problem with your garden, you can find out how to deal with the voracious critters with the information on P. 161-164.)

7. **Make a garden scrapbook** with sketches, ideas, plant varieties, and other memory trig-

gers. Or put together a Pinterest "album" full of photos (including panorama shots of your property from different angles), (Skip the glossy unrealistic garden-porn shots, or stash them in your underwear drawer.) For flower gardens and landscape, find out what blooms

when in your area. Take clippings of everything in your existing garden that you don't recognize into your local nursery or to your neighbors for identification, or post a photo on a Facebook plant ID page.

In the interests of future laziness, you may also want to estimate out how long different tasks will take. (How long to: mow a lawn, prune a rosebush, maintain a path, rake leaves, trim a hedge, pot up a flower?)

The Care-Free New Garden Unnatural, but Nice: a Moment of Philosophy

All gardens, however beautiful, will always be in a constant dialogue with terms like: "naturalized," "earth-friendly," "native," or "environmentally sound." Given that most all gardens are artificial in nature, exactly how natural and environmentally responsive can we get? More than we may think, but the methods are contained in the details that are sown liberally throughout this book.

A Process of Elimination

Gardeners often try to do too much. Some properties are blessed with plenty of natural land-

Bob sez: *There are a few plants that will take over and strangle your entire garden if so allowed, regenerating from even the tiniest bits of root, and you'll probably want to get ruthless about eliminating them or confining them to containers. Comfrey, mints, lemon balm, tradescantias, and purple loosestrife are examples of this (and let's not even talk about bamboos).*

scape to begin with. An all-too typical approach is to remove almost everything that's there, buy a bunch of topsoil and plants, and re-do the place with completely new stuff. The result is costly, far from natural, and requires a lot of effort.

So be relaxed. Don't try to grandstand Mother (or Father) Nature. Some homeowners are fortunate enough to have "inherited" naturally beautiful yard accents from previous inhabitants. Live with these a little and slowly figure out which you like and which get on your nerves (with garden gnomes, all bets are off).

Don't even think of planting permanently until you've fully realized the potential of what's already there. If it's an overgrown tangled mess, all that may be required is to selectively thin, prune or remove undesirable foliage. The idea is to sculpt your existing plants to reveal their hidden form and texture, like Michelangelo carving away bits of stone to reveal the magnificence of the David.

Plants that have survived seasons of neglect will enhance the laziness factor when you prune them and shape them into attractive growth—you know you can't kill them, and you may want to work your garden plan around them.

One gardening Golden Rule that allows you to be relaxed on several levels is to start with small steps. If you've never grown veggies before, plant a herb garden, then graduate to a cut-and-come-again salad garden (See P.36). If you're working with an existing garden or landscape, choose the easiest changes that you can make that will begin to shape it to your vision, and work up to the more complex stuff.

Mix it Up for a Natural Look

For some reason people have a compulsion to plant everything equidistant and far enough apart to match the plant's theoretical mature width—usually taken from a dog-eared favorite gardening "bible." Yet, nature seldom "plants" anything on equidistant centers, and some plants just seem to want to cuddle together.

Planting on odd intervals, without any regard to the mature width, is perhaps the first "rule" of natural planting. Let plants mingle with abandon. In the wild, few plants get to grow to their ideal, mature width. Trees grow in Darwinian mode sometimes several feet apart, sometimes in clusters of three or more. If you don't have a measuring tape; relax, you don't need one.

If you have a good-sized yard or landscape, consider planting odd-numbered clusters of trees, like small groves, in random spacing, or clusters of bulb plants, like tulips. I like to use clusters of three, five, seven, or nine to keep it from being symmetrical—a rare feature in nature.

CHAPTER 2

Permanent and Hard

Got some cash? Yes, hardscape elements in your yard cost money, but they save a lot of time years into the future. Nothing to plant, mulch, weed, or irrigate— and they provide durable places to kick back with your family and friends for years to come.

Most of us like to smoke, grill, dine, eat ("dine" means using china, "eat" means anything on double paper plates), watch shooting stars, dance, or have morning coffee outdoors. For the truly inspired lazy gardener, all these recreational uses of the garden have two important impacts: the areas and fixtures used for them (known as "hardscape") take up space that would otherwise have to be maintained as lawn or garden, and they help to define and set off planted areas.

Hardscape the Inspired Way

If you're lucky enough to inherit some of these "structural elements"—as fancy-word landscape architects call them—rejoice. The lazy aspect is that they're easier to care for than plants and lawns—usually taking much less effort to maintain. When you're planning, plotting, or retrofitting your garden or landscape, it's good to have an idea of the hardscape elements—as simple as a path, as complicated as an all-weather gazebo—you want to retain or install.

Here are some hardscape features that you might consider:

• Paths arc almost a givcn. Thcy can bc as simple as a dirt walkway edged with logs or large stones, a trail covered in wood chips, or an ornate flat construction of flagstone or brick.

• Patios are outdoor living areas with multiple functions, and are often constructed of brick or flagstones. Brick barbecue grills or a "kitchen" area for portable grills are sometimes included as a feature, as are arbors for shade.

• Decks are delightful, though expensive and difficult to build. If you don't have major construction skills, they require a carpenter or contractor—and the hassle of getting a permit. Professional help may be the easiest way to go, but always get a bid from more than one contractor.

• Arbors: Unlike decks, simple arbors can be purchased from gardening catalogs, but are shipped in parts and require a certain amount of skill to assemble. Larger ones require the same construction skills as decks.

• Gazebos are little house-like seating platforms, lovely for sipping tea, drowning one's sorrows, or making out. Again, major construction chops required, but worth it if you have the space.

• Tables: (pretty easy to build, or buy at a local hardware or outdoor-furniture store)

• Benches are also rather easy to build, or get from garden-supply stores. It's worth buying/ building for comfort, as you'll get to spend time being lazy on them.

- Chairs (that's why Craigslist exists).
- Tree swings are easy, but dangerous if you use the wrong tree. Make sure the one you choose is sturdy and sound by swinging like a chimpanzee on your designated branch.
- Water features (ponds, pools, fountains, etc.) are lovely but labor-intensive to install and maintain, and usually require a source of plentiful water.
- Kids' playground areas can be located in a spot that you have other plans for when the little rug rats grow up.

Kick Back

If you're a social being and your garden or yard isn't set up to "party hardy," you may have missed the boat. Let's start with the most lethargic part of the hardscape chairs, benches, and recliners. You know you're dealing with a fanatic gardenoholic when you visit a garden that has no place to sit down and relax, enjoy the view, or chug a few beers. It's certainly OK to be a sofa spud sometimes, so, sit on your rump and read on.

You like your padded recliner. You like being a lazy boy (or person). So, bring your reclining way into the garden. You have at least five choices:

Bob sez: *If you aren't handy with tools, and are daunted by construction projects, don't worry—skip this next part and hire a landscaper, landscape contractor, or regular contractor. They'll cost you, but you can enjoy sitting back and kibitzing while they do the work.*

1. Grab your existing recliner and use a waterproof cover when it rains. This will almost inevitably trigger the Murphy's Law of Outdoor Furniture— on the first rainy day, you'll forget to cover the chair.

2. Buy a weather-resistant resin wicker garden lounge chair with padded, rainproof cushions and stainless-steel frame. Sexy looking, but pretty expensive-sometimes 50 percent more expensive than an indoor recliner.

3.   Get a white plastic Adirondack chair — if you want your patio to look like every patio on the block. Fortunately they also come in bright colors and wood.

4.   Consider a waterproof beanbag "chair." Yep, you can relive your parents' 1970s in your own backyard!

5.   The most fun is to get automobile front seats, which allow for gazing over the garden and napping. Usually in that order. With a trip to the auto junkyard you can easily find a color-coordinated front seat, preferably Naugahyde™ so it tolerates the weather. I first saw car seats used at a community garden where the gardeners took up valuable space in their plots to provide room for social relaxation and interaction—very awesome. They even had arbors for comfortable shade.

Hammocks

It's harder to slug back your cola in a hammock than a recliner, but hammocks are much easier to nap in, so no slouch-of-a-gardener should be without one. Some come au naturel, basically woven bags without flattening bars, and are known as Mayan or Brazilian hammocks. These create a cocoon effect that's cozy, but embarrassingly awkward when you're trying to look cool while chowing down on some barbecue. So, get one with a bar at each end.

You'll need two sturdy trees 14 to 16 feet apart. Since you sure don't want to collapse the tree(s) to which your hammock is attached, fasten it temporarily and do a road test with all

your kids or your significant other to check for bending or creaking (of the trees, silly).

A hammock needs to be at least four and a half feet (or, if you're on the chunky side, even higher) above the ground because it will sag when in use. It's best to attach it so the straps at each end loop around the trunk and above a branch. The trunk should be as big around as possible. If the trunk splays much when you gingerly get in the hammock for the first time, better find another, sturdier tree.

> **Bob sez:** *Reclining on a hammock is a great way to watch your kids pull weeds, but you can bet they won't do it on their own. My dad used to pay me and my sister a penny for each dandelion we dug up. Dandelions were easy to spot with their bright yellow flowers, so off we went with visions of wealth in our heads, digging away while he napped.*

You will also need a sturdy attachment to the tree. A great kit is the "Grand Trunk Tree Sling." In their words: "Simply attach the provided nautical-grade carabineers or 'S' hooks, and you're good to go. Extra-wide straps provide greater hanging surface area and won't damage trees or posts even after prolonged use. Pre-rigged cords and slings allow for greater hang-ability even in the most widely-spaced, sparse trees or other remote locations." The kit will set you back about twenty bucks.

You can also purchase, from most stores that stock hammocks, boat-shaped stand-alone frames made of metal tubing. While not exactly portable, these do allow the hammock to be moved around to take advantages of changes of light and season.

Now if you do want to get off your fanny and walk around the yard, you'll probably need some pathways.

Walkin' Around

First, ponder where you'll be walking. Pretty simple. Look for the downtrodden lawn or worn trails in the dirt. Whatever you do, don't sit down to sketch your yard and pencil in straight walkways with right-angle turns — you'll never follow them.

Consider making the path with dirt; cheap for sure. However, this requires a mudroom in your house (to keep from tracking crud inside), and in wet weather you'll spend a lot of time bending over to clean off your shoes.

The next lazy material to consider is wood chips from a tree service, the result of running trimmed-off branches through a chipper or shredder. They come in random shapes and lengths, and often contain shredded leaves that add pattern and texture. This type of path also requires a mudroom, as the chips will decompose as the path is used. Replace them after they rot into perfect compost—and it saves buying compost.

I use wood-chips/shreddings if I can convince an arborist to dump a truckload of them at the end of my driveway. (Back in the old days—the very old days—I lured them to my driveway by putting a six-pack of beer in a cooler where I wanted the chips to be dropped. No amount of liability insurance could protect you nowadays! Keep it dry!) Besides, it now costs tree people a lot of money to dump the arbor chips at a green-waste recycling site, so they're often happy to leave them at your house at no cost to you.)

Nowadays, I look for arborists chipping within a few blocks and ask them to dump the arbor chips on my driveway. In the suburbs around my current home, it's amazing how often this can happen (especially with trees killed by occasional California droughts.)

You can also use "clean" chips from a landscape-supply center. These can be purchased in many sizes, but I like the ones that range from two to four inches. They're bulky enough to last and will settle down to make a firm path. Clean chips without additional leaves or small chips won't rot

nearly as quickly as tree-service shreddings.

If you want a brick or concrete path, get a good book devoted entirely to the process and talk to the landscape supply folks in detail. Better yet, win the Powerball lottery. Then you can buy an estate with all the walkways already in place.

Check many DIY sites such as *This Old House, Family Handyman, HGTV,* and *Better Homes and Gardens* for instructions. Some say: " A good installation consists of four to six inches of crushed rock and 1 inch of sand topped by bricks." This only works, however, in yards or gardens where the ground doesn't freeze and heave. In cold-winter areas you'll need a concrete base to have a stable path. Gophers and swelling heavy-clay soils (even contracting clay soil during severe droughts) can also disrupt a brick path without a concrete base. To avoid tedious weeding on brick/ flagstone paths (and patios), make sure you line their areas with landscape fabric to control weed seeds.

Here's a good book on the subject*: Patios and Walkways* (Taunton's Build Like a Pro), Peter Jeswald, Taunton Press, 2010.

Regardless of the material, you can make the path random widths. If you want two people to be able to walk side by side, make sure the narrowest portion of the path is at least five feet wide. You can make it even wider and plant so that some plants extend their foliage in a random pattern over the edge of the path.

Only use "hardscape" walkways if you have a pretty big yard—and a pretty big budget. Romantics often choose the five-foot width, so they and their partner can walk hand in hand.

Bob sez: *Due to too much experience with gophers, sciatica, and Bermuda grass (a tough aggressive invasive grass that regrows from the tiniest root segments and is nearly impossible to get rid of), I now garden in galvanized horse-watering troughs that are two feet deep, two feet wide, and six feet long. I drill the bottoms with holes for drainage and set them on four bricks (one under each curved corner) for an air gap—all to make sure the grass-of-the-devil never crawls inside the tub. They come in a metallic gray color that weathers nicely.*

Raised Beds

Raised-bed gardens are very popular and efficient. Although they're another element that requires some sweat to build, they often give back savings of time and reduced stress for decades. Raised beds should be considered for many reasons:

• The bottom of a boxed raised bed can be lined with wire mesh to keep out pesky gophers, moles, and voles.
• Their soil drains better in wet climates.
• Their soil warms up earlier in the spring.
• The harvest is closer to you and requires less bending over—which leads to the last and best reason for a raised bed:
• It's easier on all those Baby Boomers with sciatica or bad backs, such as writers like me. (Or to help prevent such problems for Millennials.)

The ideal height for a raised bed is at least two feet. In Figure 1, you see lettuce roots can grow down to eight feet deep, but the top foot of soil contains maybe 20-30 percent of the roots. Going down another foot snags perhaps up to 50 percent. So cultivate the most roots with a bed at least two feet deep. (Deeper is, of course, better.)

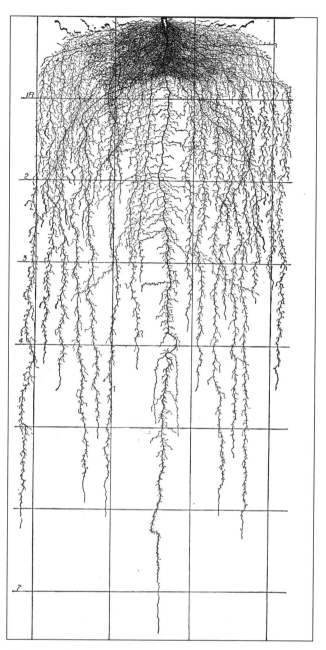

Figure 1: The roots of a lettuce plant. Each square one foot. Excavated by Dr. Weaver.

If I were to build a wooden raised bed for veggies now, I would make it three feet wide so it's easier to reach the middle. (In my youth they were four feet wide; but time has made me wiser.) The length would be six (not eight or ten) feet, so it's possible to sling compost and mulch from the ends and rake them around. When you can toss amendments and mulch from the ends, not the sides, the beds can be closer together on the long sides and save a lot of ground. The access need only be from one end, and all other paths need only be 18 to 24 inches wide. Only one end of the bed requires a path at least 48 inches wide to accommodate a wheelbarrow or garden cart. The younger you are, the longer the bed can be. Ya gotta have a strong back to build a raised bed. If you have a feeble spine, go for a collection of pots you can lift when empty, place where desired and then pot up your plants. Or, hire a football player that you supervise.

The simplest and most inexpensive way to make raised vegetable beds is to cultivate and rake soil up into a mounded shape. This type of "bed" should in no way be considered a raised bed made by the cultivation method often referred to as the French Intensive-Biodynamic raised bed. See John Jeavon's classic—*How to Grow More Vegetables: Than You Ever Thought Possible* ..... The methods outlined by Jeavons produce a proper mound of slightly-raised soil and is the best intensive, albeit strenuous, way to improve the tilth and fertility of your soil.

Many gardeners, however, prefer to construct formal raised beds framed within masonry, plastic, or wooden sides. These sides retain the soil while imparting order and efficiency to the kitchen garden and helping to define it. Formal raised beds also provide a number of other advantages:

• Enhanced drainage for better growth.
• Soil which warms slightly sooner in the spring.
• Sides which help keep soil or mulch from spilling into paths.
• A structure which allows wire mesh to be added to the bottom of a bed to exclude tunneling pests such as moles and gophers. When building garden boxes, line them with one-half-inch aviary wire, which comes in four-foot-wide rolls. One-inch chicken wire, while less expensive, may allow baby gophers to sneak inside the box. The aviary wire also has more galvanized metal and lasts longer in the ground. Even with this protective bar-

rier in place, the taproot and many other roots will be eaten at the bottom edge of the wire.
• The Cadillac version is to use one-quarter-inch hardware cloth because it doesn't rust through as quickly.
• When preparing beds for planting, be sure to work the soil with a flat-bottomed spade so you don't damage the wire.
• Provide a way that pathways between beds can be cleaned and tended without disturbing plantings.
• Raised beds also have certain limitations or drawbacks:
• A formal raised bed with solid sides will cost more and require more time and effort to construct than a simple mounded bed.
• Some gardeners find the angular geometry of the raised-bed structures unaesthetic. (Beds can, however, be masked by perennial plantings or low evergreen shrubs.)
• When watering a raised bed with drip irrigation, a little extra effort must be made to bring the water supply into the bed unobtrusively.

There are many materials which can be used to construct a raised bed. Each has its own unique mixture of attributes and imperfections:

Used Bricks (Recycled)
Pluses:
• Very good-looking; construction has character when first built.
• Since bricks are fairly narrow, the finished wall doesn't take up excess garden space.
• Wire mesh is easily added to the bottom.
• Uses recycled materials.
Minuses:
• Expensive.
• Requires some masonry skill or practice to construct.
• In areas where the ground freezes, requires a poured concrete base.

Cinder Blocks
Pluses:
• Wide enough to sit on while gardening.
• If unmortared, easier to work with than brick.
• Can be built on a base of packed gravel.
• Easy to add wire-mesh bottom.
Minuses:
• Not easily found as recycled material.
• Best used only for square and rectangular beds.
• Thick blocks take up garden space
• Looks gray and "industrial," like concrete.
• The large holes in the blocks, usually placed facing up, tend to fill with mulch and soil from the bed.
• Unless mortar and a concrete base are used, the blocks will often settle in a slightly skewed position.

Plastic "Wood"
Pluses:
• Easy to work with, like lumber. No splinters.
• Made from recycled consumer plastic waste.
• Has a long life and won't rot.
• Easy to add a wire-mesh bottom.
• Easier construction of odd-angled shapes such as octagons or pentagons.
Minuses:
• Up close, looks very fake.
• Expensive compared to lumber.
• Requires screws instead of nails for sturdy attachment.
• Must be secured more often along its length.

Recycled, Untreated Rot-Resistant Lumber
The use of the two main rot-resistant lumbers available, redwood and cedar, are controversial due to environmental issues. They are, however, still the easiest material for building raised beds. (Use of recycled wood lessens environmental impact.)
Pluses:
• Good-looking natural surface.
• Available as recycled material.
• Easy to work with.
• Easy to add wire-mesh bottom.
• Can be used to construct odd-angled shapes.
Minuses:
• If in contact with the soil, may have to be replaced within 5-20 years. (Note: redwood heartwood can last this long, but redwood with white sapwood usually rots within four years and should be avoided.)

But here's a cautionary tale: last year I once again tried to grow tomatoes in large containers (to reckon with gophers and Bermuda grass). The cost of the tomatoes I harvested, given the soil, containers, fertilizer, water, and my precious time, came to about $5 – per tomato. I learned that tomatoes are best grown in beds. (And that it was much cheaper to haul ass down to the farmer's market every Saturday morning for produce.)

Patio Deck
Now, as for true hardscapes ("structural elements"), made of wood, brick, or concrete: these generally take a lot of effort and money. But, once installed, they last for many years (your grandchildren can inherit them) and are easy to keep clean. But be careful. A buddy of mine is a weekend warrior, an office junkie who was not a landscaper by trade. But he wanted a brick patio. He built a very fine-looking one. But he ended up with carpel-tunnel syndrome and many visits to a physical therapist. (That's a lot of buts.)

To size the deck consider the amount of area each person needs. The space required to determine the size of a deck or patio is 15-30 square feet per person depending on how well the people know each other. So, if you're not a gregarious person you'll need a large deck or patio. Divorced couples need 400 square feet per person. :)

Party Hearty
When a hardscape element like a deck or patio

is finished, it means it's time to party hearty (or hard-y). Ideally, you designed the area to be big enough to hold a barbeque setup as well. My patio was also big enough to include a bean hole. If you've never heard of a bean hole (not really as kinky or weird as it sounds), see the "Yummies" chapter that includes a lot of fairly simple recipes for lazy cooks, based on plants that are pretty easy to grow.

Now, fire up the barbeque or smoker. If you're smart, you've planted the herb(s) for grilling near or next to the deck or patio. (See Chapter 4.) My rosemary shrub is planted just five feet from the grill, and I love to use this herb when grilling a butterfly leg of lamb. I also grow lavender (*Lavandula angustifolia*) plants nearby to use with lamb and chicken.

Focal Point

So many gardens I visit leave my eyes confused. They're full of color, contain lots of flowers, plenty of vegetables, and some impressive trees, but there's no place for my eyes to rest. Constant stimulation is like going to Disneyland at peak season—too much unfiltered turmoil.

A "focal point" is a plant or hardscape element that draws the visitor's eye with its drama or specialness. Sometimes it's a sculpture or gazebo. Sometimes it's a plant, like the intricate umber-red canopy of an umbrella-shaped maple. And sometimes it's a combination of the two, like a gorgeous wisteria or trumpet vine growing over an arch or arbor.

When I design a garden, I choose two or three plants to weave into the design as a unifying theme. A pattern of repeatable imagery tends to help the eye rest, as it avoids complete visual pandemonium.

For example, echiums are a plant I like to work with. (They only thrive in Zones 9 and 10—sorry, Midwesterners—but I'll use them here as an illustration.) They come in many shapes and bloom colors, but with similar foliage color and texture, usually a form of green with a milky-pale blue overtone and a hint of silver. The texture is scratchy, so this plant shouldn't go near pathways.

The pride-of-Madeira (*Echium candicans*, syn. *E. fastuosum*) is a mounding plant up to 20 feet wide and six to eight feet high, with dozens of three-foot tall rich-blue flower stalks. The *Echium pininana* sends a slender two-foot-wide tower of pale-blue flowers up to 20 feet high. The *Echium wildpretti* is the most dramatic of all. It's a biennial, and its floral display of a 12- to 18- inch-wide tower reaches three to six feet in the air with one of the clearest, most vibrant, blazing reds of any flower.

I often repeat the pride-of-Madeira two to five times around a garden (depending on the size of the planting area), usually in clusters of three to five plants (to avoid too much symmetry). For a focal point that draws the eye away from the pastel patches of echium foliage, I use the *Echium wildpretii*. The glory of the red inflorescences is worth the two-year wait. (And the bees *really* love it.) I've used echiums as an example here, but you may want to identify a similarly dramatic plant that grows well in your zone or area and use it to create a pattern or focal point in your garden or landscape.

Variegated foliage offers an attractive highlight all season long. Consider the variegated dogwood. There are species (*Cornus alba* 'Argenteo-marginata', a.k.a. 'Elegantissima') with a variegation of green and creamy white, with striking red stems during the winter.

Another deciduous shrub, the "European smoke tree," (*Cotinus coggygria*) displays distinctive dark-maroon foliage throughout the spring, summer, and fall. In the mid-to late-summer the beige-maroon wisps of its flowers provide an

attractive center point to a flower border.
In large gardens, consider the deciduous Chinese cork oak (*Quercus variabilis*). Regardless of the season the deeply cracked and fissured bark provides a year-round texture so unique that it can act alone as a focal point.

Trees & Hardscape
Trees with shallow roots
You don't want to damage that hardscape that took you so much time, effort, and/or money to build, so, here are some general guidelines on allowing for adequate space for root growth near a patio:

• It's best not to plant trees between hardscape areas when there is less than three feet of soil to grow.
• When you have a space with three to four feet between paved areas— such as between a sidewalk and a patio or a patio and the foundation of a house—choose trees that mature at less than 30 feet tall.
• If you're lucky enough to have a space of five to six feet between paved areas, you can plant trees that mature as high as 50 feet tall.
• With trees higher than 50 feet you'll need at least eight feet between paved areas.

Also, consider installing expansion joints in walkways or the patio near trees to limit large areas. You might be able to reduce heaving by building curves that avoid the area around the trunk, and installing narrow walkway sections near trees. Planning for the right tree will save you countless and expensive hours trying to fix heaved patios and walkways. See pages 177-180 for a boring but important list. Carry on.

CHAPTER 3

Ornamental Plants

Horticulturists advise: "the right plant for the right place." How about all kinds of ways to figure out the right plants for easiest growing in your garden?

Once you get your ornamental plants in place, you've begun to create a yard or garden that needs less work. Most perennials can be much easier to take care of than many vegetables, and are often more trouble-free than annual bedding plants. You may have a lawn already; if so, carefully evaluate how much turf you need. Lawns, contrary to popular opinion, take less work than most annual plants and even many perennials (See P. 24). However, sizing the lawn to your personal needs is very important; if you love rugby or softball or have lots of kids, you need lots of room. If watching the stars is your hobby, a tiny lawn may suffice. Is your only "yard" a deck, balcony, or rooftop? Then pot up some small herbal shrubs and fire up the barbie.

Annual Bedding Plants

You may want to skip them. I mean for real. You gotta get down on your knees at least twice a year to plant and remove annuals. For the laziness factor, stick with flowering perennials or shrubs.

Ground Covers

And for true laziness, skip most ground covers shorter than 12 inches; they usually need meticulous tending, because weeds grow up through their foliage.

Shrubs, Subshrubs

Since most ground covers lead to tedious weeding, you may want to move up the scale of things to shrubs. The definition of a shrub varies, but this one covers it: "a woody plant that is smaller than a tree and has several main stems arising at or near the ground, branching almost immediately."

One good example of shrubbism is lavender (*Lavandula* spp.). It also has another characteristic I prefer in a shrub—it's dense. The dense foliage blocks much of the sunlight to the ground, and the deep shade tends to eliminate weeds. It also only needs one "haircut" a year to keep it dense. (Be sure to cut it back to within one to two inches of the bare wood.)

Most of my own pathway borders are planted with shrubs that are 12"-24" (these are technically called subshrubs) or higher. In Figure 2 I show the classic ratio of height to the distance or width of the main elements of a landscape. With my approach you would skip the grass and low ground covers sections.

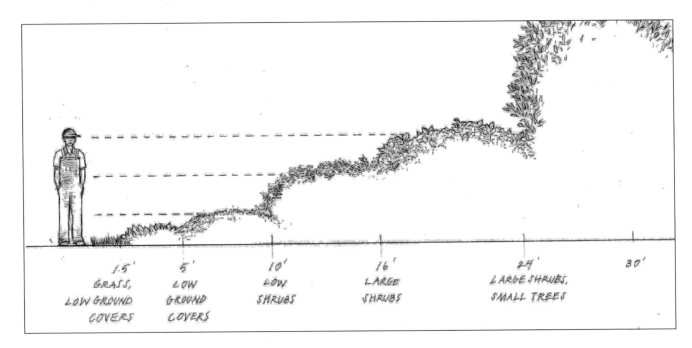

Figure 2: This ratio of plants-to-distance based on the person's height is a typical ratio from English gardens. I prefer to skip the ground cover zones and use the next low-shrub zone up to the pathway. Using the correct sub-shrubs will help reduce weed problems. I often use lavenders for this purpose.

Other examples of dense shrubs or subshrubs are:

Anemone, *Anemone canadensis* (Zones 3-8)

Artemisia 'Powis Castle' (Zones 4-9)

Bearberry/Manzanita, *Arctostaphylos* 'Emerald Carpet' (Zones 8-10)

Boxwoods, *Buxus* spp. (Zones 5-9)

Point Reyes Ceanothus/Summer lilac, *Ceanothus gloriosus* (Zones 8-11)

Dusty Miller, *Jacobaea maritima*, formerly *Senecio cineraria* (Zones 4-9)

Grevillea lavandulacea (Zones 8-11)

Heather, *Calluna vulgaris* (Zones 4-9)

Hebe, *Hebe glaucophylla* (Zones 7-10)

Hyssop, *Hyssopus officinalis* (Zones 3-9)

Jerusalem sage, *Phlomis fruticosa* (Zones 8-10)

Junipers, *Juniperus* spp. (Zones 4-9)

Dwarf English lavender, *Lavandula angustifolia* 'Compacta' (Zones 4-9)

 Bob sez: *If you've acquired a property with a lot of boring lawn, and are contemplating replacing it with edible crops, consider this: the average vegetable garden takes up 392 square feet. Most of the books on edible landscaping are done in areas with small lots and smaller front yards.*

Bob sez: *(Begin rant.) In regard to the increasing number of books saying you should replace your lawn with edibles (and/or native plants), I say they must have never been to St. Louis County where I grew up. There are miles and miles of homes with big lawns, huge lawns. Our lawn, at one-half acre, was one of the smallest. The lawns I mowed to make money in high school ranged from one-half to two acres. The average vegetable garden takes up only 4% of the lawn. Most of the books on edible landscaping are done in areas with small lots and smaller front yards. The same goes for those who would have us replace all the lawns in America with grass meadows. Give me a break. Granted, housing now is so expensive now that many houses are built on tiny lots that are so small the lawn seems to be an afterthought. (End of rant.)*

Lavandula x *ginginsii* 'Goodwin Creek Grey' (Zones 8-9)

Japanese pieris, Lily-of-the-valley bush, *Pieris japonica* (Zones 5-9)

Alpine rock rose, *Helianthemum alpestre*, aka. *Helianthemum oelandicum* subsp. *alpestre* (Zones 5-9)

Rockroses, *Cistus* spp. (Zones 9-11)

'Arp' rosemary, *Rosmarinus officinalis* (not the groundcover species) (Zones 8-11)

Rues, *Ruta* spp. (Zones 6-11)

Russian sage, *Perovskia atriplicifolia* (Zones 4-9)

Green santolina, lavender cotton, *Santolina* spp. 'Morning Mist' green santolina (Zones 8-10)

Thymes, *Thymus* spp. (Zones 5-9)

Wormwood, absinthium, *Artemisia absinthium* (Zones 4-9)

Lawns

With the reoccurring droughts in the West and Southwest, lawns are losing their appeal. Finally. In more and more areas, people are actually being paid as much as $3.75 per square foot for up to 1,500 square feet to replace lawns with drought-tolerant shrubbery. This means that at one point, if you lived within the jurisdiction of the Los Angeles Department of Water and Power (LADWP) you could have been paid as much as $5,625 to replace your lawn! Cash-for-grass is certainly the way to go. It's even been done in: Las Vegas, NV (at $1.50 per square foot); Mesa, AZ; Chandler, AZ; Tempe, AZ; Glendale, AZ; Albuquerque, NM; San Antonio, TX; and Austin, TX.

In the rest of country, removal of lawns is the trend in order to get rid of chemicals, excess fertilizers, and extra water use when compared to native plants and grass meadows.

effort. If you do buy one, make sure it has an electric starter so you don't have to squat down on a Saturday morning. Or, better yet, get an electric-powered model. If you must have a lawn, you might want to keep it as small as possible-mine was tiny, mostly for necking and watching for shooting stars. If you have kids, you may want to maintain a good-sized lawn so, when they're not playing video games, they'll have plenty of room for football, baseball, and other lawn sports.

Another reason to keep it small is that lawns generally require much more water than some veggies or some landscaping. Lavenders and rosemary, for example, can grow well with 80-90 percent less water than a lawn. And while almost all vegetables need the same amount of water as a lawn for healthy productivity, beets, celery, and lettuce are exceptions, using 10 percent less water than lawns.

If you live in an area with

Vegetable gardens can need as much as 20 hours of tending per season per 100 square feet, while lawns only need an hour of labor per 100 square feet per season. You can even pay a neighborhood kid to mow it for you, as I did in St. Louis all the way through high school.

Lawnmowers require

GROUND COVERS
Ficus pumila
Annual bedding plants
BABY TEARS
IRIS
DAISY
IVY
GAZANIA
JASMINE
AGAPANTHUS

TURF
RYE GRASS
BERMUDA GRASS
BLUE GRASS

SHRUBS
ROSE
PODOCARPUS
WISTERIA
EUGENIA
CISTUS
PHILODENDRON
BAMBOO
OLEANDER
BOXWOOD
JUNIPER
AZALEA
MAGNOLIA
CAMELLIA
GARDENIA
MAHONIA

HOURS PER 100 FT.² PER YEAR

5   10   15   20

Figure This chart shows the number of hours per plant to care for 100 square feet each year. Notice that roses, wisteria, and junipers, as examples, take much more work than lawns.

abundant rainfall, this isn't so much of a problem, but in drier areas the water bill can mount up, and/or you may run into drought regulations that will leave you with a swath of unsightly brown.

How to Kill Your Lawn

Some homeowners actually go to the expense and labor of stripping the turf off before planting when it's far easier to kill it in place. To eliminate a lawn with minimal work, simply cover the grass with one or so inches of manure or compost, and water it in. Cover with cardboard then add two to three inches of an attractive mulch (or more compost) on top of the cardboard, and wait for four to six months (or one winter) for the grass to slowly wither away. Look for appliance stores where you can get

huge amounts of cardboard in large pieces. Be sure to overlap the cardboard pieces by four to six inches in order to thwart crawling weeds. This is another example of making a one-time effort before you get back to your laptop. This mulch can also be done with thick layers of newspaper. Think ahead, and do it six or more months before you're going to plant.

However, as in life, everything in gardening is a double-sided coin. Here's the flip side of newspaper mulching, according to Dr. Linda Chalker-Scott, an Extension Horticulturist and Associate Professor at Washington State University, in her blog "The Myth of Paper-Based Sheet Mulch":

• When wet, layers of paper or cardboard can create an impermeable barrier to water

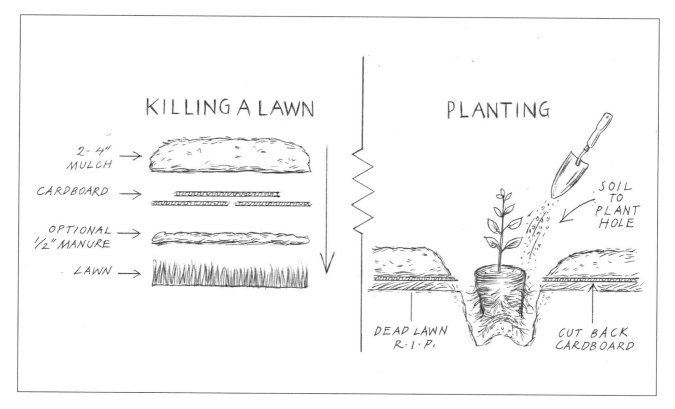

KILLING A LAWN

2-4" MULCH →
CARDBOARD →
OPTIONAL ½" MANURE →
LAWN →

PLANTING

SOIL TO PLANT HOLE

DEAD LAWN R.I.P.

CUT BACK CARDBOARD

Figure 4: Lay down the layers and wait four to 12 months. Use only as much attractive, weed-free mulch as is needed to barely cover the cardboard. To plant, pull back or puncture a portion of the newspaper or cardboard, add a bit of topsoil, and plant in the normal way. Be sure no grass fiber is in the planting hole as it will "grab" nitrogen from the added plants and slow or stunt their growth.

and air exchange.

• Garden pests, moles and gophers can hide under the newspapers and cardboard sheet mulches. In her experience, termites preferred cardboard over wood chips.

• If the paper mulch is allowed to dry out, irrigation water may sheet away rather than seep through the layers, especially in arid climates or well-drained soils.

Organic mulches work as well as cardboard and newspaper to prevent weed growth and kill turf, but it takes about six inches of mulch to do the job—two to three times more bulk than using cardboard or newspaper as an organic "herbicide." If you're buying mulch, this can really add up.

Hedges

Don't try to grow proper hedges unless you can afford to subsidize a full-time gardener — it'll be weekly or monthly job security for them. Let shrubs grow to their natural, mature size. This also means that fewer plants are needed to fill the same area as a trimmed hedge. Allowing the full-sized growth of a hedge plant means skipping countless hours of pruning when you could be reading the classics or playing games on your phone.

One solution is to use a smaller version of the same plant. Many plants have a form called 'compacta' or 'nana' or similar, indicating smaller than usual size. As an example, consider the shrub known as mock orange. (It's not at all related to citrus; the blossoms just happen to have a similar fragrance.) The botanical name is *Pittosporum tobira*—it grows to 33 feet tall and 10 feet wide. One variety, however, called *Pittosporum tobira* 'Compacta' grows 10 feet wide, but only 10 feet tall.

Another selection comes in a compact form called *Pittosporum tobira* 'Nanum' or ' '. This compact plant grows only two feet high and wide.

Yet another is *Pittosporum tobira* 'Wheeler's Dwarf' — three feet tall by five feet wide. So, you do have a choice. (There are even variegated selections of this plant — six to eight feet tall and wide.)

Trees

Trees. Artists, poets, and writers have immortalized them as symbols of fertility, sturdiness, longevity, strength, and renewal. Entire cultures have worshipped them. Some variety or other will thrive in nearly every environment and climate.

Of course, the laziest kind of tree is one you don't have to plant, prune, or otherwise manage. If you have a large yard or landscape, you may already have mature specimens in place. If you do, they can make great focal points for laying out or enhancing your landscape.

If, however, you're looking to plant some trees, thinking ahead will pay dividends. What kinds of trees do you want, and what for? Do you want to grow fruit? Marvel at spring blossoms and/or fall color? Create a shady spot to hang your hammock? Screen out an unpleasant view or nosy neighbors? How much space do you realistically have for trees without overcrowding your yard or shading out your vegetables? Figuring all this out will help narrow down your choices. Consult your neighbors, or the old guy or gal who knows everything at the local nursery.

You Can't Myth With Science

The careful research of dedicated scientists has uncovered many radical new guidelines for home gardeners. In many cases, these new guidelines are completely contrary to what we've been told—even by our own grandparents! My grandfather wasn't lying to me when he said: "Put the sprinkler near the trunk to give that tree a good drink;" he was just reflecting one of the popular myths of the day. Science and good old observation have since revealed that watering the ground at the edge of, or well beyond, the foliage canopy is far more effective and promotes the best growth. This is because tree-root systems can grow as much as three times wider than the canopy. (See Figure 5.) Occasionally, some old-time wisdom simply disappears, only to resurface decades later, well supported by scientific scrutiny. My grandmother, in her time, always insisted: "You can't prune fruit trees in the summer; that's only for late winter." After heeding this well-meaning advice for over 20 years, I found a copy of Edward Wickson's 1919 book, *California Fruits*. This was the first place I read or heard about the possibility and

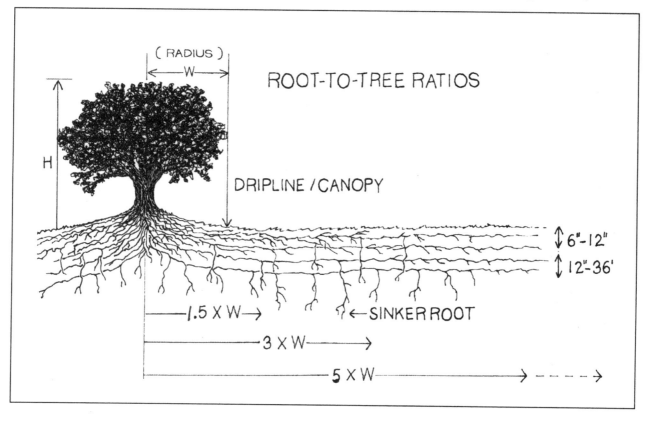

Figure 5: The root growth of a plant in relationship to the soil surface depends primarily on the type of soil in which it's growing. In compacted or heavy soil, roots will grow closer to the surface in order to find an appropriately aerobic zone. In clay soils, 90-95 percent of the roots growing in the top 12 inches of soil (and 50 percent of the plant's absorbing roots) will be found in the top four to six inches of soil. In loamy soils, 90-95 percent of the absorbing roots are found in the top 36 inches of soil, with 50 percent of those in the top 12 inches. As seen here, soil type also affects the spreading width (W) of roots. In very heavy clay soils where the clay is near the surface, roots can be forced upward and may spread five (or more) times further than the radius from the trunk to the foliage perimeter (dripline). Roots in loamy soils may spread two to three times wider (the radius) than the dripline. Heavy loam soils can produce roots that cover an area one-half again as wide as the radius. (Note: not all trees produce sinker (vertical) roots; they are most common with fruit trees.) Some people suggest the formula that the roots are as wide as the tree is tall (H). But I don't recommend this ratio.

(Illustration by Mary Jarvis.)

value of summer pruning of fruit trees—which applies to all ornamental trees as well.

Subsequent older books I discovered from England and France reinforced the concept that not only would summer pruning not harm the trees; it was the best time to prune for controlling rampant or unwanted growth. At the same time, the research of intensive orchard techniques by extension services and universities around the country was recertifying this important pruning strategy as valid and safe. The concept has come full circle. (See pages 118-121 for more on summer pruning.)

Treemendous Tenacity

Trees, especially if they're allowed to germinate and grow in an appropriate place, are amazingly hardy, tenacious plants. Even surrounded by an asphalt jungle, certain kinds will sometimes prosper and often hang on for decades. (Tree-of-heaven, anyone?) They exhibit a remarkable resilience and will grow despite monumental abuse. Conversely (and sometimes perversely), they can prove to be delicate and vulnerable in your yard. For instance, a sprinkler throwing water on the trunk of certain trees can kill an entire 20-foot specimen—if it's planted in the wrong soil or with the wrong methods.

The natural way for many trees to grow is usually from seeds sprouting in a multitude of tiny crevices—cracks in soil, sand, gravel and rock, and beneath moist rotting leaves. Some seeds require a good fire to sprout. To germinate, others must pass through the gut of just the right animal. The odds for survival are less than your chance of finding a straight-talking politician these days. For every glorious specimen we see in the forest today, hundreds—if not thousands—of tiny seeds and seedlings gave up their lives.

It would be lovely to think that every single tree is sacred. Sure, if you pay a small fortune to a landscape contractor for a 15-foot shade tree to

be transplanted by a mechanical tree spade—a large tractor-like machine that plucks the tree out of the ground, very much like a monstrous ice-cream scoop—and it dies, you'll be sad or pissed, maybe both. But nature very rarely transplants trees, and never large specimens.

The point is that losing one tree in our backyard is really no big deal in the grander scheme of things. Besides, just like the forest, you can replant. "Replant?" you say. "Yikes! That's a lot of money wasted," you say. Well—WARNING, BRAZEN SELF-PROMOTION!—you can learn how to properly plant a tree by reading my book *Understanding Roots*, Metamorphic Press, 2015. (It's simply too much to cover here.)

Let's begin by seeing how to select a bare root tree.

Naked Trees

The nursery industry sells trees in several kinds of "packages:"
1. Saplings of various ages, in containers.
2. Trees dug from the ground with a ball of dirt and roots and wrapped with burlap (known as "B&B").
3. "Bare root" trees: these are one or two years old, dug in early spring (with roots intact) while they're still dormant, and sold that same spring. Why buy a bare root tree? Price—bare-root stock is usually the least expensive of the three choices. And, planted properly, bare root trees almost always grow well and catch up within a few years to the bigger trees sold by local nurseries in containers, or balled-and-burlapped. You'll find bare root fruit trees in local nurseries only during the months that immediately precede spring bloom and leafing-out. When buying locally, avoid focusing on size, and look for quality. Many trees are grafted. Where the rootstock and the top of the tree join (the graft) you should see continuous callus (bark-free growth that "heals" grafting cuts and unites top

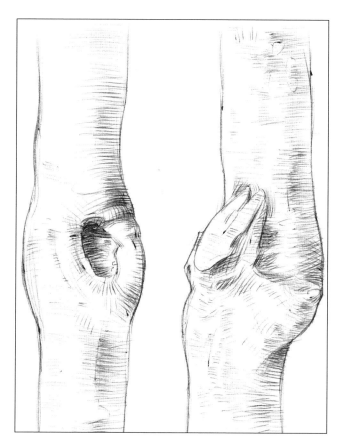

Figure 6: Look for a well-formed callus where the fruit variety was grafted to the rootstock. The graft on the left shows the rounded, circular callus of a healing graft. The rootstock on the right sticks out and should be avoided.

and bottom) — no fractures or gaps. (See Figure 6.) Next, look for a tree with little or no damage to the roots. Broken roots can be pruned, but the less pruning needed, the healthier the tree.

Exemplary trees, with their branches already formed in the ideal positions, are hard to find at a local nursery. It is even more rare to receive an ideally branched tree from a mail-order source. When ordering through the mail, it is better to request a "maiden" or "whip" tree. Such trees are merely a single trunk with no branches, and can be pruned to your vision of the perfect tree.

Trees for Solar Warmth and "Coolth"

If you have the space, trees can assist with keeping your home cooler in summer and warmer in winter. But it's much more complicated than just planting a bunch of deciduous trees along the south side of the house.

Deciduous trees (their leaves fall off in the fall) are practical for letting in southern light during the winter to help warm your home, but they also create a surprising amount of shade as well. Their limbs, branches, and shoots block out an appreciable amount of sun; you just don't notice it because the shadow "ends" before it reaches the ground. But get out a light meter and compare the reading under a tree with that in an open space nearby, and you'll see a considerable drop in light—many deciduous trees block 25 percent or more of the available light. (See Figure 7.)

But planting trees (sure are a lot of buts in this section), even deciduous varieties, on the south side of the house can often actually increase your heating bills. A study in Sacramento, CA, determined that all homes, both solar and conventional, would pay more for energy year-round if deciduous and evergreen shade trees were planted along the south side of the house.

Some varieties of trees actually doubled the cost of energy when compared to a house with no trees. In many cases, the closer to the house the shade trees, the higher the yearly utility bills. Solar houses with solar hot-water systems were the most severely impacted by shade trees near the south wall.

What all this means is that for maximum tree efficiency, you need to leave a "solar corridor" with no shade trees on the south side of your house. (See Figure 8.) To determine the area to leave free of shade trees (the example here is for areas south of the 45-degree North latitude where you find cities like Portland, OR, Minneapolis, MN, Dexter, ME, and Yellowstone, WY) extend an imaginary line due south from the southeast and

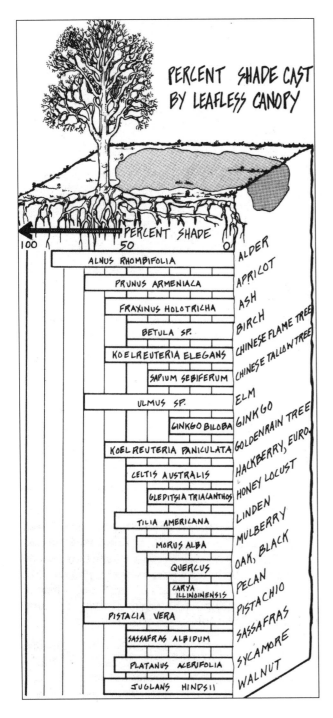

PERCENT SHADE CAST BY LEAFLESS CANOPY

PERCENT SHADE

100   50   0

ALNUS RHOMBIFOLIA	ALDER
PRUNUS ARMENIACA	APRICOT
FRAXINUS HOLOTRICHA	ASH
BETULA SP.	BIRCH
KOELREUTERIA ELEGANS	CHINESE FLAME TREE
SAPIUM SEBIFERUM	CHINESE TALLOW TREE
ULMUS SP.	ELM
GINKGO BILOBA	GINKGO
KOELREUTERIA PANICULATA	GOLDENRAIN TREE
CELTIS AUSTRALIS	HACKBERRY, EURO.
GLEDITSIA TRIACANTHOS	HONEY LOCUST
TILIA AMERICANA	LINDEN
MORUS ALBA	MULBERRY
QUERCUS	OAK, BLACK
CARYA ILLINOINENSIS	PECAN
PISTACIA VERA	PISTACHIO
SASSAFRAS ALBIDUM	SASSAFRAS
PLATANUS ACERIFOLIA	SYCAMORE
JUGLANS HINDSII	WALNUT

Figure 7: All limbs and branches block the sun, it's just not all noticable. Here we see that trees like the ginkgo and pecan only block 30 percent of the sunlight. All others 40 percent or above. And a tree like the alder blocks nearly 90 percent of the light.

southwest corners of the house, then draw a line 45 degrees east of the southeast line and a line 45 degrees west of the southwest line. The entire area between these two lines should be free of trees tall enough to shade the wall or roof. (Oh, come on, you can do the math.)

When using plants to reduce summer's heat, don't forget the east and west sides of the house. A Mesa, AZ, study indicated the importance of the east and west walls: when it comes to reducing heat, the western wall was found to be six times more important than the south side and the eastern wall was 14.5 times more significant than the southern wall and almost 2.5 times more critical than the west-facing wall. While the figures or effects may vary considerably in other climates, just remember that eastern and western windows can really tend to overheat a house in the summer. But carefully placed trees on those sides can help it keep its cool.

OK, deep breath. Enough with the science-speak for now.

Disease- and Pest-"Free" Trees

An old wise-guy once said: "The best time to plant a tree is 20 years ago, the second best time is today." If you are going to the trouble of getting off your rump, might as well pick a tree that won't need a lot of attention—one that is nearly pest- and disease-free. The first choice would be a plastic, ornamental Christmas tree. The second would be a living tree with few problems. Do some research on your iPad or laptop. Google-up some trees. Or, call your local Master Gardeners and ask them—if they don't know, fire them. Of course a reputable garden nursery will know, and stock many of them. But here's a short list to start with:

Ginkgo (*Ginkgo biloba*) Zones 3-9
50'-100' H X 20'-40'
This is my favorite choice. This living fossil—

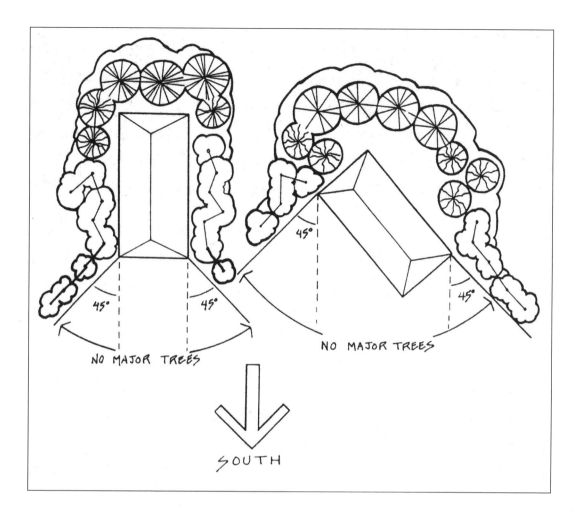

Figure 8: Trees south of the house can actually reduce the amout of solar light in the winter. To provide a corridor of winter sunlight, plant trees forty-five degrees from the southeast and southwest corners of the house. You'll need a compass to determine solar south. Then determine the forty-five degree angle. Use Figure 7 to choose the best trees with deciduous branches to let light in during the winter.

geological records show it to be unchanged over the past 270 million years—is, as far as I know, free of all pests and diseases—except deer! The blazing hot yellow fall color is spectacular, and an extra asset is that the roots are much less likely to heave sidewalks than those of most trees. The fruits of the female tree do produce an unpleasant smell; the male tree doesn't, but it's fairly high on the allergy scale. If you plan to live a long time, you're in luck—some ginkgos are thought to be over 1500 years old. (Yes, that's the correct number of zeroes.) Its positive attributes are many. As a side note, it's one of the rare deciduous conifers. (See P. 32.)

Black Tupelo (*Nyssa sylvatica*) Zones 4-9
30'-50' H X 20'-30' W
Besides being relatively pest-free, this tree is very tolerant of wet soils—even flooding, thus its roots are resistant to root rots (*Phytophthora* spp.). It's native to the central and eastern parts of America, and is often rated in the top ten for spectacular fall foliage color. Can get occasional butterfly larvae (caterpillar) damage.

Sweet Bay Magnolia *(Magnolia virginiana)*
Zones 5-10   10'-35' H X 10'-35'W
A very adaptable tree that tolerates acidic soil, air pollution, moist and boggy soils, clay soils and full or part shade. Native to the eastern US. Semideciduous, with fragrant blossoms.

Serviceberry *(Amelanchier arborea)* Zones 4-9
15'-25' H X 15'-25' W
Produces brilliant, slightly fragrant flowers that bloom early- to mid-spring. Tolerates a wide range of soils, but needs good drainage. Often called "Juneberries" for its edible dark-purplish fruits. Native from Maine to Iowa, south to northern Florida and Louisiana.

Japanese Snowbell *(Styrax japonicus)*
Zones 5-9 20'-30' H X 20'-30'W
Mildly fragrant white flowers in May/June. No significant fall color. Deciduous.

Katsura *(Cercidiphyllum japonicum)*
Zones 4-8   40'-60' H X 25'-60' W
Likes well-drained, but moist, soils. No showy flowers. The early-spring leaves are a reddish-purple color.

Persian Parrotia *(Parrotia persica)* Zones 4-8
20'-40' H X 20'-30' W
A deciduous tree often found on top-ten fall color lists. Needs well-drained soil in full sun. Its showy curled (exfoliating) bark is attractive in the winter.

Paperbark Maple *(Acer griseum)*   Zones 4-9
20'-30' H X 15'-25' W
This deciduous tree, with its especially beautiful exfoliating copper-orange bark, is very striking in the winter. Can display showy orange fall foliage. Needs some moisture in full or partial sun. Makes a great "understory" tree for planting beneath taller trees.

Other examples include: Goldenrain tree (*Koelreuteria paniculata*); Douglas fir (*Pseudotsuga menziesii*); hemlock (*Tsuga* spp.); and northern red oak (*Quercus rubra*).

 Bob sez: *Some other trees are very pest- and disease-free, BUT are also very invasive. Avoid at all costs: Chinese scholar tree* (Styphnolobium japonicum, formerly Sophora japonica)*; Russian olive* (Elaeagnus angustifolia)*; Norway maple* (*Acer platanoides*)*; and especially Tree-of-heaven* (Ailanthus altissima)*.*

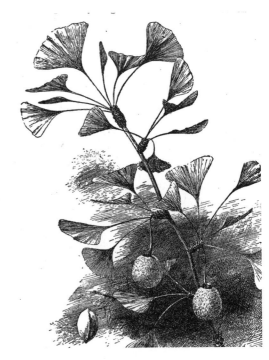

Ginkgo leaves and fruits.

CHAPTER 4

Edible Plants

Less effort, more food—it's a win/win.

In case you haven't noticed, there are a lot of books out there on vegetables, fruit trees, nut trees, and countless strange, exotic, and prolific vegetables and fruits. Some of the books, like John Jeavons' *How to Grow More Vegetables*, (*and Fruits, Nuts, Berries, Grains, and Other Crops*) *Than You Ever Thought Possible on Less Land Than You Can Imagine*, (9th Edition, Ten Speed Press, 2017), promote productive yields, but are very, very, labor-intensive. Others, like the *Square Foot Gardening* books by Mel Bartholomew require considerably less effort. If you're not serious about eating from your garden, you may want to support the hard-working

 Bob sez: *I can actually recommend another Lazy Gardener book. (How's that for a gracious move? And she didn't even pay me to say it.)* Tips for the Lazy Gardener *(Linda Tilgner, Storey Publishing, 1998.) has lots of tips for how to save time with annual vegetables. While it covers very little of what I do, it's a good manual for those that want to hassle with growing their own veggies as opposed to frequenting one of the 8,000 plus American farmers markets.*

growers at your local farmers market. Otherwise what's a dedicated but truly languid locovore to do? Consider methods that don't require much tillage, or none at all.

Got Herbs?

Edibles are usually more work than ornamentals. So, how do you slip into growing edibles? Start with herbs. You'll save an enormous amount of money by growing your own fresh herbs. Fresh herbs are even more expensive at the supermarket than dried herbs—and taste better, with their valuable nutrients, oils, and phenols intact.

As far as herbs go, consider rosemary (*Rosmarinus officinalis*) as an example. It thrives in USDA Zones 7-10 (the cultivar 'Arp' can grow, if sheltered, in Zone 6), and it's easy to grow indoors in a sunny south-facing window. In colder climates rosemary can be grown in pots and brought indoors for the winter. This plant can grow like a weed in my garden because it gets so big and wide other plants prefer to not grow in its deep shade.

At my local Trader Joe's (supposedly less expensive than "regular" stores), fresh rosemary costs $3.50 for one ounce. That's equal to $56 per pound! And this is not even organic produce! Well, that means my three-foot tall organic rosemary must be worth at least $250.) I've got mine planted in a trough three feet from the BBQ grill so it's easy to use. I live in Zone 9b, but in colder climates you can do this with basil in the summer or some perennial mints (USDA Zones 4-10).

Addicted to Salad

After you've gotten proficient with herbs, you might want to move on to mixed salad greens. A mix of several leafy greens is sold as "Spring Mix" in my area—even though it's sold all year round. Go figure. A popular method known as "cut-and-come-again" salad gardening is much more productive than growing individual heads of lettuce, and it's a great way to harvest food even from small containers.

Here's a funny cut-and-come-again salad story (and how many of those do you get to read?). For several weeks in a row, I had dropped off a half-pound of mesclun, (a French word usually pronounced as mesk'-len') salad mix at my friend Jeannie's. One day after church, Jeannie (not her real name) boasted to some friends: "Robert brought me another half-pound of mesclun, and it's so wonderful that I ate nearly half of it at one sitting!"

Some of the churchgoers turned pale and moved away from her. Finally, a friend took Jeannie by the arm and politely pulled her aside—"Jeannie, mescaline is a drug!" Jeannie's response was, "No it's not; it's a wonderful salad," and explained the difference. Her friend relaxed in bemusement; the similarity of pronunciation (the drug is pronounced as mes'ke-lin') had given the impression that Jeannie was a drug addict, not an innocent aficianado of quality salads.

Cut-and-Come-Again Salad Mix

The secret to mesclun, for the inspired but time-conserving gardener, is to plant once and harvest for many weeks by leaving a few of the youngest leaves on every plant to regrow.

The secret to a quick, simple, and efficient mesclun harvest is intensive, broadcast-seeding and frequent cutting. Unlike the ready-to-plant mesclun seed blends offered by some catalogs,

By planting small areas to one type you can cut and re-cut many more times than an area planted to a mixture of seeds. Plan which varieties of greens you want to grow. Then buy and plant separate amounts of seed, rather than the seed blends offered in some catalogs.

Planting patches of unmixed seedlings makes repeated harvesting convenient, relaxed and productive. If you plant all the salad varieties, including lettuces, mixed together, you'll only be able to harvest everything a few times at best. By separating the varieties, you can harvest most leafy-green ingredients six to eight times. Some of the greens that can be harvested this frequently include: arugula (*Eruca vesicaria)*; mizuna (*Brassica rapa* var. *japonica*); 'Red Russian' kale (*Brassica oleracea*, Acephala Group); white mustard (*Sinapis alba,* formerly *Brassica hirta*); and garden cress (*Lepidium sativum*).

The seed should be lightly broadcasted with the goal in mind of having plants on about two-inch centers. Next, water the beds immediately and, in the summer, once a day, depending on the weather, until the seeds germinate. Thereafter the beds are watered once a week, or as needed. The beds usually need only one weeding while the seedlings are young, and one thinning to achieve the desired spacing. (Naturally, any thinnings go into that day's salad mix.)

Better yet, be even more hassle-free and buy six-packs of most veggies. (Squash and tomatoes are examples of good candidates for buying in one-gallon pots.) It'll save far more irritation and frustration than the cost of the plants. Let the grower deal with irregular water needs, poor germination, late frosts, proper fertility, slugs, and damping off. I can now even buy organic veggie seedlings at the local Big Box hardware store—but I don't.

Bob sez: *Known in some circles as "That fancy California gourmet salad with weird greens and lots of flowers," mesclun, in its present evolution as an American culinary product, is a delightful blend of tender young salad greens. Adventurous gardeners like me add the succulent shoots of young edible wild plants, the small tips of various herbs, and a heavy sprinkling of edible flowers.*

Leafy Containers

Containers are a great place to grow repeating-harvest salad greens. It doesn't take a very big pot or trough to grow the 10 or more plants a person might need for salad harvesting. Containers are a great way to foil gophers, creeping weeds, voles, and (with a copper-foil band around the perimeter) snails and/or slugs.

Containers for Shade-Tolerant Vegetables

Another very nice advantage to containers: the smaller ones can be moved from shady to sunny spots on small decks, ledges or patios as the season progresses. See page 38 for ideas about how much sun leafy greens need. You may be surprised to learn that many vegetables don't need eight hours of sun to be happy and productive. For example, the mesclun salad mix mentioned above needs a mere two to three hours a day of direct sunlight to grow a decent salad.

Perennial Food Crops

Some gardeners are now promoting a perennial food crops diet for easier gardening, since the crops only have to be planted once. (Have these people ever eaten a salad?) Eating only perennial foods, however, can imply a radical shift in nutrition, disrupting dietary patterns that are very difficult to change. Let's take a look at some examples: chives, Egyptian top-set onions, garlic, and society garlic, for instance, are not very impressive options. Asparagus, sunchokes (Jerusalem artichokes), and artichokes (in mild climates) are good examples. Fruit is good but there's a limit to its nutritional value and how much you can eat—even if you're a fruitarian. Nut trees are great additions, but are often way too large for a small suburban lot. And Italian chestnut trees (at least in my area) are dying from root rot, *Phytophthora* spp., a more recent disease manifestation than the blight that almost wiped out the American species in past decades.

Globe artichoke (*Cynara scolymus*)

It's also hard to make a truly sustainable garden of perennial foods if you move a lot. The average household moves every five to seven years per lifetime. The average American individual moves 11.7 times in a lifetime. Although tough economic times will slow down moving (except for foreclosures), many people will still relocate too often to maintain a truly mature sustainable garden.

The likelihood of moving exerts a great influence on which edible tree crops the average homeowner will grow. Trees like chestnuts take up to five to seven years to begin bearing. Commercial walnut production begins in 10 to 15 years, but does not reach peak levels until 25 to 30 years have passed The temperate-climate almond is an exception, as it comes into fruition after about three to four years.

Perennial vegetables, however, take fewer years to come into harvest:

Globe artichokes – 2nd year (see previous page)

Asparagus – two to three years, four for a really decent harvest

Horseradish – year number one or two

Rhubarb – 2nd year

Chayote – 1st year

I can't live only on perennial vegetables, can you? (Although I probably wouldn't mind trying to live on asparagus. But it isn't practical once I remember the unique "fragrance" when peeing.) And if you rent or have a tiny yard, nut trees and many fruit trees may be out of the question.

Shade Tolerant Veggies

2 Hours - Asian Greens, Mesculun Mix

3 Hours - Culinary Herbs, Mustard Greens

3-4 Hours - Arugula, Kale, Lettuce, Mizuna, Spinach, Swiss Chard

4-5 Hours - Beans, Beets, Carrots, Celery, Collards, Pak Choy, Peas, Radishes, Rutabagas

5 Hours - Broccoli, Brussels Sprouts, Cabbage, Cauliflower

That said, here are 50 tips conducive to vegging out:

Fifty Laid-Back Veggie Garden Tips

1. Grow three-in-one vegetables for more impact in the kitchen with less work. Chayote is the King of the list of multiple-use vegetables. It puts out edible young shoots you can prep like asparagus. You get tasty squash-like fruits. The seed has a nice nutty flavor. And as the plant grows, it forms large tubers that can be prepared any way you cook potatoes. You can harvest pounds of tubers and there will be plenty to sprout new growth with this abundant perennial vegetable. (Actually this makes it four-in-one!) (Sorry folks, this triumph of a vegetable can only grow in USDA Zones 9 and 10.) Fava beans are another three-in-one: young edible leaves, the early-spring green beans and the

mature, hard bean that's gathered in the summer for robust fall soups and stews. In the flower kingdom, the spicy foliage of the nasturtium is used in salads, as are the flowers. Leaving some flowers to mature creates an edible, peppery-hot young green seed-pod that can be used in place of capers.

2. Two-for-one veggies include beets (leaves for salads and steaming), carrots (foliage for pesto), peas (edible tendrils), squash (edible flowers), radishes (edible flowers) and many roses (edible petals and rose hips).

3. You can save a lot of seasonal effort by planting perennial veggies only once and harvesting thereafter.

4. In the past, I've used clay chimney flues for some root crops. They make for easy harvesting of burdock and other long edible roots. (If you've never tried burdock, it's great in soups, stews, and stir-fries, with an agreeable earthy taste and an incredible level of nutrients.) I treat the inside of the flues with swimming-pool plaster to seal them so the clay doesn't wick the moisture out. Then I stack several flues and wire the bottom against gophers. (To harvest the veggies, let the soil dry some and just pull the flues up.) Do not use flues to try and control mints, as the roots will just come out the bottom.

5. No backyard? No problem. The easiest way to grow tomatoes, for example, on a deck or driveway is to buy a sack of potting soil or compost, lay it flat, slit it open and plant with tomato seedlings. You can also experiment with other vegetables like broccoli.

6. Perforated pipes inserted into a hot compost pile (if you've got one) help it breathe better and compost faster.

7. Use bottomless one-gallon plastic milk jugs as "greenhouses" or little cold frames to protect young seedlings.

8. If you want to use an olla (an unglazed ceramic jar that's buried near plants and filled with water to wick out to plants naturally) to water your veggies, you can see how to make a home-

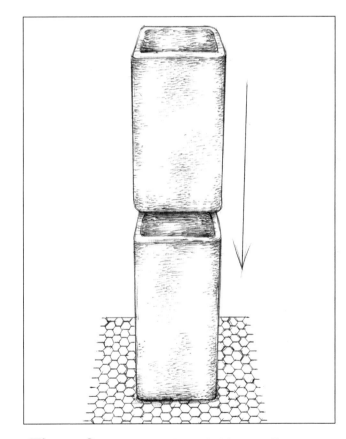

Figure 9: Set a number of chimney flues on top of each other. Grow rootcrops such as burdock (gobo) and lift the flues to harvest the roots.

made one on page 90.

9. Cats are cute—except when they mess with your freshly cultivated soil. You can lay down (temporarily) chicken wire or hardware cloth with small mesh, or stick old forks into the ground with tines up to say "Fork you, kitty!"

10. You can easily suppress weeds when growing onions and garlic by making small cuts in three to five sheets of newspaper and inserting the young bulb or clove. Cover with straw or an attractive seed-free mulch.

11. If you place large flat stones as a mulch under and around plants, you also provide extra warmth for superior growth. (This may allow you to stretch the climate enough to grow veggies that your neighbor can't.)

12. Some unusual mulches include: cocoa shells (Warning: they're poisonous to dogs); kelp; rice hulls; shredded corn cobs; coffee grounds; oyster shells; tiles or roof slate; decomposed granite; cotton gin trash; and salt hay.

13. Even more unusual: shredded paper (I met a gardener years ago who worked at the CIA. He brought home shredded government secrets to mulch his vegetables. Now they probably cross-shred them like confetti—not so good in windy places.); sheep wool (Sea Ranch, CA, uses sheep to graze down weeds and wild grasses. Their community garden is mulched with strips of sheep wool, that compacts very tightly and suppresses all weeds); and, yes, even carpets.) (See Chapter 5.)

14. When mulching, don't use shredded acacia, *Acer saccharum* (sugar maple), *Celtis occidentalis*, *Leucaena* spp. (white leadtree, jumbay, river tamarind, subabul, and white popinac), willow, walnut, eucalyptus, or redwood, as they all contain various levels of plant toxins.

15. I like to use comfrey leaves to fertilize summer vegetables (not root crops). I simply add a handful of leaves to a gallon of water, wait a week or so for it to ferment, strain the liquid, dilute the liquid 10 parts water to one part comfrey glop and use the juice as a soil drench. (Be warned, this smells VERY bad.)

16. You can save water by choosing which veggies you grow. See page 41 for the number of gallons of water it takes to produce a pound of produce. If water is tight, kiss off homegrown corn at your BBQ.

17. Lay 1/2-inch aviary wire onto seed flats or in the garden as a guide to placing seeds.

18. Some good friends use an old wooden ladder to grow climbing beans. (I think metal or plastic ladders would be too tacky. Just my opinion; they may suit your garden.)

19. Trim the branches off the trunk of your Christmas tree to make a tall stake with "handholds" for beans to clamber up.

20. In the 1970s, I lived near a brick factory that made old-looking bricks by painting them white and tumbling them, and some broke in the process. I used thousands of these broken bricks to make hundreds of square feet of paths. (At first the bricks were free. After awhile they saw a money-making opportunity and charged me one cent each.) This is surely a localized opportunity, but if you're trying to figure out what to do with a pile of bricks, they do make great permanent pathways between your raised beds.

21. I've grown climbing beans under the dense shade of willow trees. The leaves got enormous and the yields were low, but I got more green beans than not growing them there at all.

22. In the '70s I got shower doors from the

Gallons of Water Used to Grow One Pound of Vegetables

Lettuce	23 gal
Tomatoes	30 gal
Carrots	33 gal
Apples	49 gal
Potatoes	60 gal
Broccoli	65 gal
Cantaloupe	80 gal
Corn	168 gal

dump (they were free then!) and made a large greenhouse. You can also use them to make cold frames. A cold frame is a (usually) four-sided frame of boards with a removable glass or plastic top. The frame is placed on the ground and is used to house, protect, and harden off seedlings and small plants, without artificial heat.

23. Use an old leaky wheelbarrow to grow small veggies. Move it around to follow the sun.

24. And use some old boots and shoes as pots for hanging plants, like peas, or even tomatoes.

25. I need plenty of B&W newspaper every year, since I use it each spring to cover the weeds that sprouted over the winter (Zone 9a). I spread it fairly thickly, with overlapping edges and put an attractive mulch on top. The B&W papers nowadays use soy ink for the black—no heavy metals like when I first did it in 1973.

26. For keeping seedlings moist, I use a "water rose" or showerhead sprinkling can (made by Bosmere Haws). They cost a lot, around $45, but are the best way to gently water new seedlings. The tiny holes face up and the water cascades up and then falls like a very gentle rain. Figure 10.

27. If (like me) you're stuck with gophers or other burrowing/gnawing/destructive critters, use wire baskets under the ground to contain vulnerable plants like squashes. Get the largest one you can, because virtually all the roots that try to grow beyond the wire are eaten. When I make my own baskets, I use four-foot wide rolls of half-inch hardware cloth—it has the best galvanized coating.

28. Dry your herbs in the car. Place them on a towel and put in the trunk, out of direct light.

29. Use a wooden hoe handle as a measuring stick. Just mark every foot with a stroke of a file, and do it every inch for the first foot.

30. To make a hose guide to protect plants in garden beds, stab a two-foot length of steel reinforcing bar one foot into the ground at the corner of a bed and slip two clay pots over it—one facing down, the other facing up.

31. Find smooth fist-sized stones and use a Sharpie™ pen to write on them; they make great unobtrusive plant markers.

32. Do you ever use up all the toilet paper? I bet you do. Use toilet paper rolls as seedling pots by bending in the end of the tube.

33. Vertical gardens are popular but can be expensive. Use a cloth shoe rack to grow plants such as perennial herbs.

34. Buy some new disposable diapers—not used ones! Take them apart and line the bottom of a (fiber) hanging planter. Use the bottom layer with the absorbent padding facing up. Voilà! Nothing

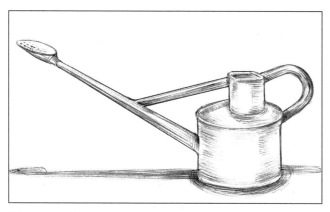

Figure 10: The Haws sprinkling can is another life-time investment. A metal one costs up to $150. It makes the most gentle spray of any sprinkler.

escapes out the bottom—water or soil.

35. Be sure to paint all tool handles bright colors so they're easy to find.

36. Fill a large metal saltshaker with diatomaceous earth (a soft, crumbly, porous sedimentary deposit formed from the fossil remains of diatoms—single-celled algae that have a cell wall made of silica). When aphids show up, sprinkle them with the diatomaceous earth which easily washes off before you eat. The diatomaceous earth has tiny sharp edges that pierce the soft skin of the aphids and kill them.

37. Use an old golf bag to hold long-handled tools. (Of course, you'll probably have to be your own caddie.) A long piece of terracotta chimney flue with a flange (flared rim) on one end works.

38. A used mailbox in garden can hold clippers, tie-tape, plant labels and pens out of the rain.

39. I had an old disk snow sled—I could have used it pull heavy items, but I left it in St. Louis.

40. Go to the thrift shop, buy old colanders and use them as hanging planters.

41. I have Bermuda grass in part of my garden, and it wants to colonize the whole thing. I cover it with cardboard, with wood-chip mulch on top, but I have to redo it every two to three years.

42. Use natural fiber twine to tie up veggies like tomatoes and beans. When the crops are finished for the season, cut down the whole mess and compost it.

43. Keep an old spray bottle full of soapy water to spray on aphids. They hate it.

44. Put up a wire line for drying herbs, and keep some clothespins handy to clip them to the wire.

45. Recycled plastic strawberry baskets turned upside down make great cloches (small covers for protecting or forcing outdoor plants) to shade tender seedlings on hot days.

46. Tomatoes will happily ramble up inside a large coil of concrete reinforcing wire—it comes with six-inch square openings you can reach through.

47. Do you tend to accumulate lots of wine bottles? Fill some with water and cluster them around tomato plants in the early spring to form a vertical greenhouse.

48. Hoe in some alfalfa pellets (from the feed store) to help fertilize your garden. Or use them as a mulch.

49. Use cuticle clippers to thin out little thickets of seedlings, leaving one baby plant behind to flourish.

50. Grow edibles like broccoli or kale (and of course, tomatoes) that you can harvest a bit over time. Pick single lettuce leaves instead of harvesting a whole head.

Fruit Trees

Most fruit trees are too much work, that is, if you compare planting and tending them to jaunting off to the farmers market. Some fruits, however, are so superior when eaten ripe off the tree that it may be worth the effort to you. My favorite example is apricots, but in my area (Sonoma County, in the California wine country) these trees have four major faults:

1 They bloom so early that the rains often wipe out the flowers.

2. Their roots are very sensitive to wet clay soils.

3. They are prone to special diseases like bacterial canker, crown gall, blossom brown rot, green fruit rot, phytophthora crown and root rot, scab and shot hole fungus. If these afflictions sound disgusting, that's because they are.

4. A good crop comes only once every four to six years.

So, back in the day, my friends and I would go 30 miles east to the exemplary organic apricot orchard of Henry Eschbensche near Winters, CA. His orchard occupies several ridges east of the coastal zones, and that location makes all the difference in the world. During the peak of the season, the flavor of Henry's apricots tickles the tongue with a rich, complex essence and delights the senses with a sweet, delicate aroma. In Henry's orchard, hundreds of pounds of fruit could be harvested in a fraction of the time it took me to tend a single tree at home.

Other fruits can be easier to grow, but each comes with its unique problem(s). Take apples for example. They're also vulnerable to a number of rusts and mildews, and apple trees are often infiltrated by codling moths. If codling caterpillars show up on your trees, forget typical spraying; it's just too complicated to kill the tiny caterpillar before it's inside the fruit. One very tedious option is to bag the fruit, which is effective but can distort the color.

Apples are pruned or shaped in part to encourage fruiting areas called spurs. Once a flowering spur is formed on an apple tree it may go on fruiting at the same place for 25 or more years.

So, what if you could nearly eliminate pruning for the sake of flower formation? Meet the spur-type tree. These are apple trees whose forebears were selected because they made more spurs (flowering buds) naturally, with no regard as to pruning. The flower spurs are also closer together on the limb, making the trees a bit more dwarfed. These trees will save you a lot of time when lightly pruning. Look for the word "spur" or "spur-type" on the label. See below for some examples.

'Arkansas Black Spur'
'Cox's Orange Pippin Spur Type'
'Compspur Granny Smith'
'Compspur Rome Beauty'
'Empress Spur Golden Delicious'
spur 'Gala-go-Red'
spur 'Red Gala #42'
'Golden Delicious, Empress Spur'
'Granny Smith, Spur'
'Iwamatsa Spur' ('Fuji' spur type)
'McIntosh, Compact'
'McIntosh, Compspur'
'McIntosh, MacSpur'
'Oregon Spur Delicious'
'Red Delicious, Starkspur'
'Spur Red Rome Beauty'
'Spur Winter Banana'
'Spuree Rome Beauty'
'Starkspur Winesap'
'Winter Banana, spur type'
'Yellow Delicious, Spur'

Spur apple trees make more fruit regardless of how they are pruned.

Standard-sized fruit trees (non-dwarf trees) take about two to seven years to come into bearing, depending on the tree. Non-dwarf pear trees take two to five years to begin to fruit. Sweet cherries, which have no very effective dwarfing rootstock (except for the genetic-dwarf cherry that is a poor bearer), take four to seven years to fruit. Persimmon trees take five to seven years or more, although the occasional tree will bear much sooner.

Some dwarf fruit trees often start bearing in the second year. Some very dwarf fruit trees, such as apples on a rootstock called M27 and M9 (originally from Malling Research Station, Malling, England), will fruit the first year, but the fruit should be stripped off to allow the tree to grow for a year or two as fruiting can virtually stop these trees from growing new shoots. For the average lazy person, dwarf fruit trees are a must. Not to mention that the care and harvesting of the shorter tree is so much easier than with a full-sized tree. Shorter is better. (I should know, I'm 5' 6".) Be aware that summer pruning can reduce the height even more.

Another problem with apple trees, most trees need to be pollinated by another variety in order to have a successful crop. Some of my favorite apple varieties are: 'Golden Delicious', 'Braeburn', 'Granny Smith', 'Scrumptious', 'Anna', 'Dorsett Golden', 'Empire', 'Grimes Golden', 'Newtown Pippin', 'Spitzenburg' and 'Northern Spy'. If your planting area is limited, plant one of these varieties to save space. (See Figure 12.)

For a more detailed list of other fruit trees that need pollinators, see: extension.oregonstate.edu/ lane/sites/default/.../c105_pollination_of_fruit_ trees_05.pdf

Trees that often need pollinizers in order to bear fruit include: apples, pears, plums, prunes, and sweet cherries.

There are a number of fruit trees, however, that don't need pollinizers. This saves space more importantly, it saves you from having to dig another hole! Fruit trees that are self-fertile are:

- Apricots
- Citrus
- Figs
- Nectarines
- Peaches
- *Sour* cherries

If you've got a hankerin' for home-grown peaches, you come face-to-face with the dreaded peach-leaf curl. Control is very difficult as timing of the spray is critical, and it requires you going out into the cold to spray in late winter and early spring. If it rains right after you spray, you gotta put on your down jacket and spray again (cursing allowed).

Figure 11: Columnar apple trees are a recent development. They stay below eight feet, and can be planted two feet apart or in large containers.

Pollen Source	Akane	Braeburn	Cortland	Empire	Fuji	Gala	Golden Delicious	Honey Crisp	Jonagold	Jonamac	Jonathan	Lodi	McIntosh	Paulared	Red Delicious	Red Gravenstein	Spartan	Tydemans's Early	Tydeman's Red	Winter Banana	Yellow
Akane		X	X	X	X	X	X	X		X	X	X	X	X	X		X	X	X	X	X
Braeburn	X		X	X	X	X	X	X		X	X	X	X	X	X		X	X	X	X	X
Cortland	X	X		X	X	X	X	X		X	X	X	X	X	X		X	X	X	X	X
Empire	X	X	X		X	X	X			X	X	X	X	X	X		X	X	X	X	X
Fuji	X	X	X	X		X	X	X		X	X	X	X	X	X		X	X	X	X	X
Gala	X	X	X	X	X			X		X	X	X	X	X	X		X	X	X	X	X
Golden Delicious	X		X	X			O	X		X	X	X	X	X	X		X	X	X	X	X
Honey Crisp	X	X	X	X	X	X	X			X	X	X	X	X	X		X	X	X	X	X
Jonagold	X	X	X	X	X	X		X		X	X	X	X	X	X		X	X	X	X	X
Jonamac	X	X	X	X	X	X	X	X			X	X	X	X	X		X	X	X	X	X
Jonathan	X	X	X	X	X	X	X	X	X			X	X	X	X		X	X	X	X	X
Lodi	X	X	X	X	X	X	X	X		X	X	O	X	X	X		X	X	X	X	X
McIntosh	X	X	X	X	X	X	X	X		X	X	X		X	X		X	X	X	X	X
Paulared	X	X	X	X	X	X	X	X		X	X	X	X		X		X	X	X	X	X
Red Delicious	X	X	X	X	X	X	X	X		X	X	X	X	X			X	X	X	X	X
Red Gravenstein	X	X	X	X	X	X	X	X		X	X	X	X	X	X		X	X	X	X	X
Spartan	X	X	X	X	X	X	X	X		X	X	X	X	X	X			X	X	X	X
Tydemans's Early	X	X	X	X	X	X	X	X		X	X	X	X	X	X		X		X	X	X
Tydeman's Red	X	X	X	X	X	X	X	X		X	X	X	X	X	X		X	X	O	X	X
Winter Banana	X	X	X	X	X	X	X	X		X	X	X	X	X	X		X	X	X		X
Yellow Transparent	X	X	X	X	X	X	X	X		X	X	X	X	X	X		X	X	X	X	O

credit: WSU Master Gardner publication C105

Figure 12: However, if you have plenty of room, here is a chart of apple trees that can be used as pollinizers:

X = Acceptable Pollinizer, O = Partially self- fruitful, but a pollinizer is suggested, o = Should not be relied upon as a pollinizer for this cultivar.

Compiled by Tonie Fitzgerald. For the Washington State University Master Gardeners. Jan. 2005.

The good news is you can cheat a little and save labor if you plant one of the nearly curl-free peach trees. The peaches 'Frost', 'Indian Free' (excellent), 'White' (best), 'Muir', 'Peregrine', 'Redhaven' (good), 'Q-1-8 White Peach', and 'Salish Summer' are all good choices.

Barreled Fruit Trees

Is your yard very small? Only got a deck, patio or driveway to grow on? Then columnar apple trees, a relatively new phenomenon, are for you. These trees have vertical trunks with no branches, and the fruit clusters along the trunk. There also are columnar pear, peach, plum, and cherry trees.

These are great fruit trees for containers—wine-barrel halves, large pottery or any kind of bigger container. One variety is even called 'Urban Apple'. The apples aren't self-fertile but the peaches and some cherries. (But cherries tend to fruit better with a pollinizer) are. Still, even planting two varieties for pollination doesn't take much space. (As another fantastic value, some columnar trees are self-fertile—so you don't need two different trees.) The apple trees are grafted onto a hardy rootstock called MM106 and grow about eight feet tall. In the ground the apple trees can be planted as close as two feet apart. Be forewarned, these new apple trees are not up to par with some other apples for flavor. Try to taste one first before buying and planting a columnar tree.

Eating only fruit won't keep you alive. But boy, is it a great way to lounge in edible paradise. For relaxed pleasure and satisfaction, I recommend at least one small fruit tree in your planting area.

The Climate is Changing, Chill Out

Fruit trees need some rest (a nap, as it were) each winter before they leaf out and fruit. This rest is called the "chill factor." It is calculated as the sum of the number of hours below 45°F from autumn leaf-fall to spring bud-break. Symptoms of not getting enough chill are:

• Delayed, reduced, or no foliation (leafing out)
• Reduced fruit set, and buttoning (Buttons are flowers which have set but never develop into full-size fruit)
• Reduced fruit quality

It's very important in mild-winter areas to know the chill factor for each tree so it gets enough cold weather to set a good crop. How do you find the chill factor for the tree you want to plant? Certain catalogs now list the chill factor of each variety, or, contact your local Master Gardeners. (If they can't tell you, fire them.)

UC Davis provides the chill factors for many of the cities in California. Here's the list for my county (Sonoma County, 60 miles North of San Francisco):

Chill, in Hours

Bennett Valley	1148
Petaluma East	2341
Santa Rosa	1184 (where I live)
Windsor	1076

Each tree's chill factor is different. Here is a range for various fruit trees, in hours:

- Apples and Pears: 100–2200
- Apricots, Peaches, Nectarines:
                                                      300–1500
- Japanese or Asian Plums: 300–1500
- European Prune Plums: 500–1700
- Persimmons: 300–600

With apples as an example, here is a short list of low-chill trees:

- Arkansas Charm: 400
- Pink Lady: 400–500
- Cameo, Fuji, Pink Pearl: 600
- Braeburn, Gravenstein, Yellow Newtown Pippin: 700
- Hauer Pippin, Sierra Beauty: 700–800
- Honey Crisp, Idared: 800
- Bramley's: 800–1000
- Golden Delicious: 700
- Jonagold (and related strains): 700–800
- McIntosh: 800

For a good list for all types of low-chill fruit, see: *Reliable Fruit Tree Varieties for Santa Cruz County.* From: News & Notes, of the UCSC Farm & Garden Issue 132, Winter 2012.

Now that the climate is changing, we need to be more accurate about the chill factor. With warmer winters, more and more trees don't get enough chill to fruit properly. If your tree needed a chill of 800 hours or less five years

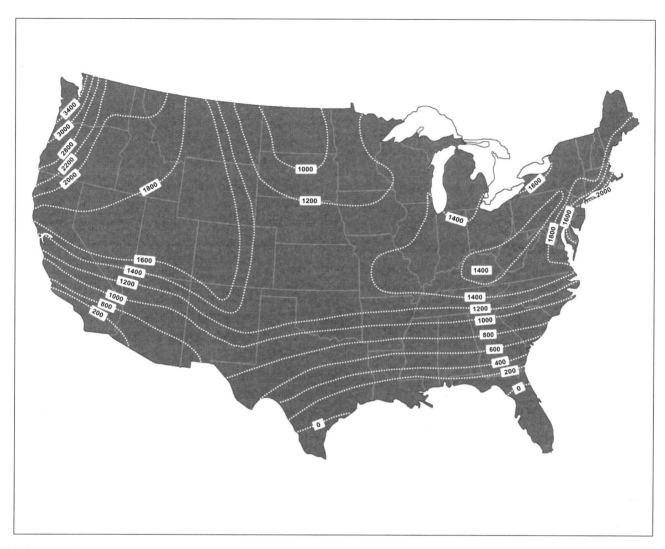

Figure 13: This is a general map of the United State's chill factors. There are many microclimates that require adjusting the chill factor. Contact your local Cooperative Extension or Master Gardeners to learn the specifics of chill hours in your area.

ago, your yard may now, due to climate change, have a chill factor of 500-600 hours now. This means that trees you planted to match the chill of 800 no longer fruit well, and you need trees with a chill factor of at least 500 hours. I plant a range of fruit trees, with a bias to planting slightly higher chill factor trees. Or plant ones with a wider range of chill hours. (See the list above.)

Good Grafting

Do you have room for a full-sized fruit tree? Do you come home from work to find 300 pounds

of ripe apples? Do you feel guilty when you don't can all of them? Be guilt-free. Graft a number of fruits onto the same tree. You'll have less fruit, but will eat guilt-free in many different seasons of the year. (See Figure 14.)

Grafting is not that difficult. Start with apple trees. For a simple booklet on grafting, look for: *Grafting Fruit Trees*: Storey's Country Wisdom Bulletin A-35; Jan 6, 1981, by Larry Southwick.

If you aren't inclined to learn a new garden skill

that requires you to stand in the sun and reach up into a tree, find someone you can pay to do the grafting. Happily for the lazy gardener, more and more nurseries are selling trees with two or three kinds of fruit on the same tree, but if you graft you can easily have more varieties than that. I grafted my apple tree produce eight types of apples, so I graze throughtout the fruiting season into October, eating a few pounds each month or so, with no guilt about not canning.

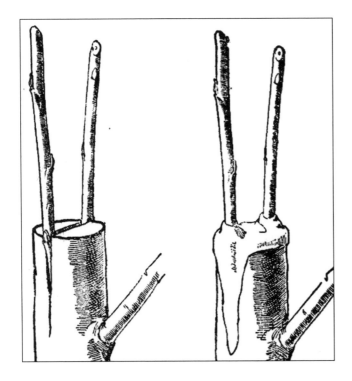

Figure 14: On the left two pieces of an apple variety (called scions) are being grafted to the branch of an existing tree. The scions are trimmed so that when placed into the branch's slit the cambiums touch. On the right is the black pruning tar that is used to seal the graft so it doesn't dry out.

CHAPTER 5

Tillage: From Some to None

**Superb soil without toil is a wonderful goal—
and you can achieve it with these correct and
thoughtful techniques.**

Double Digging – Not

Digging of any kind is hard work. Double digging is much more than double the effort. So this method would appear to be inappropriate for a book about laid-back gardening. Sometimes, however, your soil will be so bad that a few years of double digging can speed up the path to no-till gardening, then you can cruise with much less effort. Double digging can therefore be seen as a means to an end—the end of tillage.

It requires a tremendous amount of effort. Double-digging proponent John Jeavons estimates the initial preparation of a 100-square-foot bed takes six to 14 hours. Two to four of these hours are spent double digging. (Subsequent digging might take three hours.) Holy cow!! He forgot to mention how many sodas or beers you'll get through. (Although it does save you from needing to go to the gym.)

Besides, the way to properly double-dig is rather complicated and precise—beyond the scope of this book, as you'd have to really not be a lazybones to pull this off. It would be best to learn from a practioner. If you can't find a mentor, use Jeavons' book *How to Grow More Vegetables, (and Fruits, Nuts, Berries, Grains, and Other Crops) Than You Ever Thought Possible on Less Land Than You Can Imagine.*

Also, double digging is not appropriate in areas that are hot, windy, desert-like and plagued by hot winds. In such places, gardeners use sunken beds instead. (These are called "waffle gardens" by the Zuni Indians.) (See: *Extreme Gardening: How to Grow Organic in the Hostile Deserts*, David Owens, Poco Verde Landscape, 2000. And *Growing Food in a Hotter, Drier Land—Lessons from Desert Farmers on Adapting to Climate*, Gary Nabhan, Chelsea Green Publishing, 2013.)

 Bob sez: *BUT, and it's a truly big but, if you double dig, you need to live with a chiropractor or have a very good back. Don't forget good health insurance. I'm not being funny. This technique is mostly for young people in very good shape.*

Figure 15: Here we see a waffle garden as used in the Southwest. The planting areas are lower than the walkways so the hot winds are less harmful.

On the Hole...

Digging a hole (by hand; heavy machinery compacts the soil and defeats the purpose in more ways than I even want to think about) obviously requires heavy-duty, bent-over labor. Heaven forbid! But if you want, for example, decades' worth of delicious tree-ripened fruit, ya gotta dig at least once.

The Hole Scoop on Planting

Digging a hole seems like a simple task, but a poorly dug hole will have a detrimental effect on a tree for decades, or may even kill it.

Why is this? As mentioned elsewhere in this book, the roots of most trees and shrubs will, if planted in clayey soil and unrestricted, grow to be 1.5 times wider underground than the circumference of the leafy canopy (dripline), and up to 3 times wider in sandy soil. (See Figure 5, 17, 33 and 34)

Take, for instance, a wonderful shade tree like a pin oak (*Quercus palustris*) with a 40-foot canopy spread. This tree will grow its roots into an area as much as 60 feet in diameter in clay soil and 120 feet wide in sandy soil! When planting a tree or shrub, your goal is to encourage its roots to grow beyond the planting hole and into the native soil as quickly as possible, so here's the scoop: the dimensions of even a well-dug hole have little influence on the growth of the tree. (In this case, size doesn't matter.)

Dig your planting hole when the soil is slightly moist, but not at all wet. Turning over a shovelful of wet clay soil causes the plate-like structure of the clay to compress, expelling air and further destroying what little loose structure the soil may have had. The result is a stickier, more anaerobic, clayey soil—conditions tough on the young root hairs of transplants. Sandier soils can be worked when more moisture is present in them.

You can tell if conditions are good for digging when a shovelful of soil placed on the ground will crumble if tapped slightly by the shovel blade. But to actually dig the hole, use a spading fork with forged tines (for description about

 Bob sez: *A spading fork of forged metal cost me a lot—about $100. (I only buy Bulldog brand forged tools. They have over two hundred years of history making them.) Don't go cheap on this important tool that you'll be using a lot for a very long time. Cheap forks can snap off, bend backwards, and/or wind up with tines that look like spaghetti.*

the forged part, see the tool list, page 102 Figure 38). This will keep the sides of the hole cracked and irregular, and prevents them from getting slick.

Make your hole only as deep and wide as is needed to fit the well-spread-out root system of the tree or shrub. (Some researchers found that a hole much wider than it is deep is also helpful, but if your rootstock is well chosen for the soil, a wider hole isn't worth the effort.) In the case of balled-and-burlapped plants, the hole must be wide enough for you to pack the soil around the ball (and to be prudent, you should cut off any wire used to hold the root ball and the burlap together).

It's also important to remember to finish off the hole by using the spading fork to fracture the sides and bottom. This provides nooks and crannies for the young root hairs to grab onto when they're creeping out of the hole and into the native soil.

No Amendments Are Good Amendments

• Amendments are materials, such as sand, peat moss, compost, and rice hulls, that are added to a planting hole to improve drainage and keep the soil loose and friable.

• Fertilizers are substances like blood meal, cottonseed meal, greensand, and wood ashes (or, yuck, even commercial fertilizers) that are added mostly to provide nutrients. Some amendments, such as compost, also act as mild fertilizers.

One of the best studies of the effect of amendments for fertility was done at Oklahoma State University at Stillwater by Joseph Schulte and Carl Whitcomb way back in 1973-1976. They found that control plantings of trees with no additional amendments generally outperformed all plantings that had different types of amendments added as tests for drainage and fertility.

The fact is that when it rains hard, loose, over-amended soil becomes something like an underground swimming pool full of water, drowning those all-important root hairs. In addition, adding a lot of amendments only leaves the roots unprepared for the shock of what lies beyond the amended area; often they'll fail to make it out of the well-amended hole and merely circle around in the loose planting medium. Without extending roots growing out past the planting hole, trees may likely blow over in a storm. The trees most tolerant to wind are those with the widest root systems (not, to the surprise of some, those with a deep single taproot; less than two percent of trees actually have taproots).

Sandy soil can tolerate more amendments because the structure before and after planting isn't so different. However, since the fiber of the amendments tends to absorb plenty of water, adding a lot of them to drought-prone sandy soils will concentrate the roots in the moister amended area, and, again, leave the tree vulnerable to wind damage.

No Fertilizer Is Good Fertilization

As mentioned earlier, roots are relatively lazy; they feed where it's easiest, and fertilizers encourage the roots to stay in the planting hole. Compost, especially in quantity, turns out to be one of the worst additions when planting trees, because it's both an amendment and a fertilizer. If you absolutely feel you must fertilize, add the material to the soil surface way beyond the planting hole to encourage the roots to spread into the native unamended soils.

Unlike us, Mother Nature doesn't use a shovel; she builds soil from the top down with the decomposition of carbonaceous materials such as fallen leaves and decaying grasses, as well as various forms of poop. In addition, there's a lot going on, root-wise, beneath the surface of the soil that helps it improve without cultivation.

• The activities of roots loosen the soil.

• The roots of nitrogen-fixing plants add nitrogen.

• "Compost" is created as roots rot at all levels to create decomposed organic matter for the use of other plants and microbes.

• Nutrients cycle from root systems to the foliage of plants (and back to the earth again as leaf, stem, branch and trunk litter).

• Roots develop tunnels for the movement of earthworms.

• Root canals (the soil kind) help rainwater soak into deeper areas; and root exudates create a microbial "soup" that helps to liberate all manner of nutrients. (And all of this is happening while you're napping or driving to the supermarket to get some ice cream!)

Planting Success by Heaps and Mounds

Magnificent Compost Mounds

The entry path to my front door used to be a swampy spot during heavy winter rains. To re-route the surface runoff without complicated drainage piping, I began forming a mounded planting area (known as a "berm") along each side of the path and dug a shallow "creeklet" or "swale"— on the far side of the berm to carry off water during heavy rains. (A swale is a low or hollow place between areas of higher ground.)

This was originally an experiment in no-till gardening, an attempt to learn more ways to improve soil and drainage. In the process, however, I discovered that you can just construct piles of all kinds of agricultural and garden "wastes" and grow beautiful ornamentals on them.

To begin these original mounds, I piled horse-stable sweepings (mostly manure and straw) and turkey bedding (rice hulls, some sand, and turkey poop) into a shaped mound about 18 inches high and over three feet wide, and watered the entire thing thoroughly. Then I added a six- to eight—inch "cap" of topsoil —a one-time effort.

This mounding approach is like building a very large, low-heat compost pile with a safe, neutral cap of soil into which you can plant directly. Mounds are much like great heaps of "sheet compost"—thin layers of compostable materials. The root hairs of plants will follow right behind the warm decomposition and won't grow into areas that are still too hot for them as a result of composting activity. The plants also get some benefit from the heat the mound generates, much like bottom-heated greenhouse flats.

In the spot where each plant was to be placed, I made a large pocket of good mellow soil to receive the roots. Here's how to do it: simply pull back a bit of the neutral, native-soil "cap," make a small pyramid of cap soil, spread the roots over the pyramid, and cover them with soil from the six- to eight-inch cap.

After planting, water everything again, then cover the mounds with 5-10 sheets of newspaper, topped with four or more inches of composted stuff like weed-free turkey bedding.

Planting on Chips n' Chunks

As I experimented more with mounding, I started using fresh chunky wood chips mixed with green leaves and twigs from local tree-trimming services. (The best chips for this purpose are from hardwoods.) Two things to avoid:

1. Any shredded material that might easily re-sprout—willows, acacias, alders, or various vines.

2. Plants with foliage that stunts or kills the growth of other nearby plants: black walnut (*Juglans nigra*), and sagebrush (*Artemisia californica*). In certain areas of the southwest, you may need to watch out for mesquite (*Prosopis glandulosa torreyana*).

Also, if you're constructing mounds with arbor mulch, don't insert any of the roots of the new plant into the leaves and chips, as the plant will suffer from a loss of nitrogen.

Over time, the arbor-mulch chips and leaves will rot like a slow, cool compost pile. The roots of your plant will follow behind the rotting mixture and will only grow into the well-decomposed material. (To plant shrubs and trees on a fully composted soil mound, see pages 57 through 59 for the details.)

If you can't get a fresh load of green chippings, use mixed sizes of woody chips. Because the chips are so high in carbon, it's good to layer or mix them with some manure. Start your mound with the chunkiest, largest-sized pieces to keep

the bottom of the pile from settling too much. For all of the subsequent layers, use a blend of smaller chips, ½ inch to 6 inches long, and "juicy" stuff—fresh grass clippings; green-manure crops such as buckwheat, vetch, bell beans, and clover; wet kitchen garbage or scraps; and green weeds from the garden.

I've experimented with a ratio of four parts green matter to one part wood chips, and found that the more nitrogen (green material, manure, or fertilizer) you add, the faster the mound will decompose and the greater the nitrogen supply for the growing plants will accumulate. You should pile this mixture of high-carbon and high-nitrogen materials at least 1/3 higher than you want the final soil level to be. Depending on the types of materials used, the mound may settle as much as 30-50 percent.

Now make a soil cap at least four inches thick on top of all this (the thicker, the better; again a one-time digging job.) For good drainage, a normal soil temperature and good initial growth, use native soil gathered from around the garden. It's best to take earth from the area next to the mound, and create a small serpentine streambed, so that as you add soil to the top of the mound the swale (drainage area) gets deeper at the same time. This doubles the depth of the swale (for better drainage during heavier rains) as the mound is built.

Eventually, within four or five years, my "research mound" chips decomposed; the soil settled to a lower level (less than 12 inches high); the shrubs rooted fully into the native soil, and the new mound became a wonderful, curvilinear feature alongside a new little "creeklet."

So, as a result of all this experimentation, mounded plantings, which seemed to me to be a heap of contradiction at first, have become one of my preferred techniques for quick soil development. They are also a cheap way to create "instant" soil drainage, an aesthetically pleasing way to design a

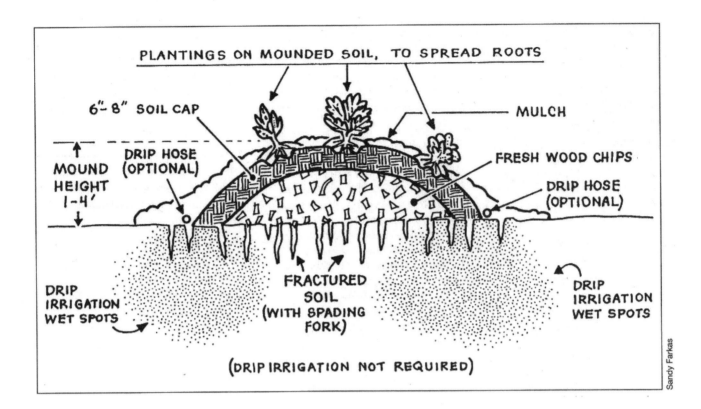

Figure 16: I use arbor chips (a mixture of shredded leaves and wood chips) to make a mound that's used to form drainage and and eventually compost. Use arbor chips as soon as you get them so they are moist. The mound is covered with four- to eight-inches of topsoil. Plant into the topsoil after making the mound. I don't need drip irrigation if I plant just as the winter rain begins.

gently meandering topography, and a great way to establish a truly drought-resistant landscape.

With mounds, I've been able to plant within the natural flow of the seasonal cycles for my microclimate. I didn't water my garden in Occidental for over 33 years—not even in the all-dry summers. And no drip irrigation, even though I wrote the "Bible" on it—*Drip Irrigation for Every Landscape and All Climates, 2nd Edition.* (Might as well boast and lure you to buy one—from my website, not from you-know-who.) Another important component of learning how to grow without irrigation was to discover it was essential to plant *only* in the fall as the rains begin, and then mulch deeply. And, of course, I had to select the most drought-resistant plants.

Planting on a composting mound is reserved for smaller plants like perennials in one-gallon pots or four-inch containers.

I use mounds most often for perennials, herbs, and sub-shrubs like lavender, but mounding is also by far the easiest way to plant shrubs and trees. (You'll trade off actual hole-digging for lots of scrabbling around with a pitchfork and scraping with a shovel.)

First off, It's important to know that many ornamental and fruiting trees are prone to dying of crown rot (*Phytophthora* spp.)—a fungal disease of the upper portion of the roots near the soil surface—without the gardener even suspecting the culprit. The fungus damages the sapwood of the tree, either killing limbs or the entire plant. Once the symptoms appear (pale-yellow, wilted leaves), it's too late to do anything. Observant horticulturists have noticed that the trees that survive this disease were either in very well-drained soil or were planted on mounds. Because the crown-rot fungus thrives in damp and warm soil, mound-planting acts as preventative engineering in climates where it rains during the summer.

Mound Planting for Trees

To understand planting, you need to understand how roots grow. Contrary to the common misconception (that the size of a tree's root structure mirrors that of the foliage canopy), the roots of a tree will often grow to extend half again as wide as the foliage canopy in heavy, clayey soils and three times wider than the foliage in loose, sandy soils. This means tree roots usually want to grow far out beyond the biggest planting hole you could possibly dig. (See Figure 5, P. 27.)

Tree roots do their "grazing" near the surface of the soil, not down deep. The top two feet of the soil provides well over fifty percent of the water and nutrients for good, healthy growth. The deeper roots gather some nutrients and moisture during droughts and help to anchor the tree. Tree roots, however, tend to dawdle; they'll feed where the eatin' is best and the easiest. If you put a big pile of compost and fertilizer in a planting hole, the roots will simply colonize the hole and happily pig out on the convenient feast. If the goal is to naturalize a tree, don't serve it a huge "breakfast" and then expect it to find lunch and dinner outside the planting hole all on its own. Save your compost for the vegetables.

(For instructions for planting a bare root tree, look here and on the next page for the part about planting on a small volcano of soil.)

Planting on a 12- to 18-inch raised mound of well-drained soil will protect roots from crown rot, insure the tree's survival and encourage superior growth. If you have sandy soil, a raised planting area isn't necessary. Even in arid areas, you needn't worry about the mound drying out and killing the young tree because, due to the natural vigor of the roots, as described above, they will quickly grow beyond the planting hole and the mound. Remember, a 12- to 18-inch planting mound is more important than a hole.

Bare Root Mound

If you're planting a bare root tree on an 18-inch-high mound, you don't even need a planting hole, but be sure to soak it in water while you're making the mound. This rehydrates the tissue and washes off any odd matter clinging to the roots.

Remove all the grass and weeds from the four-foot diameter of the mound-to-be. Then, with a spading fork, heave and crack the native soil within the entire circle—don't turn or till it. Now, scrape up good soil from the surrounding area (after the weeds have been skimmed off) and make a small cone of soil, about 24 or more inches wide and 12-18 inches tall, in the center of the circle. Then spread the roots of the bare root tree over the top of this cone. (You can use this technique with container-grown or tube-grown plants, but make sure to tear apart any well-knitted roots, knock off most of the planting mix, and spread out any circling roots on the soil cone.)

Either way, make sure some of the exposed roots are tucked into the native soil that was fractured open with the spading fork. After the tree roots are spread evenly out on the cone of soil, gather plenty of topsoil to form the rest of the mound. Cover the base of the trunk of the tree to the same depth as it was in the nursery growing grounds; this will be indicated by a marked change in color on the trunk. Tamp the soil with your shoes to eliminate air pockets that can dry out young roots.

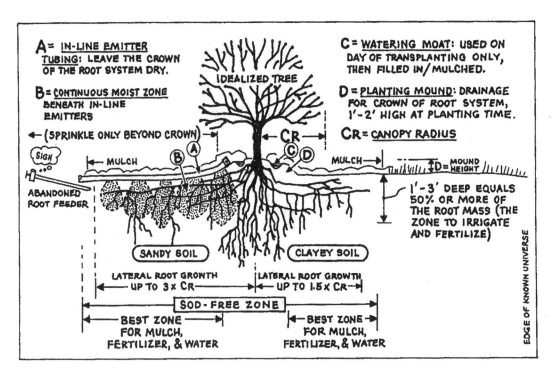

Figure 17: Inhale, breath out. Relax, this is a lot of info. But you can come back to it a number of times and get more out of it. It's important to see that the tree is planted on a mound. This also shows the root ratios—sandy soil has roots up to three times wider than the Canopy radius (Cr). In clay, it's 1.5 times the Cr. Mulch beyond the dripline.

 Bob sez: *Alas, if you have gophers, a big hole is needed to allow for a protective wire basket. The bigger the basket, the more roots you'll protect from these hungry little devils. Be sure the upper edge of the basket sticks at least six inches above the soil and mulch to keep nocturnally wandering gophers from climbing inside your secured perimeter. For the wire basket, simply dig a hole two to three feet deep and wide, put the basket in and fill the hole again—just like the Army!*

Rake the finished mound to look like a gentle knoll.

After planting, soak the entire mound once or twice, then mulch the mound and beyond about 4 inches deep, making sure that the mulch stays at least 6 to 12 inches away from the trunk.

Incidentally, the greater the drainage, the easier it is to grow plants without irrigation. My theory is that the enhanced drainage allows the roots to quickly and easily follow the dwindling moisture supply down through the earth of the mound.

Heavy clay soils are so stiff they retard the growth of roots, and the moisture can slip away faster than the roots can keep up with.

Carpet Mulching...

Hey, if it's good enough to go under your recliner in your living room, why not use it outdoors?

Knock Back Weeds!

My garden has natural-looking pathways requiring very little maintenance. How do I do this?

Used carpet controls the most stubborn perennial weeds easily—without herbicides.

Forty years ago, there were no commercial fabrics to control perennial weeds like (in my area) blackberry vines and poison oak. Since then, I've found that used carpet is more resistant to these tenacious weeds than most landscape fabrics, not to mention that carpet is free and comes in large pieces.

Synthetic carpets do contain artificial color, plastics, nylon, polyester, poly-vinyl chloride (PVC) and other chemicals. Deborah Lynn Dadd says in *Nontoxic, Natural & Earthwise* (Jeremy P. Tarcher Inc., Los Angeles, CA 1990) "if your carpet is over five years old, chances are a majority of the toxic components have already gassed out." (If you're worried about the possibility of minute traces of chemicals, only use synthetic carpet next to ornamentals.) The most "organic" carpets were/are made from natural wool with a jute backing, or from woven rags, but these will rot faster than modern synthetic carpets. (Also be aware that mothproofing pesticides are used on some recently manufactured wool carpets.)

Used carpet is the most cost-efficient. Scout out floor-covering stores where it's tossed into an outside dumpster. Rent or borrow a pickup truck, because carpet from the store's dumpster is often too bulky for other vehicles, Be sure to ask permission from the store owner to retrieve rolls of discarded carpet; most will be only too happy to have you haul it away. Some may have insurance concerns.

Harvest only dry carpet, as wet carpet is far too heavy. (Wear a good face mask to keep any unknown dusts in the trash bin out of your lungs.)

Also wear gloves and sturdy leather boots—no tennis shoes here!

Protect your back by getting someone else to help you lift the carpet. Watch out for sharp and hazardous objects—the used strips of board used to hold down the carpet at the walls are loaded with nails. As with some other inspired-laziness efforts in this book, a hassle at the beginning produces a constructive effect for decades. So, get off your heinie, grab a friend or two (or more), find a pickup truck, and locate a well-carpeted dumpster. (It may be illegal in some cities to "dumpster dive" for used carpet, so then it's off to flea markets and garage sales to find some.)

Carpets from an entire room can be really heavy. If your back is not up to the effort, go to flea market and garage sales looking for smaller carpets or some rugs. You may be able to find rugs made of cotton, isal, jute, rags or wool. Smaller carpets or rugs means you needn't scout around for a pickup truck, as they can fit into a regular car or SUV. If you're piecing together several rugs, make sure the edges overlap by six inches or more so weeds don't crawl through the edge cracks.

Rug Recipe

To prepare the area where the carpet is to be laid down, use a 2-cycle string mower, (a WeedEater® or similar machine) or a machete to chop down all the unwanted plants to the ground. Then spread one or more inches of manure over the entire area to help rot the chopped foliage. Don't even bother to dig up the root crowns of perennial weeds.

Roll out the carpet with the backing face up, and cut or trim it with a sharp garden knife or machete. Be sure to overlap carpet edges by at least one foot to keep vining and twining weeds from snaking through the places where sections join. Secure the corners and edges of the carpet with nine-inch landscape-irrigation stakes every three feet. Next, cover the carpet with four or more inches of chipped tree trimmings or a wood-based landscape mulch. Although you can use mulches other than wood chips. I like the informal woodsy effect, especially when it's achieved with free chips from a tree-arbor service.

Replenish the chips as they compress, decompose, or move around. All of the mulch options I've listed will eventually decompose. On several occasions over the years, I've use a flat-bottomed

 Bob sez: Most discarded carpets (some with some very "interesting" smells) are made from synthetic fibers which do not easily biodegrade. These were good for my paths since I wanted to suppress those nasty perennial root systems for as long as possible. Polyester and nylon carpets can resist the regrowth of weeds for many decades. The pathway at my house is 30 years old.

 Bob sez: I once rolled one corner of a carpet mulch back after about four years and found pure-white blackberry vines, still rambling around trying to reach sunlight. Now, after 40 years, not a single blackberry vine or poison-oak shrub has re-emerged. If your yard or garden is infested with such persistent weeds, the carpet method sure beats having to get off your butt and out of your air-conditioned house to dig out all the roots and counter the constant regrowth from the invasive plants' gnarly sprouting nodes or root crowns.

shovel to scoop up what amounts to almost-finished compost from my carpet-mulched paths. (Since the carpet is "upside down" the backing is usually a nicely smooth surface.) Replace the mulch with more chipped tree trimmings or bark chips.

Pull any weeds that blow in and sprout. Get them when they're young, so their roots don't get a grip on the carpet or sprout in any dust that has settled in. In areas that receive summer rains, you may try using a special propane torch to burn back the young sprouts—ideally you boil the water out of the tissue; you don't need to fry them to a crisp. This works especially well with monocotyledon seedlings. (Monocots are plants, such as grasses, with parallel veins running along the leaves.) Organic garden suppliers list products such the Garden Weed Destroyer Torch™, with a one-inch opening to work on tight places near the edges of the carpeted area. Or, if you've got Star Wars fantasies, you can get a larger model with enough flame-blast to whack back intruding weeds in larger carpet-mulched areas. (See Figure 18 for an "industrial-strength" version.)

Be sure to flame those weeds only after a rain, while the mulch is soaking wet; you should also have a hose nearby and a friend on hand to keep an eye out for and extinguish smoking embers. Be careful to not singe nearby plantings. Also be aware that the larger torches sound like a jet plane. Warn your neighbors and wear earplugs.

Carpets for Vegetables? Could Be

Now for the slightly odd but supposedly convenient gardening method called "Carpet Gardening". I stumbled across this book in the shelves of the UC Berkeley campus agricultural library in the 1970s —decades before the Internet.

The title is *The Carpet Garden* by Renee and Steve Rockmore from upstate New York, and it was published in 1978 by Harper & Row. The grandiose subtitle is *The Answer to No-Work Vegetable Gardening for Less Than $5 per Summer* (obviously 1970s prices). They came up with the $5 by averaging tthe cost of the carpet over 20 years! Great optimists.

The Rockmores' basic modus operandi was to fertilize and till the soil (they used a rototiller), rake the surface even, roll out some indoor/outdoor carpet, water the carpet and proceed to cut a long tiny 1/2- to 1-inch-wide strip for carrots and beets. They cut three-inch circular holes for crops like tomatoes, eggplant, cucumbers, kale, peas, peppers and such, planted the seed, weeded along the strip if need be, watered if needed (they live in a New York rainy, summer climate), picked the veggies, and when the last plants in the garden had been harvested, they pulled up the carpet, dried it on a clothesline, then rolled it up and put it in the garage for the winter! This is not a no-till garden, but nearly a no-weed garden. They obviously live in a cold-weather climate and don't grow any winter vegetables.

They claim that this kind of garden requires only 10% of the effort of "traditional" gardens and the yields are four times higher. The key here, I think, is that the comparison is to the old-

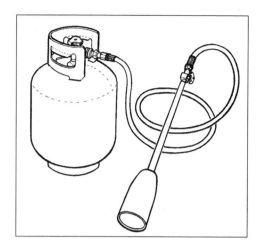

Figure 18: This is the "industrial strength" propane weeder. Kills weeds with a *lot* of flame. But it is very heavy and as loud as a jet engine.

fashioned approach, gardens with large rototilled spaces between the rows. (These two statistics were obviously arrived at before the French-Intensive Biodynamic—with its raised beds— "revolution" hit America.)

The Rockmores hate mulches such as hay, leaves, straw, and a dozen more options because they find them to be short-lived and ugly. (There's even a photograph of Renee sweeping the carpet while

 Bob sez: *I have not tried this method with vegetables other than with trailing winter squashes and for permanent use under perennial shrubs and trees. I once used a large 16' by 16' used carpet—with the backing facing up—with a hole for planting a mound with squash. This maintained a tidy area that kept the fruit off of the soil so it didn't rot. In one of my gardens with regular soil—no carpet—a gopher came up through the bottom of the fruit and hollowed it out. When I went to harvest—nothing but a pathetic empty rind! Carpet stops such pilfering while simultaneously controlling weeds.*

the plants are growing!) They used a type of indoor/outdoor needle-punched carpet called Ozite that is no longer available. The current versions of indoor/outdoor carpets come with a rubberized back, which the Rockmores claim won't work because "If you purchase a carpet with (a rubber) backing on it…you will get root rot…(and) your onions will turn to slime."

The Rockmores say, without a control study, that the carpet seems to keep pests like slugs, cutworms, and aphids away. (No mention of the dreaded earwig.) Caution should be advised. Maybe a small test area is the best way to proceed, especially in warm winter areas where pests aren't knocked back by freezing temperatures. This peculiar method might be just the right approach for the right person (perhaps someone who's a little OCD) but it would be an interesting experiment: a garden concept far, far away, where few have gone before.

Although outgassing may release many of these chemicals, (if you believe this, you may want to use the 100% polypropylene carpeting and mulch it to hide it from your organic-gardening friends); there are several alternatives: buy a new wool carpet with a jute backing (expect to pay Big Bucks, as much as $60 per square yard); go to the local flea market in search of used wool carpeting; or slink around estate sales and grab a natural-fiber rug that's too worn to use in a home. I've reserved the deployment of used carpets to create wood-chip "patios" and pathways.

Of course the Carpet and Rug Institute has another view—including the statement that formaldehyde has not been used in carpet manufacturing "for more than three decades."

Footnote: This approach will outrage a gardener with pure organic intentions. Current indoor carpeting can, according to some, come with a plethora of chemicals: volatile organic compounds (VOCs); ethylbenzene; formaldehyde; methacrylate acid ; methyl methacrylate; acrylic oligomers ; tetrachloroethylene; toluene; xylenes; acetonitrile; azulene; benzene; biphenyl; 2-butyloctanol-1; cyclopentadiene-ethenyl-2-ethylene; 1,3,5-cycloheptatriene; 1-chloronaphthalene; diphenyl ether ; dodecane; 1,4-dihydroxyacenophthene; ethylxylene; 1-ethyl-3-methylbenzene ; hexadecanol ; hexamethylene triamine; 1-h-indene; 1-methylnaphthalene; 2-methylnaphthalene; 1-methyl-3 propylbenzene; 2-methyl-4-tridecene; 5-methyltridecane; octadecenyl amine (oleylamine); oxarium; polyacrylates; 1-phenylcyclopentanol; 2-propylheptanol; phthalic esters; styrene; 1,2,3,-trimethylbenzene; 1,2,4,-trimethylbenzene; tetradecene; 2,3,7-trimethyldecane; undecane, 2,6-dimethyl to name a few. Some of these are thought to be possibly carcinogenic. (Don't let me know if I misspelled any of these chemicals. I don't care.)

Bob sez: *A local carpet salesman recently told me that he takes home carpet samples for his raised beds. So the loose glue, primary backing seems to be no problem in his garden.*

No-Till Gardening

You can kick back even more by getting your garden to the point where you don't have to till it. Tilling (preparing and cultivating soil for crops) is usually done with shovels, hoes, plows, rototillers, harrows, etc., and it greatly affects the amount of much-needed nitrogen in the soil. Too much roughing up your dirt causes its stored nitrogen (the result of natural soil processes) to convert to a gas and escape into the air. Most of it, as the adjacent chart indicates, is found in the upper layers of the soil, vulnerable to tillage methods. (The first six inches of topsoil, well within the reach of a shovel or rototiller, contains 52% of its nitrogen.)

Each spring seems to proclaim: "Get thee outdoors and cultivate," but here are at least three reasons why gardening methods that depend on tilling can be harmful: tillage releases surplus carbon dioxide (a climate-warming gas); cultivation and compaction destroy beneficial soil fungi; and the over-application of nitrogen fertilizers—even manure and compost—can result in their leaching into freshwater supplies. While we assume a plow, shovel, or rototiller is required for a good crop, actual "tillage" seldom happens in Nature. The only natural models are really just spontaneous phenomena like landslides or frost heaving.

There are plenty of advocates for no-till gardening. Many say it mimics nature's way of improving soil from the top down, while others maintain that they're relying on earthworms to do the "tillage" at the speed of nature.

Here's an interesting fact: tilling by artificial means can actually impede the storage of moisture in the soil. Research by Dennis Linden, soil scien-

Bob sez: *Any garden can have a well-laid carpet. At the very least, it's a great way to force certain stubborn weeds into submission. Let your personal view of what's safe in your garden be the guide. I hope I'm just giving you some informed choices.*

tist at the USDA Agricultural Research Station in St. Paul, MN, found that the common earthworm (*Aporrectodea tuberculata*) working under tilled soil forms a pattern of meandering tunnels that slows the absorption of moisture. Worms wiggling around under plots with no tillage, however (in this study), formed "a network of vertical burrows (from night crawlers), and depressions, (from common earthworms), (that) tends to funnel water

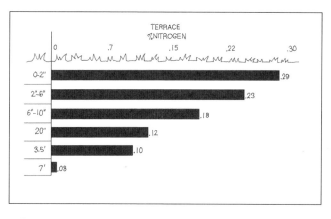

Figure 19: The percentage of nitrogen in the first two inches of the soil is .29. Going down to the two- to six-inch zone is a drop of eight percent. From the six- to 10-inch zone it's another eight percent drop. This shows how important the upper soil is. Tilling the top six inches of soil can release 52 percent of the soil's nitrogen into the air.

Bob sez: *If you ask me, all gardening, especially food gardening, is an unnatural process. Nobody is "healing the Earth" by cultivating and fertilizing vegetables, and such gardens may be among the most environmentally damaging land interactions (OK, not so bad as agribusiness, strip mining, or clearing the way for condominiums, but still). The gardener may be having fun, getting some exercise, and harvesting tasty, nutritious vegetables and fruits; but the best situation, as far as Nature is concerned, is probably no gardening at all. (Just sayin'.)*

rapidly downward through (and into) soil layers."

According to Linden, who (bravo!) cares for his own garden with layers of organic mulch and compost made from his household food waste, the use of no-till methods "means the soil absorbs water faster, and encourages keeping it in the soil as a reservoir. This stored moisture in the soil provides another measure of drought resistance..."

Here's another fact to support the value of no-till gardening. The earth's soil naturally contributes ten times more carbon dioxide to the atmosphere (60 billion tons of carbon per year) than all of humankind's activity—this odorless gas comes from the myriad of creatures which inhabit the soil—microbes, pill bugs, worms, fungi, and algae—as they breathe, "pass gas," and expire.

Until recently, the increase in carbon dioxide gas produced by small-scale tillage was compensated for by the natural reabsorption of plants. Now, according to Professor of Biology Tyler Volk at New York University, tillage is a large contributor to the current surplus of carbon dioxide in the earth's atmosphere. When soil is stripped of its living cover in order to grow crops, up to one-fourth of its stored carbon is lost in the form of carbon dioxide and, with today's agricultural methods,

most of this squandered carbon is never replaced. The warming of the bare soil by sunlight also speeds up the activity and death of soil microorganisms, thus increasing the outgassing of carbon dioxide.

Many gardeners try to compensate by adding large quantities of organic matter or manure purchased or gathered from outside sources, either to make compost or to be tilled directly into their garden plots or flowerbeds. In reality, however, most of these sources (the plant matter, compost, or manure) are really just stored carbon imported from some other place.

To minimize the loss of carbon dioxide from your own garden, there are many types of no-till gardening you can experiment with—deep mulch, sheet composting, straw bales or various methods of mixing native and domesticated edibles and/or wildflowers.

Here's how to ease your way into no-till.

Shallow "Tillage"

A gentler way to garden is known as surface cultivation, and only requires partially bending over and scraping the soil just two to four inches below the surface. No heavy digging or spading. The main tool for this approach (in addition to using your hands to pull weeds or vegetable plants), is in England a "scrapper," (not a typo) which is known in the U.S. as an onion hoe. While most readers will not be growing a marketgarden, I did discover (in 1976!) a fine example of the efficient use of surface cultivation in a commercial setting, which indicates that it can in fact be adapted to a larger scale of planting. With a little creativity, these techniques can be adapted to your garden, and it's a wonderful way to transition to no-till gardening.

This anecdotal evidence was collected from an organic market garden in England with 12 years of experience in surface cultivation. The market gardeners firmly state that "...Preparation for the following crop is one operation with the (scrapper), with the occasional use of a rake, and it should not penetrate the soil more than three-and-one-half inches to four inches for any purpose. "The scrapper is always pulled toward the gardener at a 45-degree angle to its path. The tool is used only to pull, not push soil." The rationale is that "True aeration of the soil is achieved in undisturbed soil..." This is not a pure form of no-till gardening, but comes pretty close.

This garden was not only successful but "Sales were on a competitive basis." The book about this remarkable market garden is entitled – at great length—*Intensive Gardening, using Dutch Lights, Surface Cultivation and Composting for the Commercial Production of Crops, and Introducing a Motion-Study Routine*, by Rosa Dalziel O'Brien, (Faber & Faber Limited, London, UK. 1956.)

The secret of this style of gardening is this: Instead of digging, you'll need to make compost. Compost, compost, and more compost.

O'Brien mentions that it took about three years for the new market garden to make the transition from harboring obnoxious weeds like docks (*Rumex* spp.), thistles, and dandelions to lesser noxious weeds such as nettle, groundsel (a European weed with small yellow flowers, *Senecio vulgaris*) and wild chamomile (probably the low-growing weed *Matricaria discoidea*, not the kind used for tea (*Anthemis noblis*). It took about that same amount of time for the compost and surface cultivation to enrich the soil, increase its population of beneficial bacteria, and enhance its aeration in a natural way. Obviously in this case, patience is a virtue. But hey, no strenuous, sweaty digging needed, and more relaxed gardening over time? It's a win.

O' Brien's compost recipe does include very small amounts of lime, charcoaled wood, and a compost inoculant to speed up the process; also imported, as needed for certain crops were some seaweed,

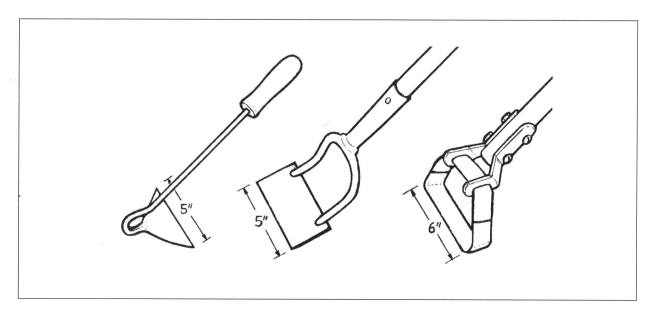

Figure 20: From the left to the right, a scrapper (UK spelling), Dutch scuffle hoe, and Hula Hoe™ (oscillating hoe). The scrapper hoe is called an onion hoe in America. The onion hoe is used with surface cultivation techniques.

old domestic soot (from coal-fired chimneys), granite dust, and silver sand.

One significant one-time "import" into this garden included the purchase of so-called "Dutch lights," panels of glass built to a standardized cold-frame form and set up like tiny greenhouses; these were a traditional feature of Dutch commercial horticulture. This was a crucial aspect of the market farm, as the Dutch lights allowed for an earlier harvest and extended the harvest time beyond that of crops grown in the field. Dutch lights or their equivalents wouldn't be needed in your home garden if you didn't want to push the natural growth cycle of the vegetable.

If a truly sustainable garden is one with virtually

 Bob sez: *No S**t. Amazingly, O'Brien's garden was maintained without the use of any manures. (She was a vegan.) With its limited number of imported items and its calculated non-use of manures ("...(no) animal products or by-products, not even eggshells, were included.")—the fact that this market garden was commercially competitive is truly astonishing. Vegan surface gardening is another way to eliminate tedious, tiring trips to the horse, goat and cow stalls for stinky manure, or schlepping home heavy sacks of manure from the garden center.*

no "imports," surface cultivation as practiced by O'Brien comes pretty close. And she was doing it many decades before the word "sustainable" was "invented."

A Fickle Way to No-Till
Barb Fick, formerly a community horticulturist with the Benton County office of the Oregon State University Extension Service, says she's maintained her large vegetable garden by the no-dig

method for many years. Not only does it use less water, she says, it also discourages weeds, improves the soil, and reduces labor needed for both tilling and weeding.

In Fick's experience, as described in the article *Mulch is a key to no-till gardens* of the OSU Extension, "The crux of no-till gardening is to pile on enough mulch to keep weeds from germinating and growing up through it. If you use leaves, grass clippings or straw, you might need as much as eight to 10 inches of mulch. If you start out on the bare ground with some-

 Bob sez: *If you haven't much extraneous plant material in your yard or garden, offer to take your neighbors' unwanted grass clippings, leaf rakings, non-woody trimmings, and other good potential composting materials off their hands.*

thing more solid, like cardboard or 10 sheets of newspaper, you'll need fewer inches of leaves or grass clippings on top. Whatever you use, don't skimp on mulch—it keeps the underlying soil moist. Since you're not tilling, you're not bringing old weed seeds up to the surface where they can germinate."

To start a new no-till garden, carefully lay out the paths between the spaces marked out for the beds—the path soil will be compacted by foot traffic, and that helps reduce weeds. (Don't forget to make the paths wide enough to mow.) Lay the beds out so you can easily reach any part of them from a nearby path. Avoid stepping onto the bed area—it compacts the soil.

Mulch lavishly, as described above. When planting time comes around, pull the mulch layer to the side of the space in which you want to put your seeds or vegetable transplants, and add some soil or compost directly to the soil where you want to plant (during the first year, you may also need to pull out dead roots). Incorporate any dead vegetation into the mulch layer, and water under the newspaper and mulch with drip irrigation.

Barbara Fick notes that: "Over time, the mulch layers you keep adding will form enough soil to support your garden., and the soil formed by the addition of so much organic matter will likely be loose, full of earthworms and teeming with

the healthy microbes that make nutrients available to your plants."

Yikes! Another citation: In a paper published in Rome in 2005 (*The Importance Of Soil Organic Matter, The Key To Drought-Resistant Soil And Sustained Food And Production*, by Alexandra Bot, a Consultant for the Food and Agriculture Organization of the United Nations, and José Benites, FAO Land and Plant Nutrition Management Service), found "a 200–300-percent increase in population size of root nodule (nitrogen-fixing) bacteria in a zero-tillage system compared with conventional tillage."

It's simple: when you till, you tear up roots. Most of the nitrogen-fixing bacteria are found on the upper part of the root system—the top 12 inches or so—and tillage can disturb the roots as far down as eight inches, When you dig, plow, or rototill, it's goodbye to many of the beneficial nodules (they can repopulate the roots, but it takes awhile).

Ruth Stout's No-Till Method

Ruth Stout (1884-1980) was known in America as the grande dame of no-till gardening with the use of deep-hay mulching. She published three classic books of gardening instructions and anecdotal musings; her first was *How to have a Green Thumb without an Aching Back: A New Method of Mulch Gardening*. New York: Exposition Press, 1955.

Stout, however, had a dirty secret. She actually had stoutly tilled and manured her garden plot for 14 years before switching to her till-free technique of applying a deep mulch of spoiled straw.

Check out *The Ruth Stout No-Work Garden Book: Secrets of the Famous Year-Round Mulch Method*, Emmaus, PA: Rodale Press, 1973. On page 24 she says: "For about 12 years, [I did] about everything experienced growers told me. ....[my plot] was plowed each year." On page 117: "For the first 14 of my gardening years I covered my asparagus with manure, cultivated it each spring..."

So go ahead and till your soil—even double-dig it if you've got the back for it—if the ground is clayey, has a hardpan barrier near the surface, or in any situation where a few more years or seasons of dig-and-till will contribute to soil that requires less frequent tillage while maintaining good yields. Although soil compaction, carbon loss, and nitrogen depletion are still issues, there is a lazy advantage to tilling for a few or more years: it speeds up the process of getting to an effective no-till regime.

Ruth Stout's Method

First, ya gotta get naked. Ruth often gardened naked, which was fairly easy, since she didn't use a shovel. (People driving by, however, often got a quick unexpected show through a gap in her hedge.) If you're not inclined to work naked in general, at least try to do it on the first Saturday of May, as that's World Naked Gardening Day. (Yep, check it out.)

Anyway, her technique was quite simple:
• Lay down eight inches of hay.
• Pull the mulch back to plant seeds and leave it there until they sprout.
• Pull the mulch back to put in transplants and then replace the mulch up to the stems.
• That's it. Very simple. (And she was able to write three gardening books about it!)
In 1975, in Australian named Esther Dean, was 60 years old and still showing gardeners around her no-till garden, which she maintained with a technique that she had "developed" around 1964. In 1977, she published *No-Dig Gardening and Leaves of Life*, (HarperCollins Publishers (Australia) Pty Ltd, October 24, 2001).

 Bob sez: *Love that synchronicity. It's fascinating that two older women halfway around the world from each other were innovating a mulched style of food gardening at about the same time. Whether you're naked or not, once your soil is up to snuff, no-till techniques pamper your back and yield as much food as just about any garden. You can begin to wean yourself from tillage to no-till methods when the top few inches of your soil is loose enough to crumble in your hands. (If you're blessed with a sandy or sandy-loam soil, you can probably start no-till right away.)*

The suggestions in Dean's book are just a bit more complicated than Stout's:

• On a lawn or other ground surface, spread .25 inches of overlapped newspaper.
• Cover the newspaper with "flakes" of lucerne hay. "Flakes" are handful-thick layers of a hay bale.
• Sprinkle on a thin layer of organic fertilizer or chicken manure.
• Add eight inches of straw and sprinkle with some fertilizer.
• Add three to four inches of compost to the top.
• Be sure to moisten all layers.

This created a garden (in the '70s no less) with a process much like what we now call "sheet mulching" or, occasionally, tongue–in-cheek, "lasagna gardening."

Straw-Bale Gardens

Don't have a yard? Got a driveway? A tennis court nobody ever uses? Straw-bale gardening is the perfect perennial solution for those without soil. (I think it's the single best way to improve soil without too much work.) Growing annual vegetables or ornamental annuals on straw bales is also the easiest way to add lots of compostable organic matter to the soil surface in a short period of time, not to mention a great way for the intelligent (yet lazy) gardener to progress to no-till gardening.

Here's the recipe I used in 1978:

1. Place six or more bales of straw (with more carbon than green nutrients) in a cluster. Cluster the bales in a square pattern to conserve the most water. Place the bales with the end grain facing up, and leave the strings/wire on them. (They're heavy, so cut yourself some slack, open your wallet, and pay the high-school football player down the street to move them. Be sure to direct his or her every move safely from your recliner.)

2. Thoroughly soak the cluster of bales.

3. Add several inches of fresh manure to the top (in this case, the exposed end grain) of the bales.

4. Add four or more inches of loamy soil to cap off the top of the bales. (All right, I know this requires some digging. Or, buy some potting soil. But it's only a one-time effort to start off a remarkable process.)

5. Water all the layers again.

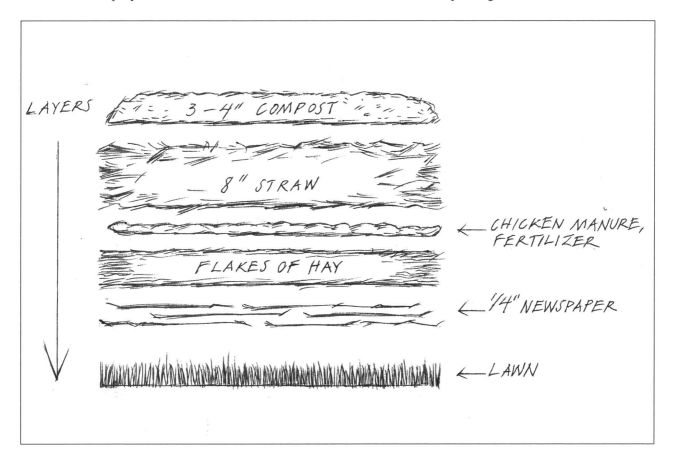

Figure 21: Esther Dean's method is very similar to Ruth Stout's way to garden. The difference is that Dean layered more materials. Her depth of hay and manure is much more like sheet composting a.k.a. lasagna gardening. Like planting after killing a lawn, pull back or puncture a portion of the newspaper or cardboard, add a bit of topsoil, and plant in the normal way. Be sure no grass fiber is in the planting hole as it will "grab" nitrogen from the added plants and slow or stunt their growth.

6. Plant and cover with plenty of loose straw on top—six inches or more.

7. Keep the plants and bales moist —you can use drip rrigation.

Et voila! The bales will grow plants up above the ground where no gophers can get to them—at least the first year! Then you can go back to sheet composting, mulching and/or layering with finished compost on top of the (now nicely-broken-down) bales.

BUT (Oh, no! It's another big butt), if you live where there are no summer rains, this can be a very water-intensive method; to water a fresh, dry bale in the summer in drought-prone areas takes a tremendous, tremendous amount of water. Only get your bales (they come cheap, too) from sloppy farmers and slovenly stable-keepers that have allowed rain to soak them. But be prepared, the bales are very heavy when wet. All the garden books on this simple technique were written in the summer-rain Midwest or New England. In the arid West, it's best to get your lighter straw bales in the fall and let the winter rains soak them with no effort.

I gotta get something off my chest. None of the people with recent books on straw-bale gardening "invented" the method. Nether did I, even though it's described in my 1986 book *Designing and Maintaining Your Edible Landscape – Naturally*, nearly three decades before the current heap of books on the topic. I found out about it in the mid-70s in the agricultural library at UC Berkeley.

There I was, wandering around the stacks—long before the Internet, when they still let you look at the shelves—and stumbled on a book from England. It described how they had been growing tomatoes in greenhouses for years on top of fertilized straw bales. When the crop was over, they simply pushed the spent bales out of the greenhouse to a compost pile, scrubbed the concrete floor with bleach or another disinfectant, and brought in more bales. (This is a very easy way to break the cycle of any pests or diseases.) Leave it to the English to invent such a useful technique.

 **Bob sez:** *Bale your way into maximum fertility.*

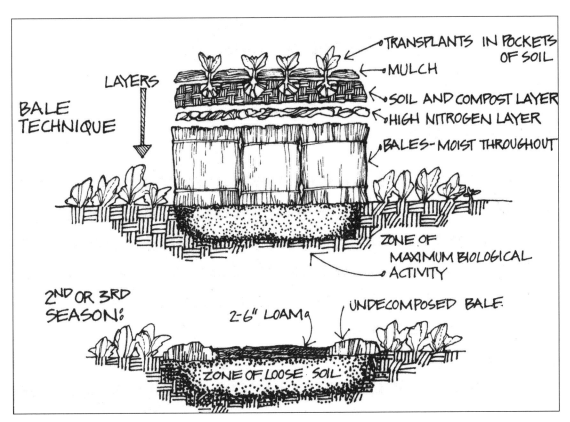

BALE TECHNIQUE

LAYERS

TRANSPLANTS IN POCKETS OF SOIL
MULCH
SOIL AND COMPOST LAYER
HIGH NITROGEN LAYER
BALES - MOIST THROUGHOUT
ZONE OF MAXIMUM BIOLOGICAL ACTIVITY

2ND OR 3RD SEASON:
2-6" LOAM
UNDECOMPOSED BALE
ZONE OF LOOSE SOIL

Figure 22: I think straw bale gardening is the fastest way to develop good soil. It's also the best way to garden on cement driveways or patios. The English developed this technique in the '60s to grow tomatoes in a greenhouse. After growing a crop of tomatoes, the bales are pushed out of the greenhouse and the concrete is sanitized. Then another batch of bales are added. Very cool. Do not use hay.

CHAPTER 6

Compost & Fertility

**"Compost, compost, compost" used to be the
first commandment of organic gardening
(followed by mulch, mulch, mulch). But
moderation is the gentle way to grow.**

Seen many hot compost piles lately? You know, the ones that are put together as if with a recipe, achieve temperatures of 140F⁰, and decompose even the starchiest cornstalk within four to six weeks? Bet you haven't. While plain old heaps of garden refuse are hidden away in the dark corners of most gardens, active composting has slipped rapidly into obscurity in the 21st century. Some ardent proponents of composting have survived in gardening backwaters—but many former "Captains of Compost" have let their active piles dry up.

This is more than OK for a budding lazy gardener. In reality, nowadays if we're not nursing a bad back, most of us are just too busy trying to support ourselves. I mean, how many small-scale or part-time gardeners have the time and energy to make labor-intensive hot compost while working to pay off mortgages and student-loan paybacks in amounts we thought only the national debt could achieve? Not to mention that fewer people have ready access to the manure that used to be an important ingredient of hot compost piles.

Moreover, an evil groupie of the "Kings of Klassic Kompost" has appeared: it's called symphylan (*Scutigerella immaculata*). These little ¼-inch-long critters in the garden look like very fast-moving, tiny white centipedes. Symphylans (they even sound like a "Dr. Who" villain species) thrive in tilled soils with large amounts of

organic matter and regular moisture levels—the same conditions many people strive to create in their organic vegetable gardens. The voracious varmints munch on the delicate root hairs of many vegetable plants, stunting or killing them, and are nearly impossible to banish by any organic method(s). (They are, however, easily controlled by adopting no-till methods.)

Some organic gardeners and farmers think perhaps symphylans become a problem when too much unfinished compost is added to the soil in great quantities. In some places the heavy-composters are seeing more and more of this horrible pest, yet it also invades other gardens with well-managed compost. When symphylans are identified as the cause of wholesale death of whole areas of plants, the usual first response is panic. Once you're able to see the damage—stunted, wilted and dead plants—it's too late to do anything but re-plant or turn the area into a fallow spot where no food crops are grown for awhile. Research has pointed to some possible ways to deal with symphylans, but there is no silver bullet. No organic pesticide has been shown to be worth-

 Bob sez: *One way to test for these creatures is to put pieces of cut potatoes on the soil at night. In the morning, lift the potato pieces up and look for the centipede-like symphylans chowing down on them.*

while in controlling these little beasts that can burrow seven to ten feet deep into the soil. There are a number of organic control options promoted: the abovementioned fallow period; 'Wheeler' rye, 'Monida' spring oats, 'Micah' barley, used as a winter cover crop, have been effective at reducing symphylans in some studies. "Aggressive" soil tillage to disrupt the pathways they use and packing the soil after transplanting to collapse the tunnels they move through, while logical ideas, are not effective, especially if you have symphylan levels high enough to prevent seedlings from forming roots.

What does work is to adopt nature's method of creating healthy soil with good structure and a balance of micro and macro-organism predators—in other words, the magic of no-till. Symphylans are found throughout the continental US, Hawaii, and the United Kingdom in both forest systems and prairies. So why aren't they killing the forests or grasslands? The simple answer is that nature, for the most part, doesn't till—she mulches. Tilling disturbs the permanent burrows that predatory insects and organisms use to find and capture invasive and harmful prey.

Many pests reproduce much faster than predators, so when you till the soil you favor the pests—in this case, symphylans. Simply stop tilling and mulch with some fully decomposed compost. What was barren soil due to severe symphylans feeding on plant roots will become a verdant paradise—and think of all the hard work you're avoiding as well.

Try to keep the organic matter of the soil at around five percent. Send some soil to a lab (some states offer soil tests via the Agricultural Extension, others require a commercial lab) that does soil tests. Check with a lab report for the organic matter content. Inspect all potted plants, compost, and soil you bring into the garden. All this may help keep things under control, but you'll most probably always have a few symphylans noshing

Bob sez: *I propose creating a "cold" compost pile. That is, make a heap hidden somewhere in the background of the garden—out of sight and out of mind. If you want to save your garden waste instead of putting it out for the garbage collector, simple pile it up and let it rot over the years, removing completed compost from the bottom.*

in your garden.

As a practical and laid-back gardener, you may also want to check out the option (if applicable in your area) of putting garden waste into the appropriate bin of the local garbage service and then buying back finished, high-quality compost. While it may get a little expensive (up to as much as $54 per cubic yard in my area), you get a jump on the garden, get to recycle green waste, and don't risk stressing your back by repeatedly turning over a compost heap.

But beware: commercial bulk compost is often turned or churned, but because of the surface area required in the composting yard (and sometimes because the demand is so high) it is usually not cost-effective to properly turn and age the compost. Thus commercial compost can be in an unfinished state. For instance, if you have a load delivered and it's still hot and steamy, you'll want to allow it to "mellow" until it has a dark, loamy feel. Cover it with a tarp to hide the charmingly distinctive smell. If you have the room, you can let it digest and mature for as much as a year. If you don't have the room, don't feel guilty—just buy a few sacks of aged compost. Don't get the imposter stuff made with redwood or fir chips (often called "nitrolized wood shavings") as there's usually not enough nitrogen in it to fully digest the wood content. It'll steal nitrogen from your soil, especially in a container planting.

The Smokin' King of Kompost

And compost can go awry for another unexpected reason. Tim Dundon, aka "Zeke the Sheik," the Compost King of Los Angeles County, loved compost so much that he made and accumulated it over a 17-year period. Eventually his pile was 40 feet tall and 200 feet long, easily big enough to cover a house. Twice in one month the heap spontaneously combusted, and the fire department had to be called to douse the flames and smoke. While Zeke defends composting as "the key of energy that will eventually set mankind free from misery and gravity," I'd say his pile shows what happens when a zealous intellect elevates a natural process to unnatural proportions, turning a beneficial practice into a hazard.

Now, how about some techniques that use green "waste" without the effort and hassle of hot composting? Grab a soda or glass of wine (or even herbal tea!) and read on.

The Realities of Worm Culture

If you don't have room for even a cold compost pile, worms may be for you. I spent nine months living and working with Ken and Barbara Kern (of *The Owner-Built Home* fame), who were major proponents of worms as waste digesters; they used them to devour garden waste as well as animal and human manures, and frequently extolled their virtues as decomposers and for the speed at which they consumed wastes.

I constructed a simple worm bin solely for my kitchen scraps, using an abandoned Army-surplus drum with a tight-sealing lid. I layered a foot of straw in the bottom, added six or more inches of horse manure (or a thin application of a sack of chicken manure or a thick application of coffee grounds), capped with a six-inch layer of straw mulch, and moistened the entire bin. After the manure had started to compost the straw, I added a large coffee can's worth of Red Wiggler Manure Worm Bin Substrate (a purchased mixture of

manure worms and their poopy castings). Shortly thereafter, I started adding kitchen scraps on a daily basis.

The first lesson I learned was that I should've waited for a while, until my population of worms had increased, because there just weren't enough worms in the bin to digest each day's waste. After several months, the worms had gotten busy and increased their population enough to quickly consume each day's scraps.

The thoughtful "wormologist" feeds new worms manure, coffee grounds, or nutmeats for a period of time to build up the population before introducing kitchen scraps. (Contrary to many guidelines, I feed my worms all the scraps left over from BBQs. No problem, except that the bin with its accumulated castings winds up full of bones; I sift them out so my garden doesn't look like a mass grave.)

Then tragedy struck. I had a large BBQ party and the worm-bin lid was left slightly open. The larger amount of scraps from the party, combined with the larvae of flies, caused a literal "meltdown"— the bin turned into a stinking near-slurry of castings, drowned worms, and fly maggots (enough to make you lose your lunch). I drained the surplus liquid off by puncturing small holes in the bottom of the drum, but it took more than four months for the worms to re-populate the bin and the fly larvae to die off.

Bob sez: *Some people (especially kids) comment, "Eeew, worms—how gross !" To these people I say "Worms are one of nature's grand cultivators and decomposers, incredible creatures with fascinating habits and phenomenal capabilities. Get with the program—learn to love your worms!" Once you learn to appreciate the slimy little critters (you may have to coddle them a little, but you don't have to cuddle them), your garden will be happier, and your recycling of kitchen scraps will be easier than any method I know of.*

Then another tragedy struck: my landlady had the large tree that shaded the drum cut down. The first hot spell turned my drum into a baked-worm casserole. Yuck! Again, it took months for the few wormy survivors to re-colonize the drum. Many months later, I was back to a healthy, happy drum-full of wiggly, hungry worms, and I fervently hope that I've been through all of the Murphy's laws of worm culture!

Using worm poop (castings) as a fertilizer and starting soil improvement with straw bales are the two most important and easiest ways to accelerate the soil's friability and vitality.

Sheet Composting

Sheet composting has nothing to do with woven percale or thread counts, but refers to the use of thin layers of compostable material laid out over the soil like a thick mulch. It's another nearly hassle-free no-till way to improve your soil without strenuous digging. The technique is akin to Esther Dean's deep-layered mulching practices (see page 68.)

By layering high-carbon wastes with nitrogenous plant refuse, you're essentially constructing a low, flat, wide compost pile. Use a blend of dry brown leaves or woody stems (chipped, chopped,

or not); fresh grass clippings; "green-manure" crops such as buckwheat, vetch, bell beans, and clover; wet kitchen garbage or scraps (no meat scraps, as they'll tend to attract hungry animals and/or smell bad); and green weeds from the garden before their seeds ripen. Experiment with a ratio of one part green matter to three or four parts dry dead matter. Water the dry materials as you're layering. At each intended planting location, make a large pocket in the native soil to receive the roots of your transplants.

NOTE: Since sheet composting doesn't generate enough heat to kill weed seeds, diseases, or pathogens, you'll need to water everything again after planting, then cover the area with five to ten sheets of newspaper, and cover the newspaper with a weed-free mulch; this will often take care of the nasties.

Sheet composting has several benefits: it slowly helps improve soils from the top down while allowing the gardener to quickly dispose of large quantities of compostable materials and avoid unnatural tillage. The sheet-composted area will require more irrigation the first year or two as the roots grow into the uncultivated soil. So, more water, but less drudgery—not too bad of a trade-off.

Surplus Nitrogen

Most gardeners (even those who use manures) squander nitrogen at rates even higher than the worst farmers. Kate Burroughs, Certified Crop Advisor with the Society of Agronomy in Sebastopol, CA, estimates that most homemade compost contains 0.7%—or less—actual nitrogen once all the turning and layering is done. In general, to equal the nitrogen farmers apply to their crops, Burroughs recommends raw steer or horse manure or compost spread only one-quarter to one-third inch deep over the soil for tree crops.

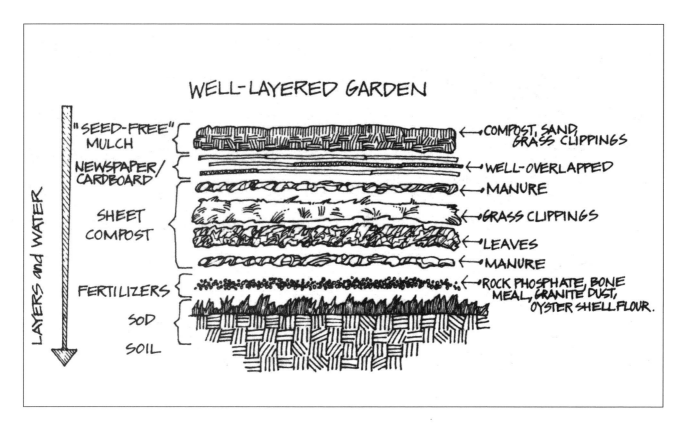

Figure 23: Sheet composting is the old-fashioned term for lasagna gardening. Use layers of green, brown, and manures. No need to cut the grass as the depth of the sheet compost and the cardboard will wither and kill all grasses and most weeds. Skip the minerals and fertilizers if your soil test says all is pretty-well balanced—less work, less cost.

She uses the same guideline for crops like homegrown sweet corn and lettuce. (Broccoli and pear trees need only 1/12- to 1/9-inch of raw manure or compost to equal farmer applications. Burroughs also commonly recommends such a "light dusting" for these crops and for apple trees—"if the apple trees need any additional nitrogen at all.") I often observe gardeners applying manure and compost far more thickly than these rates. Apply it any deeper, according to Burroughs, and you're wasting money and nitrogen. Bottom line? Don't waste valuable compost by guessing. More is not better. Besides, you save time and money.

Too much of a good thing can be counterproductive and wasteful. Whether manure or compost is over-applied in a synthetic or an "organic" form, excess nitrogen quickly escapes our gardens as a gas or leaches away toward fresh water supplies. Applied nitrogen can also set back the productive and effortless activity of VAM (See P. 78), the beneficial fungus that pumps phosphorus, nitrogen, and other nutrients into root cells. Surplus nitrogen tends to stimulate juicier but weaker plant growth, making crops more prone to pest and disease problems. In addition, yields may be reduced, because with too much nitrogen the plant's concentration of activity is converted to growing foliage rather than producing stems, tubers, or fruits.

Roots

Mother Nature (like Ruth Stout) doesn't use a shovel. Like Ruth, she gardens naked, and builds soil from the top down, with the decomposition of carbonaceous materials like fallen leaves and decaying grasses, as well as various forms of poop. In addition, there's a lot going on root-wise, beneath the surface of the soil that helps it improve without cultivation.

• The activities of roots loosen the soil.
• The roots of nitrogen-fixing plants add nitrogen.
• "Compost" is created as roots rot at all levels to create decomposed organic matter for the use of other plants and microbes.
• Nutrients cycle from root systems to the foliage of plants (and back to the earth again as leaf, stem, branch. and trunk litter)
• Roots develop tunnels for the movement of earthworms.
• Root canals (the kind created in soil by growing roots) help rainwater soak into deeper areas,
•Root exudates create a microbial "soup" which helps to liberate all manner of nutrients

And just think, all this goes on while you're napping or driving to the supermarket to get some ice cream!

Super Fungi

Here's my favorite reason for trying no-till gardening: in the soil under many trees, perennials, and some annual vegetables lurks a mostly unknown but very beneficial and hard-working

fungus called vesicular-arbuscular mycorrhizae (thankfully, researchers and writers generally use the abbreviation "VAM"). VAM forms a

 Bob sez: *"Athletes' foot" is gross, but there are plenty of benevolent fungi that can help your garden prosper. Favor their growth with reduced compaction and no-till gardening.*

most remarkable cohabitation and symbiotic relationship with plants, and is completely non-parasitic (they're just very good friends). The microscopic filaments or mycelia of the mycorrhizae fungi actually grow into the cells of the root hairs, providing nutrients—mostly phosphorus, potash, zinc and copper—to the plant, and receiving carbohydrates.

It's a powerful partnership; here are a few examples. When VAM was added to otherwise untreated or sterile soils: jack pine seedlings increased their weight by 28 times; oats were 80% heavier; corn yields up 14-306%; onions increased from 48-3155%; and strawberries improved by 250%. Compared to citrus trees growing in sterilized soil (using methyl bromide), VAM-grown trees grew 1600% larger. (Impressive, but true.) Most trees, in fact, can't prosper without this symbiotic association.

Most natural undisturbed soils have plenty of VAM, but it's frighteningly easy to kill off. Tillage; removal of the

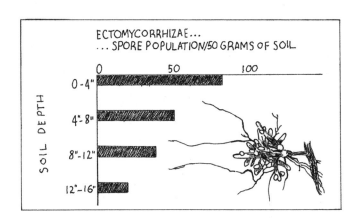

Figure 24: These beneficial fungi live in association with the roots of over 90% of plants. They pump phosphorus into the roots, along with other nutrients. They prefer the upper soils.

natural litter (duff) beneath and around trees; stripping away topsoil to build a house; compaction (even by foot traffic); over-fertilization with phosphorous and nitrogen; and greenhouse or container culture with sterile soil mixes will injure or kill VAM.

Figure 24 shows that much of the VAM prefers the upper four inches of soil. Since tillage also does tremendous harm to the mycelia (tiny roots) of plants, that's yet another reason for switching to no-till gardening.

To prevent compaction, keep permanent pathways away from trees; use deep mulches for paths used only occasionally; allow some fallow areas in your annual beds from year to year; and rotate your crops with root systems of different depths to help keep untilled soil friable. If possible, keep annual crops as far from trees as possible (1.5 to three times the width of the tree canopy) to leave the VAM undisturbed.

If you had to purchase topsoil or potting soil for your garden, there's no need to purchase some of the new mycorrhizae inoculants being touted. The existing naturally occurring mycorrhizae will inoculate the plants' roots for you.

Mulch

Like people, mulch comes in many forms— some chunkier or juicier than others. If you're mulching with really coarse woody chips, they may need to be six or more inches deep in order to settle down to form a dense enough barrier to smother weeds. When using straw, I often layer

it up to twelve inches deep; this compacts itself into a tight, dense three to six inches over time.

With most other mulches, anything deeper than four inches is a waste of money if you're buying it, and a waste of time and resources if you're making it. (I didn't guess this; it's the summary of an extensive thesis on mulching by Michael McMilen in 2013.)

In another study (*Influence of Pure Mulches on Survival, Growth and Vitality of Containerized and Field Planted Trees*, by G.C. Percival, Evangelos Gklavakis and Kelly Noviss:) "Establishment rates of difficult-to-transplant tree species such as beech can be improved from 10% to 70% [by mulch], while fruit yields of young trees can be increased by 100%." Be sure to mulch well beyond the dripline (leaf canopy edge) of a newly planted tree. As mentioned earlier, the roots of trees grow 1.5 to three times wider than the foliage.

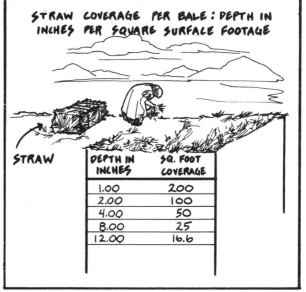

Figure 25: Use this table to determine how much straw you will need.

CHAPTER 7

Not Zeroscaping

**Got a dry spell? Got a genuine drought?
Bolster production and beauty with less water
and more smarts.**

The other day I was talking to an herb-gardener friend, and mentioned that I design what used to be called "xeriscapes." I must have slipped back into my St. Louis drawl, because her immediate response was "What, a landscape with nothing? That sounds really boring and ugly!"

"No," I quickly replied, "Not a zero-scape. Xeriscape is just a fancy term for designed drought-resistant planting."

The word (the correct pronunciation is ZEER'-uh-skape) is based on the Greek xeros, meaning (no surprise) "dry." Drought-resistant landscaping, dryland plantings, drought-hardy plantings, xeriscaping-—all are terms that refer to growing plants that require little or no extra irrigation and thus conserve precious freshwater supplies.

A xeriscape doesn't have to be like one of those strange garden-substitutes—often seen in dry-area suburbs—that feature various geometric patterns of colored gravel, large expanses of tinted pavement, a potted tree or two, and maybe a few plastic flamingos. No, a well-designed xeriscape can be just as beautiful as any other landscape, and comes with added benefits: while saving water, it also saves you many hours of maintenance gardening and the price of costly fertilizers. Some extra effort up front can mean lots of time and exertion saved for many years to come. By having a portion, if not all, of

an ornamental landscape devoted to a xeriscape, you can minimize the labor of seasonal gardening without sacrificing beauty.

The trend toward xeriscaping has also increased as more and more growing communities face limited water supplies. Sadly, with additional years of climate change, more parts of the country may soon also be experiencing water shortages. Sporadic droughts will continue to be common in many areas of the country and are a part of nature's seasonal pattern in other climates. I suspect that the landscape trades, in an attempt to gloss over the fearsome concept of "drought," have adopted the term "xeriscaping" in order to glamorize the image of drought-resistant landscaping, and

listed below are most appropriate for much of the West and Southwest, where I've done the majority of my gardening and landscape work, but many of the design strategies and planting guidelines are applicable to diverse climates.

Some Golden Rules of a Drought-Resistant Landscape

Rule # 1 – A drought-resistant landscape can be as beautiful as any "real" landscape.

I believe that many of us, especially in dry areas of the country, have been brainwashed by glorious full-color books, mail-order catalogs, and magazines about herbaceous flower borders. Just about all of these are written and published in the rainy, humid areas of the US, or in England. This has produced a kind of collective tyranny of aesthetics that the natural order of much of the West can't (and shouldn't have to) match.

I can, however, design a drought-resistant garden or landscape with a riot of spring and early-summer color that rivals that of any other herbaceous flower border, but the types of plants would be totally different. One significant difference in my garden is the preponderance of woody shrubs and herbs, not the typical soft-wooded herbaceous plants found in New England and Midwestern borders.

In my landscape, a large part of the year-round color scheme is dependent upon foliage of different hues (a good aesthetic strategy in any garden). Since the forest that surrounds my landscape is predominantly evergreen, it's only fitting that I plant a range of steel-gray, blue-green, and dusty-white foliage—also called "glaucous" plants, providing visual appeal throughout the year, over and above the colorful accents added by seasonal flower bloom.

If you live in climate other than California-Mediterranean, you may well be able to grow the

interest gardeners in trying the concept without spooking them with the "D" word.

In writing and speaking about this subject, by the way, I usually prefer the term "drought-resistant landscaping," though I do make use of the words xeric and xerophytic, which refer to, respectively, dry or desert-like conditions and to plants structurally adapted to growing in same.

Having worked with many drought-hardy plants over the past 40 years and having designed many very drought-tolerant landscapes, I've come to recognize a few "golden rules" pertaining to their concept, planning, and implementation. Those floral displays found in those wishful-thinking gardening books, but be wary of installing too many herbaceous perennials, that die back to the ground in the fall and need more care than some perennial shrubs.

Rule # 2 - All droughts are not created equal and all native plants are not equal.

The subtleties of the distinction between various "native plants" within one state or region can be a bit difficult to grasp. The state lines for California, for example, represent an arbitrary construct that has little relation to natural ecological boundaries. Its ecosystems range from the lowest, hottest desert in America to lofty, chilly alpine-meadows.

Often, however, someone will proudly point out to me a particular new specimen in his/her garden as "a native California plant." I've seen gardeners in Los Angeles show off a new planting of wild ginger (*Asarum caudatum*), yet I know that this native ground cover naturally thrives best within the foggiest coastal zones and near shady, riparian (creekside) habitats. Planted anywhere else, it requires periodic irrigation.

In Occidental (60 miles north of San Francisco in wine country), the rains only come during the winter months of October through March or April, but the average seasonal total is 58 inches. When my landscape gets wet, it really gets wet—which has great implications with regards to fungus and root rots.

For example, the *Eriogonum giganteum* (St. Catherine's lace) is native only to the Santa Catalina and San Clemente islands off the coast of southern California, some 400 miles and many ecosystems south of where I live. With a winter rain of less than 45 inches, St. Catharine's lace is drought-resistant, but unable to survive my area's winter deluge. This plant usually dies from crown rot, a water-stimulated fun-

Bob sez: *Drought-resistant gardens require less work if you choose the right plants. Plant for beauty and to save water with a mix of appropriate native and exotic plants. Such gardens can be as lovely as any other garden. Be sure to plan for the length of your "average drought." (A drought in my native St. Louis was four or five weeks without rain, at which point people started to panic.)*

gus of the upper portion of the root system, thus it's a native California plant that really doesn't belong in my part of California.

Elsewhere in the country, draw upon lily-of-the-valley plants that prosper within your local zone. For example, Lily-of-the-valley (*Convallaria majalis*) herbaceous perennial thrives in the USDA zones 2 to 7. They flourished at my Grandma's house in St. Louis with no supplemental irrigation and little care. Such a choice can really save you time and resources. (Alas, they're defined as an invasive plant—don't let them escape from your garden.)

Rule # 3 - Many drought-resistant landscapes don't need any supplemental irrigation.

Oddly enough, many definitions of xeriscaping refer to reducing outdoor water use by "up to 75 percent." Yet, by my working definition, the ultimate goal is to design, install, and maintain an ornamental landscape with plants so well adapted to their environment that no supplemental irrigation is required.

One of my "test plots" was a small planting of various varieties of lavenders, santolinas, rosemarys (*Rosmarinus* spp.), a richly-colored 'Bronze' fennel (*Foeniculum vulgare* var. *azoricum*), a low, prostrate form of summer lilac (*Ceanothus hearstiorum*) and a single, glorious specimen of the warmly-glaucous *Osmanthus* 'Silver Jubilee'. This small planting was watered

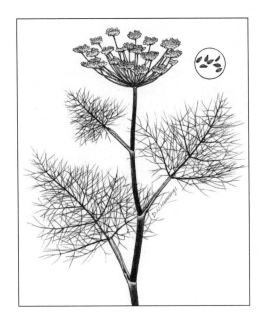

Figure 26: Bronze fennel (*Foeniculum vulgare 'Purpureum'*) is a xeric, colorful, and edible herb that also attracts beneficial insects.

only once a month the first summer after planting and received only two irrigations the second year—and this was during the second year of a significant drought. No water after that. This saves a lot of resources *and* time. You don't even have to pay for a timer.

Where it does occasionally rain, many native plants are drought-resistant in that they have adapted to the climate's sporadic rain.

Rule # 4 - Drought-resistant plants must have good drainage.

Most xeric plants must have absolutely perfect soil drainage—sandy, or rocky soils with a low clay content. The best drought-resistant plants that I grow are also the least able to withstand frequent irrigation in the summer or thrive in heavy clay soils that easily become waterlogged. Contrary to popular belief, xeric plants actually seem, at least in my experience, to grow better with less water and actually thrive with no supplemental irrigation.

Truly xeric plants should be planted in a very gravelly soil with very little clay loam or organic matter, and each plant must be planted on a raised mound to further encourage drainage. I avoid placing mulch near the base of the plant so as to prevent stem or trunk rot, especially during the rainy season. Any summer watering should be by drip irrigation applied some 18 to 24 inches away, outside the planting mound, from the base of the plant.

In all climates, providing good drainage is a precaution to various root-rots. Planting on a gentle mound—as explained on pages 54-58—will keep you from worrying; peace of mind is an essential part of lazy-ass gardening.

Rule # 5 - The best drought-resistant landscapes are planted by home gardeners.

The techniques that I've learned are best suited to the sensibilities of owner-built landscapes and are much more difficult to implement in a landscape-business setting.

As a professional landscaper in Northern California, for example, I couldn't save up all my installation jobs for the short period each fall when planting is ideal.

Drought-resistant landscaping is rightfully the dominion of the inspired, conscientious, and thoughtful home gardener, because only the homeowner can easily work within the pattern of nature's seasons to install a truly drought-resistant landscape. Professionals have to plant all year to make a living. This is a good example of a situation where personal landscaping is superior to commercial landscaping.

Rule # 6 - Native plants are not always the most drought-resistant.

One of the myths to crumble as I landscaped through the California drought of 1977 was the idea that native plants are superior in their drought-resistance. While certain California desert plants are among the world's most drought-hardy, they won't survive our local winter rains and frost. As I watched plant after plant die in 1977, I began to realize that some of the exotic, non-native plants were doing the best. (Lavenders were one of them. Thus began my love affair with this shrub that led to my 2000 book *The Lavender Garden*.)

There are a handful of Mediterranean climates throughout the world besides California—the Mediterranean basin, of course, the middle elevations of the Chilean mountains, portions of South Africa, the Canary Islands, and parts of Australia. Most of these climates are cousins to our Californian Mediterranean ecosystem and droughts are often more severe and the rainfall considerably more sparse. Plants from these areas will adapt to many other aspects of the climate and soil and still retain their superior drought-hardiness.

An article entitled, "A Trial of Drought Toler-

ance", in *Pacific Horticulture* magazine, discussed the observations of horticulturalist Barrie Coates, who stated, as a result of studies of native California xerophytic plants: "It is more sensible to choose plants for their adaptability to the site than for their area of origin. Except in the hands of an enthusiast for California native plants, a drought-tolerant planting will probably be more beautiful and satisfying if well-chosen exotics are included."

The "winners" of this small trial were:
* Numero uno - *Echium candicans* (pride-of-Madeira, a.k.a. *E. fastuosum*) (somewhat invasive)
* *Lavandula dentata* (French lavender)
* *Phlomis fruticosa* (Jerusalem sage)
* *Cistus parviflorus* (rockrose)
* *Epilobium canum*, formerly *Zauschneria californica ssp. latifolia* (hummingbird trumpet, a.k.a. California fuchsia)
* *Agonis flexuosa* (peppermint tree)
* *Cistus salvifolius* (Salvia cistus)
* *Hypericum coris* (hypericum)
* *Tristaniopsis laurina* (water gum—go figure)
* *Arctostaphylos manzanita* 'Dr. Hurd' (a California native manzanita).

CHAPTER 8

Elegant Irrigation

Drip, drip, drip your way to garden, landscape, and/or orchard abundance. Irrigate while you sleep or watch a movie.

Getting the irrigation of your garden or landscape worked out is one of the key aspects of Inspired Laziness. You can waste a lot of time and energy dragging hoses around to hand-water or setting up and moving sprinklers, especially if you're dealing with a lot of growing area. Getting the right amount of water to the right place at the right time, not to mention dealing with weather, soil conditions, and seasonal change, is a challenge for any aspiring lazy-ass. Fortunately, there are ways to set up your watering system for maximum efficiency and ease.

Pore Space, not Poor Space

To begin with, here's the real dirt on why getting the water right is so important. Healthy soil contains enormous numbers of beneficial critters: worms, bugs, microbes, algae, mycelia (the vegetative parts of fungi), etc., each with its own small but vital role in making soil fertile and workable. Most of these helpful little organisms need oxygen; they also need to be able to exhaust slightly toxic gases—kind of like teeny little farts—that result from their metabolic activity. To allow this normal venting of gases, the soil needs healthy pore spaces.

Pore spaces are minute channels within the soil—distorted, contorted mini-tunnels (see Figure 27) that allow nitrogen and oxygen to enter the soil, and gases to escape. This underground network is essentially the result of humic (soil-generated) acids binding particles of the soil together.

Healthy pore spaces make for better soil. They reduce the amount of watering needed, hold soil moisture longer, and promote better and more productive growth—all while you sleep or play tennis.

Humic acid (found in that broken-down organic stuff known as humus) is a byproduct of the decomposition of organic matter. It's a relatively stable material that binds to inorganic particles (sand, clay, etc.) and creates in them a sort of suspension or web. See Figure 27 for a close-up view of humic aggregates creating minute voids between soil particles; these are the pore spaces, and they are what makes good soil feel friable (crumbly) to a gardener.

Once created, pore spaces require air in order to survive; too much moisture in the soil (and it doesn't take much) will fill and clog the spaces

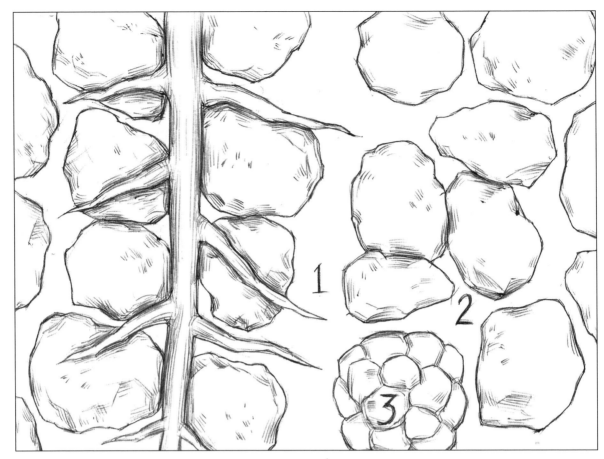

Figure 27: Number 1 and 2 are two sizes of pore space. The water can drain down without flooding the soil if you don't irrigate too long. Keeping the pore spaces from flooding allows nitrogen gas into the soil to form solid and soluable nitrogen on the roots of legumes. It also allows toxic gases to escape from the soil. Numbers 3 represents the humic aggregates found among the pore spaces. These aggregates transfer nutrients to root hairs.

and prevent the exchange of gases. When this happens, the former aerobic (air-charged) environment of the pore spaces soon becomes anaerobic (lacking beneficial oxygen). The top four inches of soil is, ideally, very aerobic, and more important to root and soil life than any other four-inch section below.

There are some forms of soil life that can tolerate anaerobic soil without dying or going into hibernation. That means they're not available to convert inorganic material (such as minerals) into soluble organic forms that can be absorbed in minute amounts of moisture, (as opposed to pore-clogging water) by root hairs (See Figure 28). Root hairs are the single-cell extensions of tiny roots, and they do most of the absorption of nutrients.

Once a source of over-watering is removed, it takes time for the soil pores to drain and the aerobic activity to begin again. Pore space is easily "drowned," and the heavier the soil, the slower the pores drain. Clayey soils have the fewest pores, while sandy soils have the most.

Sprinklers, while relatively easy to use, are likely to flood the pore spaces of the soil by completely saturating its upper layers. This oversaturation, if continuous or repeated regu-

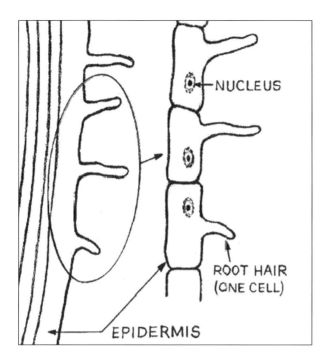

Figure 28: Each root hair has one nucleus and lives for only one day. A root hair requires a friable soil for maximum absorption of nutrients. The epidermis is the single-celled outer layer of a tiny root. (Illustration from my book *Roots Demystified: Change Your Gardening Habits to Help Roots Thrive*, Metamorphic Press, 2008.)

larly, may kill some of the soil life. If the soil is allowed to drain and dry, the remaining soil life can repopulate the soil, but only if unimpeded pore space is allowed to re-form. On the other hand, if the soil is allowed to dry out too much, the pore spaces will also dry out, enough to kill off some soil life because of oxidation. You see the problem?

Going back and forth between soil that gets over-saturated and is then allowed to drain and dry can create a too-wet/too-dry yo-yo scenario that can stress plants enough to slow their growth. The plants will still grow, but not at their ideal rate.

The only way to use an oscillating sprinkler

properly is to turn it on only for very brief periods of time, say 15 minutes, then off, then on again for a short while. (The same amount of time.)This allows the water to drain through the pore space. The "off" period is to make sure the soil remains somewhat aerobic and that the soil life doesn't drown. Automatic sprinkler systems that can be programmed for doing this are rare, and manually turning oscillating sprinklers on and off or moving them around is way too much work for most people.

 Bob sez: *When I was growing up, my Dad left oscillating sprinklers showering fan-shaped water on the lawn for hours almost every summer day. (Back then, in St. Louis, Missouri, water was cheap—a flat fee meant you could use as much as you wanted.) The soil got saturated, even squishy. The lawn grew, but proper irrigation would have created less stress and allowed for even better growth with less water. (Which could have increased the number of times I had to mow the lawn each week. Yikes!)*

Micro-sprinklers, with a finer spray that distributes less water than typical lawn sprinklers, are somewhat less harmful to growth, but will also clog surface pore spaces if left on too long (even though an amazing amount of the misty water blows away if it's windy out).

Going Natural with Ollas? (Only if You Make your Own)

Based on an irrigation technique introduced to the Southwestern Native Americans by the Spanish, the olla is a vase-like unglazed pot that's buried with its wide mouth open at the soil surface. Each olla is then periodically filled with water that oozes though the porous clay to irrigate nearby roots. The water can usually permeate about18 inches or so in all directions, depending on the soil.

In contrast, it takes, let's say, two or three hours to

Bob sez: *Ollas (see below) became the rage in gardening circles in the early twenty-first century; I have no idea why, as they're extremely inefficient and cost-prohibitive. Don't get me wrong; if you're trying to garden in a hot, dry area without electricity or running water, ollas may be your best bet. Not everybody has the luxuries many of us take for granted. That's why this section is here. But if you don't make your own, these suckers are expensive; a one-quart olla nowadays will cost you about $22. A two-gallon one will set you back 50 smackers. To irrigate a sizeable garden, you'd probably have to to take out a home equity loan. (And one source even says: " Your OLLA will last several years.") For that amount of money I could buy up to 55 emitters for drip irrigation. And water a huge area—at least 50 square feet. And automate it so I wouldn't have to refill the ollas every few days. And I could then go back inside and watch the newest Marvel movie.*

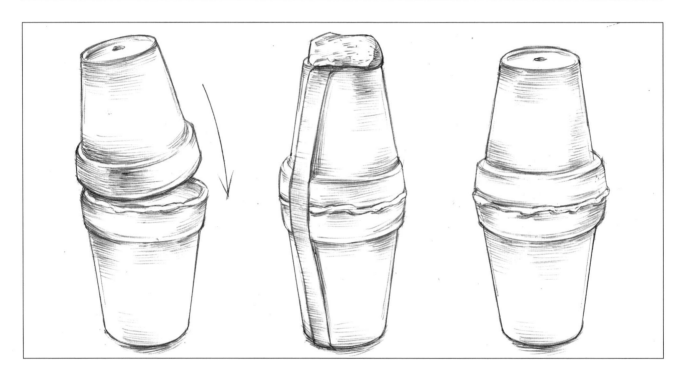

Figure 29: If you still want to experiment, there's a sneaky way to make your own olla for just a few bucks, but they still require a lot of ongoing manual labor. On the left, we see Gorilla Glue being applied. Cover lower hole with a glued rock. (And, no, I'm not a shill for Gorilla Glue that is used here.) The middle pot shows duct tape and a rock to hold the pots together until the glue dries. Adapted from *The Suburban Farm*, on-line. https://suburbanfarmonline.com/2010/08/09/make-your-own-ollas/

install that 55-emitter drip system. That may seem like a long stretch, but it's a fraction of the time you'd spend making (see Figure 29) and filling a bunch of ollas forever, or dragging sprinklers and/or hoses around. So, just another example of how a small bit of well-spent time upfront can save many hours down the line—the drip line.

Drip Irrigation

Yep, drip irrigation is technology. Yep, it takes some scheming and planning. Yep, it costs more than a hose. Yep, it is harder to install than an oscillating sprinkler. BUT, it has SO many benefits:

• First and foremost, you get greater yields,

bloom and growth than with any other type of irrigation.

• It saves time and labor. One twist of the wrist, or better yet the activation of an automated electric valve, and you can water hundreds of plants

• It stimulates fewer weeds in dry-summer areas.

• It provides better water distribution on slopes, especially with pressure-compensating emitters. (These emitters are designed so that even with a 250-foot-long line, the water coming out at the end is exactly the same amount as the flow at the beginning.)

• It promotes better soil structure.

• It's more economical than permanent pop-up sprinklers.

Emitters for the Best Application of Water

Drip-irrigation emitters slowly dispense tiny amounts of water. This distribution rate is measured in gallons-per-hour (gph). Emitters are rated at various flow rates. All ½-, 1- & 2-gph emitters can be punched into solid drip tubing or encased in in-line tubing. Instead of external emitters, in-line tubing incorporates internal emitters built inside the tubing at regular intervals (See Figure 30)—usually nine, 12, 18, or 24 inches apart, depending on which interval you buy.

The most important aspect of drip emitters is that the water is released from them so slowly. On the surface, a drip-irrigated plot looks like a series of wet spots surrounding plants, with dry soil in between. The dry area between the emitters is very deceiving however, because below the surface those wet spots spread sideways and merge. (In sandy soil the wet spot is something like a carrot shape. In clayey soil, it's more like a fat wide turnip.)

The pattern of the merging of wet spots is also shown in Figure 31. This is an important consid-

eration when planning a drip system, as it demonstrates how drip irrigation can irrigate an entire root system without the continuous saturation of pore spaces that occurs with sprinkler use.

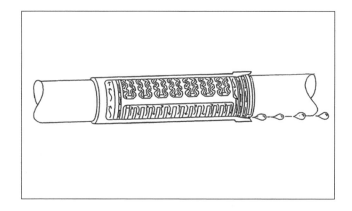

Figure 30: I only use in-line tubing (12" spacing) It is the most elegant and time-saving drip system because all you do is roll it out, flush it, and cap it. There're no punched-in emitters to break off. A view of the inside of an emitter.

How Emitters Increase Yields

This is the most important revelation of this whole spiel: unlike sprinklers, properly placed emitters create only minute amounts of anaerobic soil, very close to the emitter, as seen in Figure 32. Very little of the pore space around an emitter is flooded; soil beyond the small anaerobic wet spot is moist, but the pore spaces, due to the capillary movement of moisture, don't get saturated, and the soil life remains active and viable. This explains why, with properly installed drip irrigation, plant yields can increase while you're actually conserving water. In one study on the subject, a chili-grower in India who switched to drip irrigation reduced her water use by 38% and harvested 48% more chilies. Of the one-hundred-plus studies that I've been able to find, the average increase in yields is at least 20%.

(A company called Netafim now has a new type of in-line emitter tubing—Techline® HCVXR Landscape Dripline, with copper oxide built into every emitter. The copper prevents root intrusion, so it's a great tubing to use for sub-surface installations. This is assuming you don't have a gopher problem—they love to nosh on drip tubing.)

Daily Versus Infrequent Watering

Perhaps the biggest debate about irrigation is how often to water. The choices range from daily, to weekly, to monthly, even.

For my money, daily irrigation is the best and promotes the greatest growth and yields. This is considered radical by many gardeners. Once the soil is at a proper moisture level (NOT anywhere near wet) a daily irrigation with very tiny amounts of water, especially in arid or summer-dry climates keeps "the tank topped off." Where there are periodic rains, the system would only be turned on once the soil has returned to an ideal soil moisture level. (Take a fistfull of soil, throw it six or so inches high. If it crumbles when it hits your fist, it's about the correct amount of moisture.) This means that, in dry weather, the drip system is turned on every day for a very short time.

When I was landscaping I often got great results by using these eight simple steps :
1. Prep the soil and rake it out to the contours you desire.
2. Lay out the in-line drip system with emitters every 12 inches, and stake it in place.
3. Water the entire landscape with an overhead oscillating sprinkler.
4. Return to plant after the soil becomes slightly moist, no longer wet.
5. Transplant the plants into a loam soil, placing each plant halfway between emitters. (In my

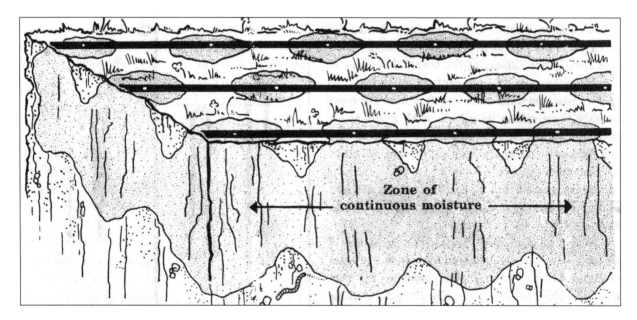

Figure 31: The dry spots around the dark-wet spots on the surface are misleading to many. In reality, the moisture widens as it moves down. Some distance below, the moisture merges together. This means the entire root system gets irrigated. To do this the emitters need to be close enough and the lines of tubing reasonably close. The distance is determined by laying out a short length of in-line tubing, running it for an hour, dig a trench along the length of the tubing, and look to see where the moisture merges. Place the tubing half-way between the merged moist spots. Clay soil has wider moist spots than loam.

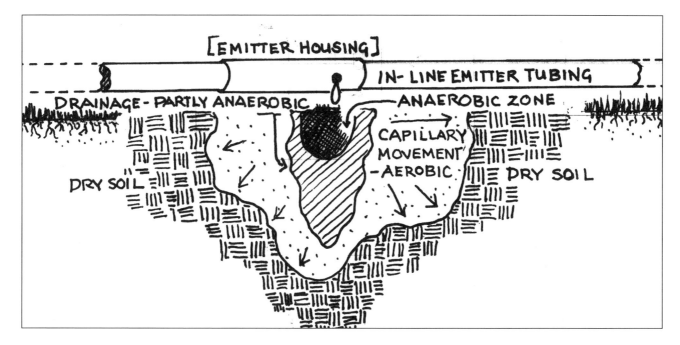

Figure 32: Drip irrigation is the best way to water plants because there is a much smaller area of anaerobic soil that floods the pore space. The anaerobic soil is much wider and deeper with sprinkler irrigation. With drip, the anaerobic zone quickly moves via capillary action to irrigate adjacent soils while keeping the soil's pore structure open for the adequate exchange of gases. The capillary action moves in all directions to irrigate many of the roots.

case, I was usually planting drought-resistant Mediterranean plants.)

6.   Water the transplants in by hand.

7.   Mulch all plants heavily (a maximum of four inches.)

8.   Turn on the drip system (I often used one-half gph emitters) on day one. In my experience, because the soil was pre-moistened, and the plants watered in and mulched, the drip-irrigation time was two minutes per day—mere tablespoons of water per emitter.)

If, however, you want to water, say, once a week, just apply the water at seven times the daily rate. For example, in my dry summers the recommended amount of water for a new fruit tree is around one gallon per day. So, on Saturday night you can lounge in the garden with your favorite beverage while the drip system soaks each tree with seven gallons of water. Or, to be really slothful (but efficient), turn on

 Bob sez: *Want to spend a lot of money that's money well spent? Then get an ET-based irrigation controller. ET stands for "evapotranspiration." That's a combination word meaning moisture lost from evaporation from the soil plus moisture that transpires from the leaves. An ET-based irrigation clock measures the weather to adjust the time the system is on. It's far more accurate than just guessing. And since it's automatic, you can also go to the Bahamas or to Burning Man and get your watering done.*

the drip system for 14 hours (2 times 7 gallons because you're using 1/2 gph emitters) if you're using one emitter per or tree. If you have more emitters, divide 14 by the number of emitters to get the run time in hours. (For example, eight emitters per tree equals 1.75 hours.) Exhale. (And remember to get the prssure-compensating-emitter tubing so the amount of water coming out is identical from the faucet to the end of the line.)

There's a reason my drip-irrigation book title reads...*Every Landscape and All Climates*. Even if your drought is only four weeks long, drip irrigation used between rains to keep the soil ideally *slightly* moist (not wet) will keep your plants growing impressively and, with vegetables, promote the greatest yields.

How Deep?

Deep. People always say, for example, to water trees deeply. But how deep is deep? It turns out that over 50 percent of most trees' roots grow in the top 12-18 inches of soil. (See Figures 33 and 34), so that's how deep. In fact, 12 inches deep is probably all that's needed for your emerging orchard or shady planting.

Inspired Laziness

Permanent and Hard

This large permanent fence, a key hardscape element in a Napa, CA garden, acts as a background to the garden through all seasons and planting cycles.

A terra-cotta Ben Katz sculpture adds a vertical line to the planting area and acts as a focal point. Two more are lined up with it to delineate solar south.

This arbor at Preston Vineyards in Healdsburg, CA offers a view into an edible landscape I designed. The terra-cotta fountain at left is centered in a symmetrical view from a different view of the garden.

Here's an asymmetrical view of a garden designed by Kate Frey for Lynmar Winery in Graton, CA. Simple mulched paths meander throughout, and the flower arch and umbrella act as focal points and lures to the eye.

I built this deer fence and arbor for Sonoma County resident Myra Portwood in 1998. The second four-foot-high fence, covered in honeysuckle vines, is nearly invisible behind the first. Notice how the slats get taller as they approach the double-gated arbor. No deer has ever entered this garden, and they won't eat the lavender outside of the fence. This costly setup is worth the effort—not only does it work, but it also avoids the ugly penitentiary-like look of eight-foot wire fencing.

Sunset magazine's edible-landscape and test garden, planted with fruit trees among colorful ornamentals, was designed by the Homestead Design Collective, and is located at Cornerstone in Sonoma County, CA. The arched arbor draws the eye into the next "room" of the garden, as does the path shown on the right, which meanders towards a metal tree in a nearby art garden.

The focal point of this hardscape arrangement is the glorious red bench. Sitting areas remind the gardener to slow down, while providing a place for visitors to relax and enjoy the view. This photo was taken in Rosalind Creasy's edible landscape in her front yard.

The majestic *Gingko biloba* is a truly diverse tree. Its leaves turn a blazing hot yellow in the fall. Its roots seldom heave concrete or brick paths. It's virtually pest- and disease-free. It's a narrow tree (20'-40') that can fit into relatively tight spaces. Brave people can eat the nuts from the female trees. BUT (and it's a big but) the fruit smells like dog doody and can make a mess of your yard or patio. Select your tree in summer in order to avoid the fruiting females of the species.

The hummingbird salvia (*Salvia spathacea*). Blooms for months from spring to summer. Does what it's name implies—attracts lots of humming-birds. Grows under California native oak trees. Is drought and deer resistant. Zones 8-11.

A five-foot-tall purple kale (above left) is an edible and ornamental annual. The native California buckwheat sub-shrub (*Eriogonum umbellatum*) (middle) blooms for many weeks and attracts beneficial insects. The flowers of Biennial mullein (*Verbascum* spp.) (right) glow hot yellow in western light. I let mine seed out so it can "walk around the garden."

All of the perennials, herbs, and shrubs in Ros Creasy's edible landscape combine into a very ornamental view. Ros is better than anyone I know at mixing ornamental annuals and perennials. The edible petals of the yellow rose add color to salads. Here a squash plant decorates the arbor. (photo by Ros Creasy).

A boatload of tomatoes and a table and chairs for garden dining grace the yard of Yeffi Vanatta and Philip Manela.

A galvanized tub (shown here filled with annual and perennial edibles) will protect your plants from foraging mammals and invasive grasses. Be sure to drill plenty of holes in the bottom for drainage.

A mixture of perennial herbs and lettuces at the Preston Winery is irrigated by in-line emitter tubing.

Contrasting colors of lettuce enliven cut-and-come-again mesclun salads.

Fig and persimmon trees make fruit on the new season's growth. If pruned heavily or not pruned at all, they make lots of fruit. Great for espaliers.

Tillage: from Some to None

Raised beds, as shown in Preston Winery's edible landscape, can be constructed with wooden boards or other hardscape materials. They can also (photo on right) be formed with the soil itself, as at Douglas Hayes' garden in Calistoga, CA. Neither of these gardens now require actual digging— the beds can be lightly prepared with surface cultivation. Both methods encourage good drainage and earlier warming of the soil in the spring.

The Sea Ranch, on the California coast, uses sheep to graze down grass and other fire hazards; extra wool is used to make a virtually weed-proof mat in gardens.

A permanent mulch, at least four inches deep and extending at least to the dripline (canopy edge) of ornamental and fruit trees, can protect them from soil compaction and weeds.

C 7

These white nodules are on the nitrogen-fixing roots of a legume, in this case, a bean. If you don't see these on legume roots, get an inoculant to start the process. A pink interior indicates a healthy nodule, brown a dead one.

Crimson clover (*Trifolium incarnatum*) is a gorgeous nitrogen-fixing plant—it can produce 2.6 pounds of N per 100 square feet. For the most nitrogen, however, it should be tilled in or composted before the flowers bloom.

This is Doug Lipton's cover crop of fava beans, grasses, and yellow mustard in Healdsburg, CA. Fava beans provide fixed nitrogen; the grass adds far more fiber than a legume can; and the mustard has a fairly aggressive taproot that penetrates hard clayey soils. All of these increase soil fertility.

This is my dad when he was the "King of Kompost" in Olivette (St. Louis, MO). His bin was a massive 20 cubic yards to contain fall leaves, and he added horse manure to speed up the composting process. He never actually turned its contents—it was more like stirring.

Not Zeroscaping

My summer-dry deer-resistant garden (in Occidental, CA, 60 miles north of San Francisco) has never been irrigated for 30 years. Each plant was watered *only* the day I planted, and only if I was planting in the early fall before the winter rains began. I mulch it heavily every season.

The lovely bush anemone (Carpenteria californica) is an evergreen shrub that can grow to be six feet tall and five feet wide. The flowers bloom for up to three months, and the cut flowers last for weeks.

The drought-tolerant plants shown here are monkey flower (upper right) and California poppies, with the silvery foliage of California buckwheat in the foreground.

A view of the outside of in-line drip irrigation tubing. Because the interior of the emitter keeps any silt in suspension, the hole on the outside can be very large.

This is the interior of a pressure-compensating in-line emitter. Two black flaps control the flow of water, so that the amount coming out at 200-plus feet is exactly the same as the flow from the nearest emitters. As far as I'm concerned, it's the only kind to use; I prefer the ½-inch version.

A length of in-line emitter tubing waters a lettuce plant. Cover it with mulch and it may last you 25 years.

Drip-irrigation tubing creates a pattern of wet spots on the surface of the soil, leaving large areas of dry soil near the surface—great for limiting weeds. This is misleading, as the wet spots spread out beneath the surface (see drawing below).

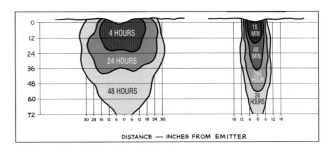

If you run the drip-irrigation tubing at even intervals across the landscape, all the roots get watered.

This drawing shows the pattern of wet spots below the soil surface (clay on the left, sand on the right). Because sand drains so easily, its wet spot is fairly narrow. The opposite is true for clayey soils; the clay resists the movement of the water and spreads it sideways.

Practical Pruning & Shaping

Use clothespins to spread young shoots to a 90-degree angle. After the first summer, the tips of the shoots will spring up, bringing them closer to the ideal 40-60 degrees.

You can also use one or more clothespins to weigh down young shoots. The outer part of the curve this creates will produce more fruit than an uncurved shoot. The shoots are shown here clipped to a trellis wire.

For the greatest yields, use spreader boards to position older limbs to the ideal 40-60-degree angle.

It's not dead... merely napping.

You can measure the angle of a shoot with the "Rule of Finger." If you see a triangle of space below your finger (top photo), the spread is too narrow. If your finger nestles in (below), the angle is ideal.

Rainwater Catchment

Give tanks for the rain! You can capture it in large tanks or in a series of smaller barrels. Rainwater is the best drink for all plants, and especially for house-plants.

The Good, the Bad, and the Bugly

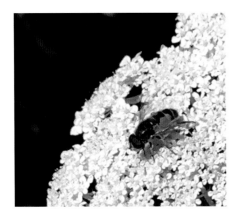

A syrphid fly resembles a bee, but unlike the bee, it can hover in place. They're harmless, and their larvae eat lots of aphids.

Here's a syrphid fly larva chowing down on an aphid. It will eat hundreds before becoming a fly, but people often squish them, thinking they're slugs.

While honeybees are important, they're different from syrphid flies in that they don't eat pests, and they can't hover. Also, the pollen on their legs gives them away.

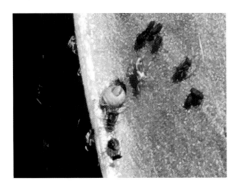

Aphids parasitized by wasps bloat up into round brown orbs. Notice the small "hatch" where the wasp has exited its prey.

C 12

Although there are many beneficial wasps, some do sting people. The dreaded yellowjacket kills caterpillars, but you don't want it anywhere around you.

Ants herd aphids together to "milk" their edible (for ants) feces, and thus may indirectly start or spread an infestation.

A ladybug faces off with an ant, maybe telling it to round up some aphids for her (and her larvae) to feed on.

These are the eggs of a ladybug. Don't squish them out of ignorance, as each larvae eats up to 5000 aphids before pupating. (Ironically, here there is an aphid crawling on the eggs.)

Ladybug larvae look ugly and a little scary, but don't kill them; a single ladybug larva will eat thousands of aphids—some say 50 per day— during its larval period.

Sweet alyssum (*Lobularia maritime* syn. *Allyssum maritima*) is a low-growing perennial in warm-winter areas. (It also blooms in the late fall and early spring here north of San Francisco.) Alyssum is very good at attracting beneficial insects (syrphid flies, bees, minute pirate beetles, parasitic wasps, tachnid flies, and lacewings), and is often planted in strips next to or near an edible crop for that reason. The plant does not have to be mixed in with the crop. (From *The Biggest and Best Insectary Plant List in North America*—see my website)

This is yellow yarrow (*Achillea millefolium*), a plant I'm easily able to grow in Sonoma County without irrigation. It's drought-resistant, deer-resistant, and comes in many colors, including yellow, orange, pink, white, and red. Like alyssum, it's a great attractor of beneficial insects—bees, chalcid wasps, braconid wasps, aphid parasites, minute pirate beetles. ladybugs, syrphid flies, parasitic wasps, tachnid flies, and lacewings. (From *The Biggest and Best Insectary Plant List in North America*)

Eccentric Gardens

Me after writing this book.

The Basket Tree by Erlandson at its final home in the Gilroy Gardens Family Theme Park, Gilroy, CA in 2011. This photo was graciously provide by the Theme Park, gilroygardens.org.

Axel Erlandson's "Basket Tree" is composed of six American sycamore trees (*Platanus occidentalis*) woven together with approach grafts to form a symmetrical cylinder. What's most amazing about this living artwork is the matching diameters of all the limbs, a horticultural feat that only a *very* few people have ever managed to come close to duplicating.

All of the photographs on these pages (except for the Gilroy Gardens Family Theme Park photo) are from 1985.

The "Squat Curvy Scallops Tree" defies gravity. When Erlandson died in 1964, he took all of his secret techniques to the grave. Only his artworks remain. (And they ain't telling.)

Two symmetrical arch-grafted American sycamore trees form the entrance to the "Tree Circus," a remarkable collection of living tree sculptures by Axel Erlandson.

The "Heart Tree" (center), is flanked by (left) the "Sideways Rope Rectangle," and (right) the "Three-Two-One Circles Tree."

Here are two views of what I consider to be the most remarkable specimen in the Tree Circus, the "Needle & Thread Tree." No one else has ever been able to approach the level of grafting skill displayed here. (NOTE: 25 years after this photo was taken, the openings have just about filled in.)

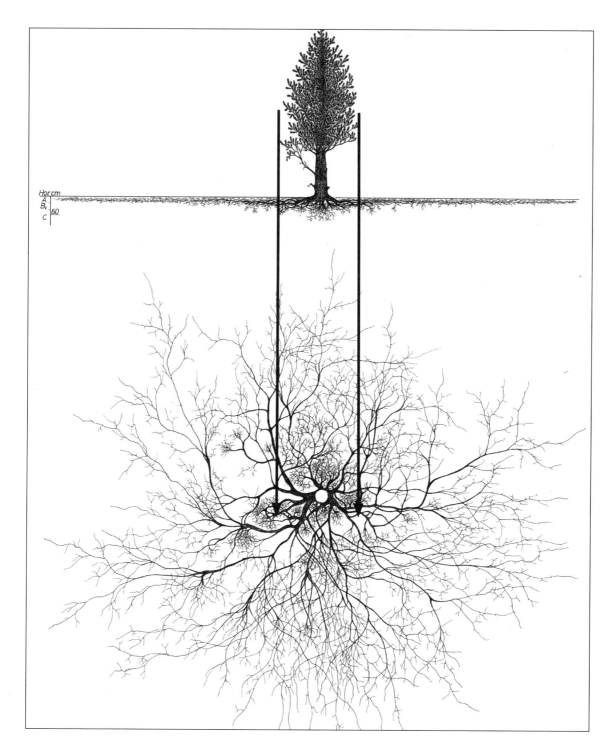

Figure 33: The shallow roots of a Swiss stone pine tree (*Pinus cembra*). There is no taproot, as less than two percent of all trees have a taproot. Notice how far the roots grow beyond the dripline. (Marked with the black lines.) These roots easily extend up to five times wider than the foliage. (60cm = 24".)

Tree and roots from: *Wurzelatlas mitteleuropäischer Waldbäume und Sträucher* (Root Atlas of Middle-European Forest Trees and Shrubs) by Lore Kutschera and Erwin Lichtenegger.

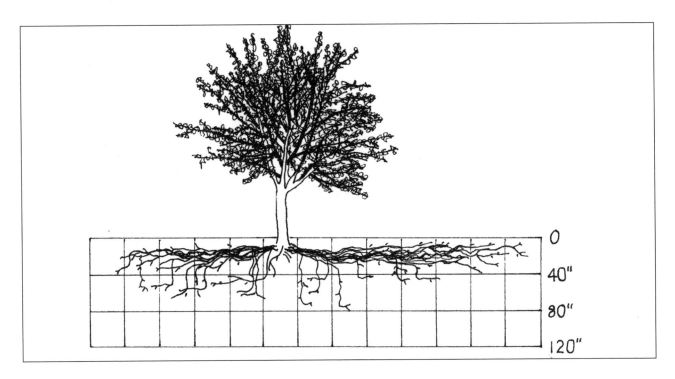

Figure 34: Here are the roots of a 30-year-old wild (ungrafted) apricot tree. Most of the roots (76.3 percent) grow between the eight- and 24-inch levels. I think the lack of roots in the eight-inch zone is due to tillage to keep weeds down. This drawing is based on a 1986 Hungarian book, published in Budapest, by Janos Tamási. He spent his entire professional life digging up and mapping only fruit tree roots. These roots extend up to nearly three times the width of the canopy on one side. This shows that roots don't always grow symmetrically. (Unlike the Swiss stone pine on the previous page.) The roots growing down are called sinker roots. They are more common on lateral (horizontal) fruit tree roots than other trees.

CHAPTER 9

Handy Tools

**Money spent now on a good tool saves a lot
of time and frustration forever.**

Here are a number of my favorite garden tools and accessories. The lazy gardener's goal is to have enough of the right tools to get work done the most efficiently and quickly (another case of money up front for savings and more leisure down the road). I don't represent any manufacturer, but if you're a tool company that likes my choices and wants me to do "product placement," feel free to contact me—I give great quote.

A List of the implements I Use the Most (In No Particular Order):

A Beverage and a Comfortable Seat
As the cover of the book shows, sitting in a wheelbarrow is very comfortable and puts you in touch with the earth—all that lovely crud and dirt gunking up the bottom and sloughing off the sides. A great place to relax and sip a drink, whether (like me) you choose a G&T or go for the soft stuff.

Hat
Your gardening headgear should be a real cover-up—the floppier the better; melanoma is not a good look on anyone. Try one of the new hats with UV-blocking technology, or one with a piece of cloth waving over the back of your neck. As a kid I mowed lawns with carefree abandon—hatless. In my fifties, I got skin cancer— luckily the not-too-dangerous kind—right where my third eye should be. Until it was cut out I thought I was having spiritual experiences, but I guess it was just the joy of gardening. Wear a hat.

Cell Phone
It's great to take before-and-after photos to see what you've achieved over the years, and panorama shots are great to share with friends online. I use my iPhone Plus 6 because I'm a Mac man with a MacBook Pro. Any other phone with a camera is fine. Some Galaxy phones may have even better cameras. (NOT product placement) If you want to, you can photograph or video all aspects of your garden—even in slow motion or time-lapse or panorama— to augment a garden logbook or in place of one. (You might also want to keep a paper record in case you crash your photo files.)

Computer
This is an essential tool for the inquisitive gardener; it allows you to Google ideas/facts/research papers/images, and to access information in the form of YouTube videos. Just remember that the information in many "professional gardener" online videos may be just wishful thinking or erroneous or sneaky advertising. There are some topic-oriented groups on Facebook, but again, a lot of

information there is inaccurate at best, or based on assumptions, not science-backed information. Many blogs are, alas, either very simplistic, or just well-meaning repetitions of false information and outdated gardening myths.

My preferred research method is to Google an assumption or concept for peer-reviewed papers. This means that a scientist or group of scientists have researched a theory, and their written results have been reviewed by other experts in the field before publication, so they're not just talking out of their assumptions. Owning a laptop means that you can do all this while lounging in your recliner.

Actually Calling People

I'm amazed at how many scientists are pleased and grateful that you're interested in their work, and are willing to talk on the phone and discuss it at length (the only way to reach some of them, however, is via email, so keep that computer or laptop handy). I've emailed professors in Scandinavia with a question or two and received in return dozens of pages of PDFs of more research along the same lines. I've almost never been turned down by a scientist or scholar I've asked for information, especially if I demonstrate that I've read his/her work and ask intelligent questions—they're usually happy to learn that someone knows their work and takes it seriously.

Hori-Hori

Many gardeners say if they had to choose one tool to have it would be a hori-hori (translates from Japanese into "soil knife" or "weeding knife"). This is a multi-faceted tool with a very sturdy handle and a seven-inch-long "blade" that offers great adaptability and ease of use. The blade is forged of very durable metal, and is curved so you can dig with it. It's serrated along one edge to cut through roots and clayey or gravelly soil. Some hori-horis also have a ruler etched onto the blade, so you can tell how deep to plant bulbs (see Figure #37). According to Genevieve Schmidt, writer

and reviewer for a great website called North Coast Gardening, the best model is the "Pro Gardener's Digging Tool" by Garrett Wade. This is how and why she recommends it:

• "Offset blade. The offset blade feels like it's doing some of the work for me, and after testing the two soil knives side by side, I found that the Pro Gardener's Digging Tool (about $50) caused less wrist fatigue than weeding than my old one.

• "Tough alloy steel. The tough alloy steel of this digging knife has proven resistant to even the worst types of misuse. I even left it out for two weeks, and no rust developed on the surface.

• "Rounded handle. The handle is another area where this digging knife blows the competition away. It has a smooth, rounded grip that's comfortable and makes it easy to control the knife. It's perfectly formed to the natural grip of your hand and is comfortable even for long days of weeding. Plus, the entire handle is made of metal.

• "Serrated blade really means it. You may have seen the cute little serrations on other hori-horis and tittered to yourself about how sharp they looked. But you haven't seen sharp yet. The teeth on this Pro Gardener's Digging Tool are downright lethal to even the most congested root systems."

You can read more of her great tool reviews at NorthCoastGardening.com.

Hula Hoe

The best stand-up weeder, and the easiest to use, is the Hula Hoe. With its long handle you don't have to bend over—bitchin'. The beauty is that it cuts in both directions, doubling the speed at which you can murder unsuspecting weeds.

Hand Mattock or Japanese Hand Mattock

One of the top four tools I use is a 1.5 lb. Tiller

or Rockforge mattock with a 16-inch fiberglass or American hickory handle. This is a serious tool for serious weeding, but you need a strong wrist. I have to hold it further away from the top of the handle every year as my wrist weakens with age. The Japanese hand mattock is a lighter-weight version and holds a sharper edge.

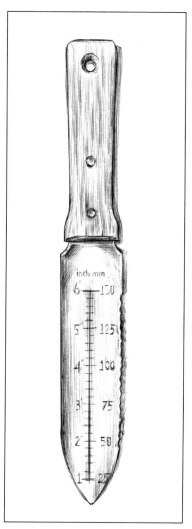

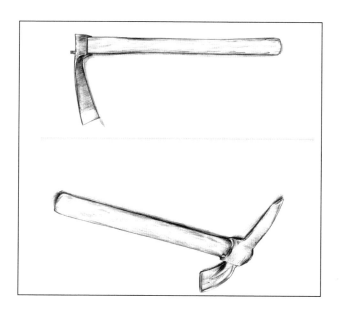

Figure 35: I use the lower mattock, but I still have strong wrists. The upper Japanese mattock is best for those computer jockeys with weaker wrists.

Figure 37: This Hori-Hori is much like many varieties on the market. Most have a ruler on the blade to assist with planting bulbs.

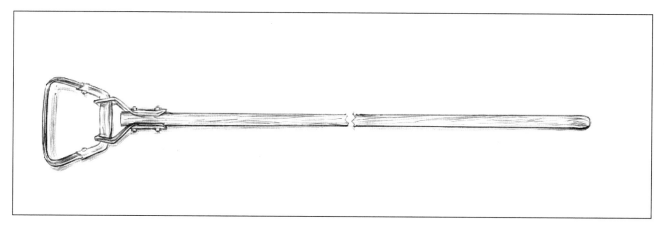

Figure 36: The Hula Hoe has a long handle. Here it is shortened to fit into the page. The long handle allows you to weed without bending over or slouching. More weeding, less effort. Cool.

Spading Fork

I use a D-handled spading fork a lot to heave the soil instead of digging it up and turning it over. This not only saves a ton of energy, it's also good at getting a heavy tap-rooted weed out of the ground. I never met a weedy dock (*Rumex crispus*) I couldn't handle with a forged spading fork. I like the Bulldog brand, but be willing to fork out a lot of money—$75-$100 bucks—for a forged one with a hickory handle. As I've mentioned elsewhere, cheap forks are a false economy. They can can snap off, bend backwards, or wind up with grotesquely twisted tines, all from normal use.

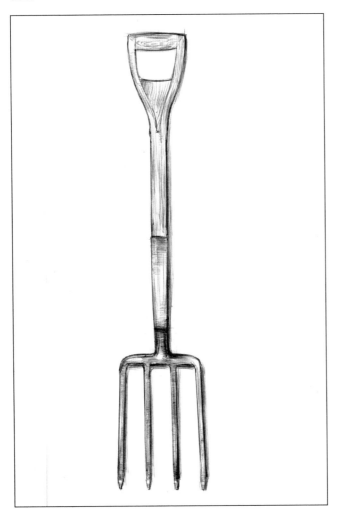

Figure 38: This forged fork will easily last a lifetime. Mine is nearly 35 years old. Some now have fiberglass handles that make them lighter. Mine has a wooden handle because I'm old-fashioned.

Hoses

There is no such damn thing as a hassle-free hose. All hoses are a form of mental torture for the gardener, not to mention a reliable source of profits for hardware stores, nurseries, or Big-Box-store garden sections—you'll always have to return to buy another one. Hoses kink, they develop leaks, they split, and they're hell to drag around. You just have to live with them and polish your vocabulary of cuss words. If you find a kink-free hose, email me, and I'll amend this page. (rkourik@sonic.net)

(Actually, rubber hoses are about the strongest, perhaps longest lasting, and are less likely to kink or fall apart in the sun, but they can be expensive and hard to work with.)

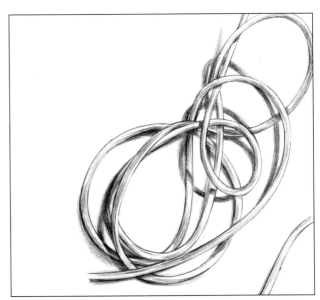

Figure 39: The usual status of many garden hoses. Get a sturdy rubber hose to avoid the Medusa effect.

Trowel

I have a trowel that's 43 years old. The paint has worn, but the forged scoop and shaft are still very much intact. Spend some extra moola—up to $30—and get a forged trowel. If your present trowel is too difficult to use, get one of the new ergonomic kind that are kinder to your hands and wrists.

Pruning Tools

I do a lot of pruning, and here are some of my favorite pruning tools.

The Felco #8 bypass pruning shears are comfortable, with three important ergonomic improvements: the handle is curved to the actual form of your slightly closed hand; the lower handle has a jog in it to keep your hand from slipping off the

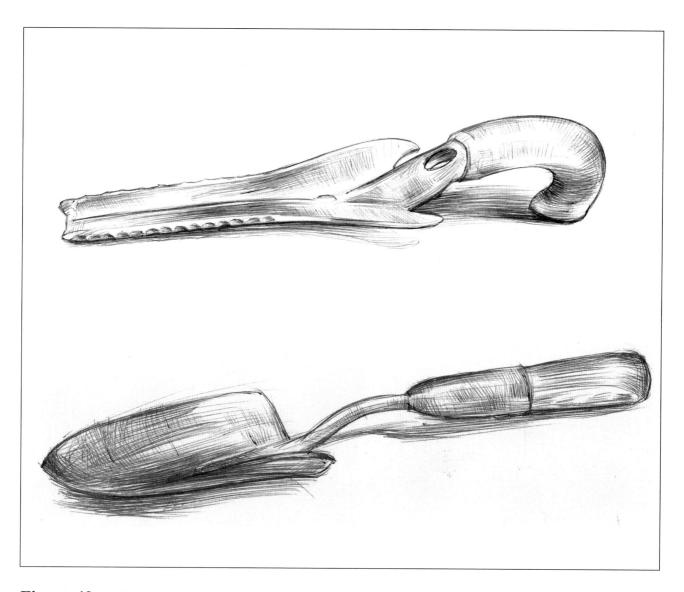

Figure 40: After 40 years I still have and use my forged trowel pictured above. For those with weaker wrists choose an ergonomic version like the weeder at top. Blade widths vary by the manufacturer but most have similar wrist-friendly handles.

handle when you're pressing forward into a cut; and the blade is angled slightly down to reduce the forward, and straining, rotation of the wrist. They're light, sturdily built, and easy to maintain and sharpen. As far as I know, Felco is the only manufacturer to x-ray its pruning blades to inspect for tiny fissures that might cause the blade to shatter when in use.

If you have weak wrists or arthritis, the Felco #7 has many of the same features, plus a rotating finger-grip handle that requires 30% less effort. Even though I don't have either problem, this is my favorite bypass pruner. The Felco rotating handle does save time and effort, but it'll flush out your wallet for sure. These puppies will set you back more than 75 bucks, so you'll want to take good care of your Felco pruners so your kids can inherit them.

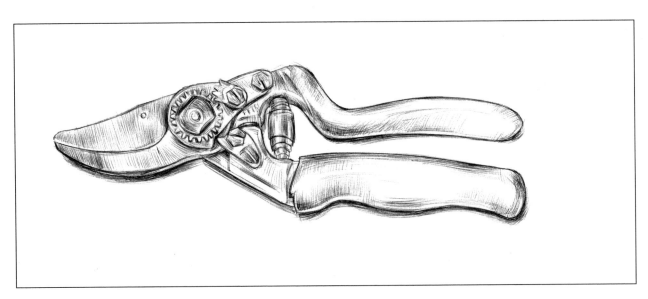

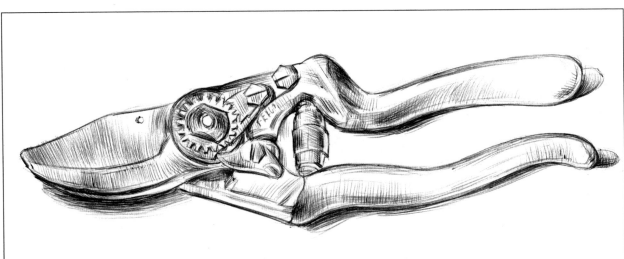

Figure 41: Two Felco bypass pruners. The lower one is more like a conventional clipper. But the handle and blade are tilted at an angle to make it easier on the wrist. The upper clipper also has a rotating handle that saves 30 percent of the effort. Great for weak wrists or long days of pruning. I use these exclusively.

Loppers

If you're restoring a slightly abandoned tree, or pruning an ornamental one, you may need a specialized pair of shears called a lopper. Choose either the 16- or 24-inch aluminum-handled Felco F-20 or F-21.

Pruning Saws

If you should need a pruning saw, a 12-inch bladed folding saw will probably be the only one you require. Make sure you get one that has a locking mechanism for the open position. Good brands are the Felco #61 and the ARS #210-DX. Japanese handsaws are known for being very sharp and staying sharp for a very long time. They're a good option for a pruning saw, and some companies make a folding version. Silky is an excellent brand that offers many options.

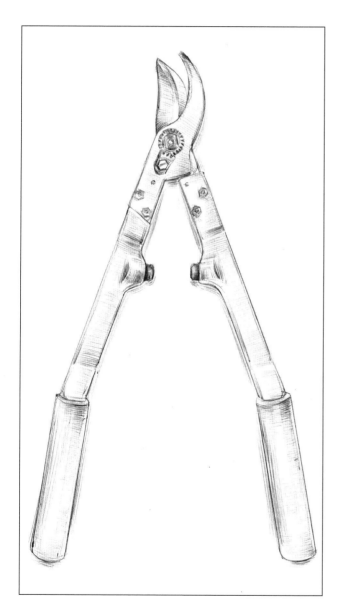

Figure 42: I like the 16-inch lopper. It allows me to be in the tree and easily work close to hand. This assumes the tree has been pruned properly from birth.

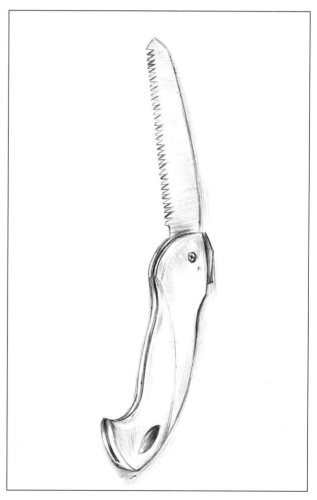

Figure 43: There are hundreds of models of folding saws. Be sure to get a Japanese model as I think they have the best blades that stay sharp for a long time.

Figure
Pruning "Stick"

This is a lopper-on-a-stick kind of gizmo that's a great tool for pruning eight feet or more from the ground (you activate the cutting mechanism by pulling on the cord, where the upper, left hand is pictured here); it saves a lot of time, and you don't have to haul your lazy butt up a ladder. Or fall off of one. I use mine a *lot*.

Figure 44: Keep your feet on the ground while you prune without fear of falling.

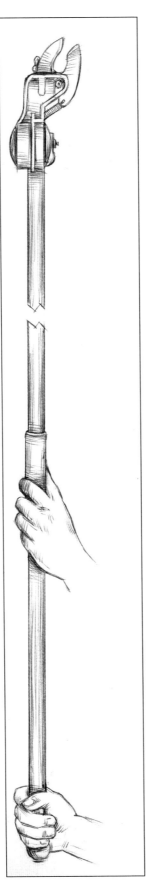

Figure Speedy Sharp Sharpener

This sharpening tool is small enough to carry around, and to fit into the "mouth" of any by-pass pruner. It's inexpensive ($11.19 as of this writing) made in the USA, sharpens any kind of blade, comes with a lifetime warranty, and is made of something called MICRO 100 SUPER. CARBIDE. Such a deal.

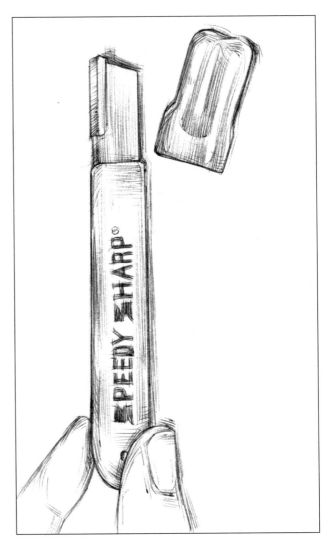

Figure 45: A super sharpener.

 Bob sez: *Don't be afraid to spend a lot on the higest quality tools so they last a lifetime. You'll save a pile of money in the end.*

Some Other Tools I Use, But Not As Often As I Do The Ones Previously Mentioned:

Figure Shovel

(A Note on Choosing a Shovel—Learn From My Experience)

In 1975, when I started landscaping professionally, I bought cheap long-handled shovels at the flea market. In 1979, I moved to the Farallones Institute Rural Center, an appropriate technology community where biodynamic intensive gardening was practiced with a fervor akin to religious ecstasy. I was swept away by the enthusiasm of the disciples of Alan Chadwick (the high priest of intensive raised-bed gardening) for short, D-handled spades, so I finally shelled out a lot of money for what many considered to be the Rolex™ of digging implements.

But in spite of the praise by my gardener friends and by a certain mail-order catalog—which had gained fame in great part from its eloquent, even romantic, praise of these heavy handmade forged tools—I kept returning to my trusty long-handled shovels for most tasks. Finally, I ran across research on tool ergonomics that confirmed what my body had already whispered—light, long-handled shovels are best for most garden tasks. At best, D-handled spades are only suited for work literally "in the trenches."

Ergonomics is the science of adapting tools and physical working conditions to suit the worker, which often involves redesigning tools to better fit the human body. In practice, much of ergonomics means rethinking what sometimes turn out to be arbitrary designs of common everyday tools.

Ergonomic researchers recommend a shovel weight of between 3.3 and 3.96 pounds. Unfortunately, most of the English-forged spades weigh from 4.5 pounds to as much as six pounds. One researcher even found that long-handled shovels increased productivity 25 percent over short-handled shovels.

There is one task where the short-handled spade was rated better, by 10 percent, than a long-handled shovel—in the confined workspace of a coalmine. So, if you've got a lot of coal to excavate, the short-handled shovel or spade may be just the tool for you!

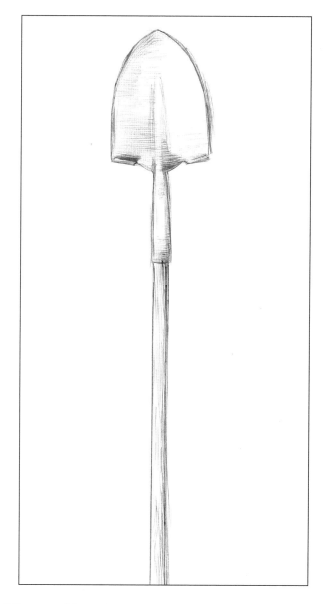

Figure 46: A long handle lends efficient leverage.

Wheelbarrow

You can now buy cheesy plastic wheelbarrows, but I like the old-fashioned metal ones. As you can see on the cover, they make a great place to sit and eat a sandwich, rest, and slug back a drink. I've only needed two in my 45-year-old gardening career. Considering what I paid for them back in the day, that works out to about three dollars a year. Like the cover illustration, get one with a single tire, they now have tires that don't deflate—grab this one. I like wooden handles for the feel, but metal handles last longer. When not using the wheelbarrow, tilt it onto its side so water doesn't stand in the bottom and rust the metal prematurely.

Figure 47: A sturdy wheelbarow can support decades of moving experiences in the garden. And, as the cover shows, support you while relaxing or eating lunch. If your terrain requires a lot more stability, consider a garden cart with two, three, or four wheels for hauling stuff around.

Bob sez: *Gloves are for wusses. I prefer the leathery skin of my hand, with warts, scrapes, and scabs to prove, with each hearty handshake, that, by golly, I'm a gardener. But seriously, you can buy gloves for just about any level of garden work, ranging from barely-there flowered cotton mitts for daintily dead-heading your petunias, to cowhide gauntlets for thrashing around up to your elbows in blackberry bushes.*

Yes, many gardeners love the feeling of getting their hands into the soil, and prefer the dexterity of unglovedness, but if you work, say, at a public-interface job for which you need to preserve your manicure, glove up. You'll probably have to road-test a few pairs until you find a level of protection and flexibility that suits your needs. All gardening centers and many hardware stores sell a variety of gardening gloves.

Clogs

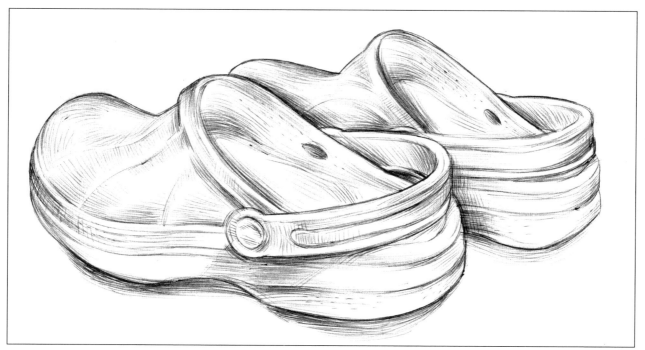

Figure 48: You'll probably want to run out into the garden from time to time to check on your ruta-bagas or read the rain gauge. It's a hassle to put on regular shoes in a hurry, and you have to bend over to tie the laces! Assert your laziness by getting a pair of slip-on garden clogs. If you do want to wear them for longer periods of time, many of them come with a strap for holding your foot snugly inside the clog. They are easy to clean with a spritz of the hose.

Figure Watering Can

I used to use classic watering cans, especially for delicate plants and seedlings, but have switched to one of those hose-heads that can be adjusted to six or eight different spray patterns. It gives me lots more choices than one single sprinkling can.

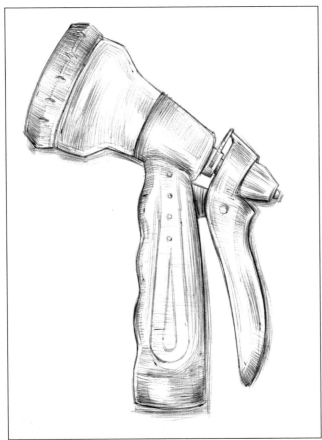

Figure 49: An adjustable nozzle for your garden offers a wealth of ways to water.

For the Ambitious

If you're a bit more ambitious than the ordinary garden bum, you can acquire the following:

Shipping Pallets

There's recently been a wave of interest in using pallets in the garden for an amazing number of projects. Examples include; raised beds, compost bins, vertical planting walls, and even garden furniture. New pallets cost between $95 and $275, depending on the size and quality, and even those made from recycled wood can cost $140-$200. In case you're wondering what the heck a pallet is, here's Wikipedia: "A pallet is a flat transport structure that supports goods in a stable fashion while being lifted by a forklift, a pallet jack, a front loader, a jacking device, or a crane." (Pallets have traditionally been made of wood, but nowadays some are constructed of metal or plastics.)

Don't be a big gluteus maximus. Many store-owners have little use for pallets after receiving the merchandise that's been delivered on them. If you ask politely, they'll often let you cart them off for free, or for a nominal fee, which saves them the trouble of breaking them up and disposing of them. But be aware: pallets used for international shipping are treated with methyl bromide, a nasty chemical that is about to be banned from agricultural use. Check for the MB stamp burnt into the pallet.

Figure 50: Free (or cheap) is good, but watch out for wood that's been treated with nasty stuff.

Well-Oiled Sand

Fill a five-gallon bucket 50-75 percent full of sand and add about a quart of used motor oil. This is where you can stick tools like trowels, shovels, and spading forks after you've hosed them down (let the tool dry) or wire-brushed the bulk of the dirt off of them. The oily sand does the final cleaning and coats the metal with a thin rust-protective film.

Grafting Knives

Victorinox™ makes a grafting knife and a budding knife. The grafting knife is used to graft in the winter or spring. The budding knife is for summer grafting. You really should learn grafting as it gives you lots of creative options for fruiting trees. (See P. 47.)

Figure Rain Gauges

I have a simple but very accurate rain gauge—the "Professional Rain, Snow and Hail Gauge" from Wind & Weather. It'll set you back a lot of yuppie beer, but it lasts, holds up to 12 inches of rain before it has to be emptied, and measures the rain in one-hundredths of an inch intervals. In 2018 it cost $60. Ouch! It's not connected to a computer, and I like that. Remote gauges for computers can be a real hassle.

You can also get a simple self-dumping remote rain gauge so you don't have to waste time going outside to read and empty one. Two good sources of remote, computer-connected rain gauges and complete weather stations are Oregon Scientific and Davis Instruments. Others are available at WeatherShack.com. Weather Snoop is one model for my Mac.

Or, make a "Kourik" weather station. The Kourik weather station is a rope fastened to any protruding tree branch or porch eave with a rock tied onto the free end. This is how you check the weather:
• If the rock is moving, it's windy.
• If the rock is wet, it's raining.
• If the rock has ice on it, it's really cold.
• If the rock has sunlight on it, it's not a cloudy day.
• If both the rock and rope are shaking, it's an earthquake.
• If covered with little white things stuck to the rock, it's snowing.
• If you can't see it, it's nighttime. (Or, you've gone blind.)

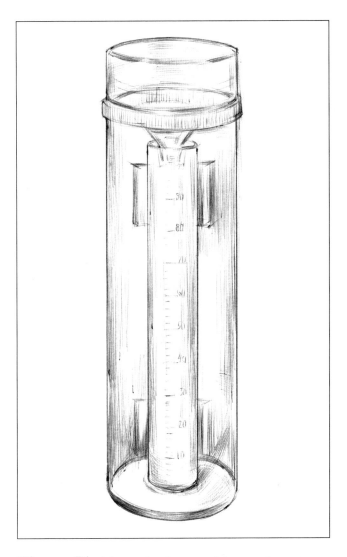

Figure 51: If you don't want this weather station, you can always use your smartphone app connected to a weather service.

Figure Rose Pruning Guard

I don't grow roses as the deer eat them with abandon. But I do have to, on occasion, remove blackberry vines. These are wonderful for protecting my arms up past the elbows from the devil thorns. They are super-resistent denim.

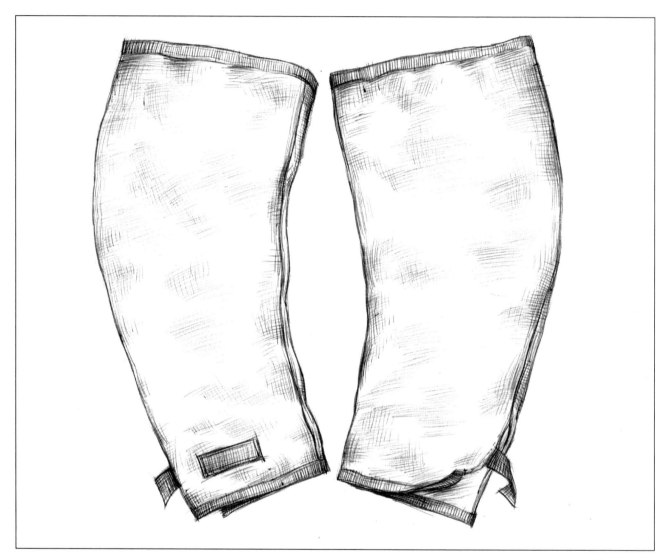

Figure 52: These sleeves go up past the elbow to nearly the armpit. This protects virtually the entire arm from wicked thorns. These are designed to adapt to whtaever gloves you use. Most arm guards now come with gloves built in.

Figure Grain Shovel

If you have a lot of mulch to move, use an aluminum grain shovel to scoop up a huge pile with each swoop. The scoop itself is very light, won't rust, and is the best tool for heaving around bark mulches, wood chips, and leaves.

Figure Pitchfork

Another tool to move wood chips and leaves. Again, purchase only one with forged tines. There are newer models with fiberglass handles that are lighter than wooden versions.

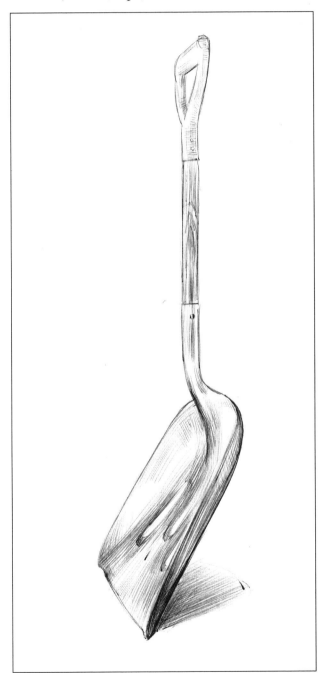

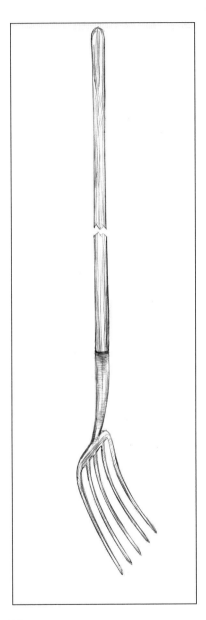

Figure 54: Use a pitchfork to toss loose, clumpy stuff like hay, straw, and leaves.

Figure 53: A grain shovel's large scoop lets you make speedy work of loose lifting.

All tool drawings by Lori Alemedia.

CHAPTER 10

Practical Pruning & Shaping

Learn to focus the magic of plant growth to produce bountiful harvests and encourage elegant ornamentals.

The forest "prunes" its trees and bushes naturally, using gravity, ice, snow, the growth cycle, and the wind. We prune our trees and shrubs by clipping, sawing, and lopping. Like any gardening task, pruning can be either a hack job or a healthy way to nurture plants. When your pruning follows Nature's lead, it helps promote healthy trees. Even if you don't have trees or shrubs to prune, you may find yourself fascinated by the almost-mystical interrelationship between the accomplished pruner and plant biochemistry.

Bob sez: *If you really want to watch your favorite YouTube concerts, why prune at all? In fact, you'd get more apples by slouching back into the couch. As Figure 55 shows, during the youth of the tree more fruit is actually produced on unpruned trees. The only problem with this laissez-faire attitude is that this early fruit can be rather small. To produce a good-sized eating pear or pie apple, you really need to get out there and prune or shape your tree.*

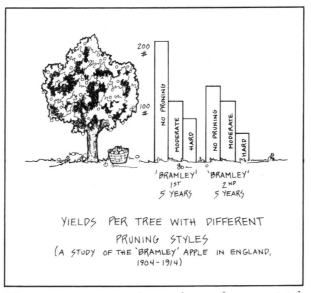

Figure 55: Apples from unpruned trees are much smaller, but good for making cider.

A Short Sidestep - Basic Tree Growth (Or, What Every Pruner Needs to Know)

Tip Bud

The large fat bud perched on the tip of each shoot is called the "apical bud," "terminal bud," or "tip bud." It's very important to know that each tip bud sends a constricting hormonal signal down the shoot to stop all the buds below it from developing into new shoots or flower buds. At the same time, the tip bud grows rapidly skyward. (This is why you'll see unpruned fruit trees with shoots bristling like the spikes on a hedgehog.) Both the limiting and vertical-growth effects are very much dependent on gravity, or at least on the position of the shoot.

Buds that haven't yet made up their tiny minds as to whether they want to become a shoot (vegetative growth) or a flower bud (fruiting growth) are called "dormant" buds. Pruning is a big deal because it can guide a dormant bud to produce either branch or fruit.

Spur-Type Flowering

An apple or pear "spur" begins, as all blossoms do, as a single flowering bud on the fruiting tree. It takes apple and pear trees an entire spring and summer to convert dormant buds into young flower buds growing on second-year shoots. They do this by diverting specific foods and hormones to the dormant buds. Without pruning, some of the nutrients and hormones randomly accumulate in a few dormant buds. But pruning, and especially shaping, can help make more dormant buds become fruitful. The critical difference with spur-type plants such as apple and pear trees is that they continue to flower at the same spot on the branch or limb for many years thereafter—as much as twenty years or more.

As a general rule, tip buds on shoots that are growing vertically have the most stifling influ-

ence on lower dormant buds and attain the most length per season (thus the hedgehog effect on unpruned trees). A tip bud growing at a lateral angle of 45 to 60 degrees (usually referred to as a "lateral" shoot) delivers much less hormonal impact; some dormant buds below it will either become new lateral growth or flower buds, and at the same time tip growth will slow.

A tip bud on a lateral shoot that's growing horizontally, on the other hand, causes most of the dormant buds on the horizontal shoot to "wake up" and become new vertical shoots. At the same time, nearly all tip growth on the horizontal shoot stops. Pruning new growth to the ideal zone of position (45° to 60° from horizontal) will promote more laterals without extra pruning and

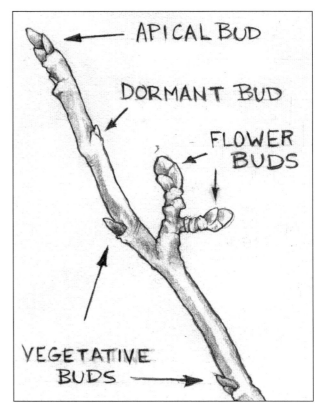

Figure 56: The bud at the tip of a branch is called the apical bud. Below there are dormant buds that can be shoots or flowers and trace buds. Dormant buds that are beginning to form shoots are called vegetative buds. *

make some flower buds that will become fruiting spurs.

Nurture by Pruning

When shaping fruiting or ornamental trees, the foremost guideline is: prune out the three "D"s—dead, diseased, and dysfunctional shoots or limbs. It's important to remove all dead tissue as soon as you spot it, because it can harbor pests, rots, or diseases. Pruning the dead wood usually ensures that these nasties won't progress any further or burrow inward to kill the entire plant.

Next, remove all diseased growth. Nature has equipped most plants with various chemical zones to fight the progression of dying tissue, and to compartmentalize rot by "walling it off" from the inner portion of the tree. The gardener who prunes before these conditions travel further back into the plant will assist nature in curtailing diseases and rot.

How can growth be "dysfunctional?" Sometimes two or more shoots, branches, or limbs will cross, causing a "raw" wound as the branches rub

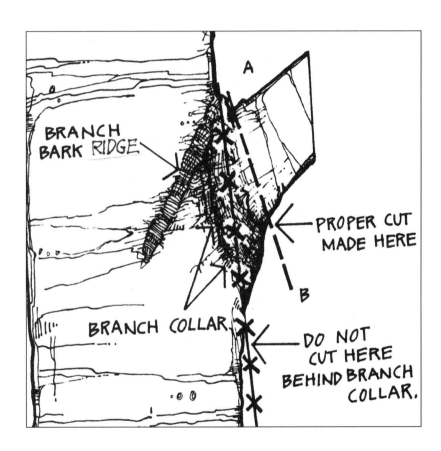

Figure 57: The branch bark ridge helps you decide how to prune a limb. Sometimes A to B is not as visible as here. Simply take the angle between the ridge and the vertical trunk and "flop" it over to indicate the approximate place to cut. The important point is the leave the branch collar intact for a healthy cut.

against each other. In this case, one of the two should be pruned off at its base, as such a wound will often let insects or pathogens enter the plant.

Another common suggestion is to remove any weak growth. Practice and trial and error will help you distinguish growth that is too slender or slight (weak) to bear the weight of fruit.

Finally, you should remove all true "suckers"—those quick-growing vertical shoots that emerge from the roots at the base of the tree.

Summer Pruning

Want to get a tan while pruning fruit trees? Want to spend less time pruning altogether? Then summer pruning is for you. Summer pruning is very helpful in: 1) producing more fruitful trees and 2) controlling unwanted growth on ornamental ones. It also offers more control of shoot growth, which means that far less pruning will be needed in the winter. Plus, you'll be able to prune in a T-shirt (and other clothes, please) and avoid freezing your buns off. While most people prune almost exclusively in the late winter or early spring, I prune mostly in the summer to control growth, promote fruiting and shape the foliage.

For "Popper" (my grandpa—and I have no idea how we came up with this nickname), tree pruning, especially of fruit trees, was exclusively a winter task. "The trees will bleed too much if you cut them in the summer," was the prevailing wisdom. In my youth, I never questioned his word, but as I got older and spent more time gardening, I noticed that windstorms in the summer did as much damage to tree limbs as ice, sleet, wind and snow did in winter. So, I reasoned, nature must be used to healing such damage in any season.

Then I ran across an amazing out-of-print 1919 book entitled *California Fruits*, by Edward Wickson. Inside I found this intriguing passage: "... Fruit bearing is promoted by pruning after the chief growth of the season is attained. Summer pruning to check the too exuberant wood growth [what are called suckers and water sprouts by many gardeners] of some kinds of trees is employed...[in cases where] the vegetative [leafy] process...seems fairly to run riot."

From another favorite old (1911) text, *The Pruning Book*, by L. H. Bailey, I found an answer to "Popper's" concern about trees bleeding—"Fruit trees rarely bleed to any extent, and on trees which do bleed, it is doubtful if any injury follows." Walnuts and certain ornamentals, such as elms and maples, will bleed when pruned in the summer, but with no apparent harmful effects.

My experience with fruit trees has proven the efficacy of summer pruning. Over the past 40 years, however, I've learned that if you prune too early in the summer, the effect is much like winter pruning—new side-shoots will form and growth will be stimulated. Wait to prune until the burst of spring and early-summer growth has tapered off. Summer pruning is the best way to control rampant growth, including those "water sprouts" and "suckers." It has a mild dwarfing or stunting effect, but is not debilitating.

Still, it's hard to tell if summer pruning stimulates more fruiting (it doesn't cause less), in spite of Wickson's assertion. I prune my fruit trees almost exclusively in the late summer (late August), after the harvest if I can, to control any growth that is too vigorous. Summer is also the best time to remove leafy growth that's overly shading the tree and resulting in slow ripening and poor fruit color.

Summer Pruning's Shortcomings

Pruning trees in leaf makes it harder to see and shape their branching patterns. The main and secondary limbs may get sunburned when shading growth is removed. (When pruning in hot summer areas, cut with discretion, leaving enough foliage to protect the main trunk and upper branches.) If you prune on older limbs before harvesting fruit trees, some fruit may be knocked off.

Summer Pruning Can Curtail Disease

Summer pruning affects the balance of nitrogen in the tissues of trees and shrubs; this helps form sturdier shoot growth. Healthy growth is more resistant to powdery mildew, a disease that infects apple, pear, plum and prune trees as well as rosebushes. In California, my experience has shown that a schedule based exclusively on spring pruning can actually encourage powdery mildew. This disease may have a harder time getting a foothold if you're not forcing succulent growth with dormant pruning but, although I hate to admit it, sulfur-based fungicides are much more effective than pruning in controlling mildew.

Three prominent diseases—Cytospora canker, bacterial gummosis (One of the major troubles encountered in cherry and apricot orchards. The same disease may attack peaches, plums, and prunes. The tendency toward gumming is common in all stone fruit trees. The gumming is due to the formation of cankers.), and bacterial canker—can also be reduced by summer pruning. Canker is a real bad guy, a fungal disease of fruit trees that results in damage to the bark or, if unchecked, the death of the tree. The term can also apply to an open lesion in plant tissue caused by infection or injury.

These afflictions can also enter through pruning wounds when it rains, especially in late winter through early summer. You can avoid these troublesome diseases—especially in dry-summer climates—with summer pruning, and disinfecting your clipper blades with a dip in a 10% bleach solution after every cut.

Other diseases enter open pruning cuts. The fungal disease anthracnose causes cankers and enters cuts during fall rains in the west. To avoid it, don't prune too late in the summer, and allow plenty of time for a callus to form. (A callus is a healing buildup of wood and bark around an area that's been pruned off) Check your local Cooperative Extension Service and its Master Gardener Program or an arborist for other diseases that are specific to your area.

 Bob sez: *If you have an abandoned tree, it's best to use mostly summer pruning to "rehabilitate" it—and you'll save time. (Paid gardeners often instinctively prune only in the winter; all that subsequent rampant growth gives them job security.)*

Make Modern Cuts

As with all modern pruning, cutting flush to the limb or trunk is no longer advised. The safest way to prune requires identifying two parts: the branch collar and the branch bark ridge. The branch collar often appears as a slightly swollen base or shoulder-shaped lump where each shoot, branch, or limb is attached. (Conifers usually have a prominent branch collar.) Prune to leave the branch collar intact, see Figure 57.

Can't spot the branch collar? Just don't leave any long stubs that can be colonized by diseases and fungi that may subsequently enter the heart of the branch or trunk.

Thinning and Heading Cuts

Summer pruning involves using mostly thinning cuts—cutting the current year's growth all the way to its branch collar. A heading cut, which is used in the winter to stimulate side branches lower on the branch, is the partial removal of a branch—not to the branch collar, but further out on the branch, above the side shoots you want to encourage.

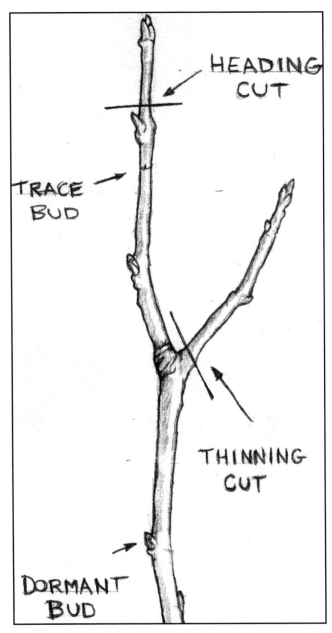

Figure 58: There are two major pruning cuts. A heading cut takes off part of a shoot or limb. A thinning cut removes all of a shoot or limb to it's point of origin. Heading cuts stimulate shoots, here the dormant bud above the trace bud. Thinning cuts can control growth. *

Summer Pruning Any Tree or Shrub for Shape and Bloom

Many plants need seasonal pruning to look good. If the crown foliage of your flowering bush was too rangy this past summer, don't spare the pruning shears. Shrubs and perennials that bloom in mid- to late summer will form their flower buds after a summer pruning and before going dormant in the winter. If you don't prune, each season's growth gets further and further from the center of the plant and will begin to look rangy and ugly. Thin back the crown after bloom. The more you prune the crown back, the more densely it will grow next summer.

Limb Position for Flowers
As a general guideline, the best position for a shoot that naturally favors a flower bud is, again, between 45° and 60° above horizontal. At these angles, flowering and branching are stimulated, and a reasonable amount of new tip growth remains so the plant doesn't become too narrow. Pruning new growth to this ideal zone of position will promote greater ornamental beauty (and with tree crops, more bounty).

When to Summer Prune
As with good comedy, timing is everything. Pruning too early in the summer may act like a dormant-season pruning and force growth. Prune too late in the summer, and any new growth is vulnerable to early hard frosts and winter's deep freezes.

If you're trying to restrain a vigorous tree or shrub, pruning is best done in the summer to continue thinning out unwanted growth. Some pruning all season long is best for a balanced approach to caring for trees, shrubs and perennials.

This doesn't mean I've cast aside all winter pruning. Winter pruning invigorates a tree, stimulating new growth. I use it to encourage side shoots where there are bare areas in the

 Bob sez: *Don't forget columnar apple trees. (See page 44.) They are almost completely free of pruning, as they have few or no branches to orient. The fruit grows on spurs along the trunk— almost effortless.*

tree's branches; for cutting back tall, unbranched young trees to help form side branches exactly where I want them; and to force a new side shoot to grow in any desired direction by pruning the branch off just above a bud which faces the preferred orientation.

Toothpicks

I bet you were wondering if I was ever going to get around to those toothpicks. Here's the scoop: if a 45-degree angle of a branch is ideal for a balance of growth and fruiting, why not give shoots an early start? A toothpick can be used to carefully spread a young four- to 10-inch shoot to the ideal angle—see Figure 59. Stick one end of the toothpick into the branch of origin, and the other into the new shoot so that it's braced at 45-60 degrees, then release. At the end of the summer you can flick the toothpick out with your finger, and the new shoot will stay at about a 45-degree angle. The more you use toothpicks the less pruning for fruit you'll need to do in the future, not to mention that you can use any extras for getting barbecue out of your teeth.

Clothespins

The next size up in spreading devices are those old-fashioned clothespins with a coiled spring in the middle. (See Figure 60.) I use them to weigh down tender young spring shoots about six to 12

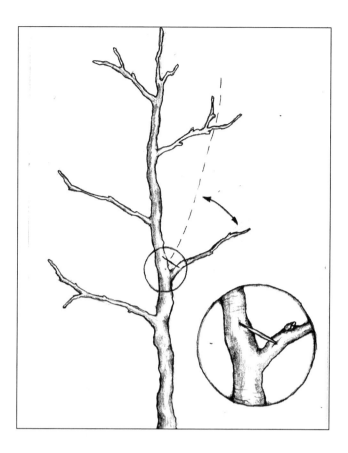

Figure 59: I like to use toothpicks when a shoot is very young to encourage the 45- to 60-degree angle that promotes fruiting. *

inches long; this slows down the tip growth and encourages fruiting buds—as shown in Figure 60. Bending down the tip bud means that not so much of the hormone (known as the apical (tip) dominance hormone) that favors vertical shoot growth gets through, and the tip stops growing or slows down considerably.

For young short growth, it only takes one clothspin to get the tip to dangle downward, but if the shoot is longer and less flexible, clip more clothespins on the outer curve. I've used as many as four or more clothespins to gently but firmly reduce tip growth. Once the shoot is bent over, buds on the curve nearest the branch of origin "germinate" into fruiting buds. The following

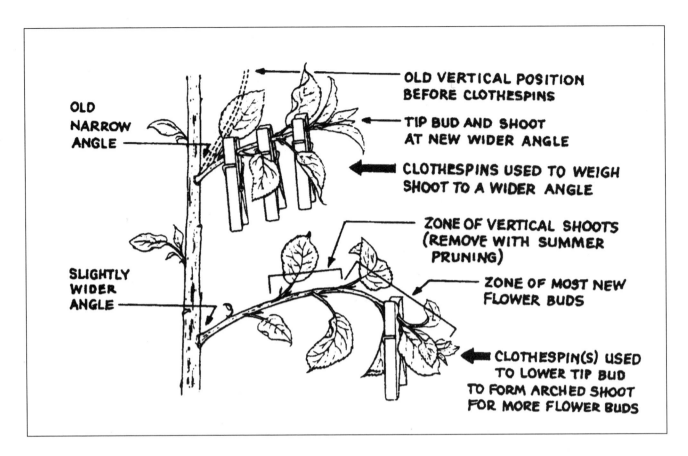

OLD NARROW ANGLE

OLD VERTICAL POSITION BEFORE CLOTHESPINS

TIP BUD AND SHOOT AT NEW WIDER ANGLE

CLOTHESPINS USED TO WEIGH SHOOT TO A WIDER ANGLE

ZONE OF VERTICAL SHOOTS (REMOVE WITH SUMMER PRUNING)

SLIGHTLY WIDER ANGLE

ZONE OF MOST NEW FLOWER BUDS

CLOTHESPIN(S) USED TO LOWER TIP BUD TO FORM ARCHED SHOOT FOR MORE FLOWER BUDS

Figure 60: I use clothespins to place a young shoot into the angle that tends to promote fruit buds. If the new shoot is very supple, it may take only one clothespin to draw the tip down to favor the buds in the outer zone of the shoot to become flowering buds. Older shoots may be stiff enough to require more than one clothespin.

year, some of these buds make fruit. At the very top of the curved shoot a bud may sprout into apical dominance, but you can just rub it off once in late summer.

This approach to making fruit is so simple and so easy that it only takes 20-60 minutes at several different times to shape 40 trees—the number of trees in my test orchard. (And once you've shaped the curve it stays in place, and you can unclip the shoot and use the clothespins over again.)

Spreaders

Spreaders are used for older limbs. If you didn't use a toothpick or clothespin in the youth of a

Bob sez: *If you use clothespins on trees wired to a trellis, a technique known as espalier (an espaliered fruit tree or ornamental shrub is one whose branches are trained to grow flat against a wall, supported on a lattice or a framework of stakes) you can easily clip the shoots to a wire. Pruning them in the fashion of traditional espalier methods takes many hours for the same effect. The clothespin approach means your tree will be much wider than traditional espaliered fruit trees, but I'll take it any day. Growing wider trees in favor of saving many hours of pruning is my cup of tea. I used only 100 clothespins over and over again to tend 40 trees (and the rest of the box to hang up my tighty-whities).*

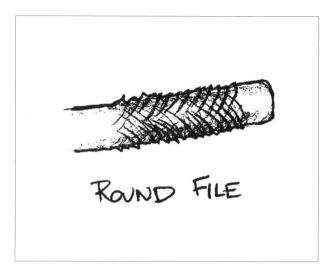

ROUND FILE

Figure 61: A round file, also called a rat-tail file, is used to notch dormant buds to produce either a shoot or a fruiting spur. *

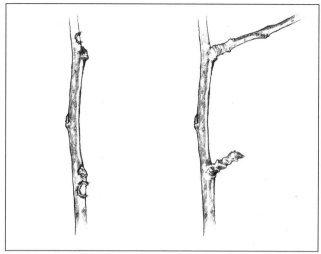

Figure 62: A notch (on the upper left) above a dormant bud makes a shoot. A notch below a dormant bud stimulates a fruiting bud (young spur). *

sprout you have to catch up by repositioning more mature limbs with one-by-one-inch sticks of different lengths, known as "spreaders." Hammer a nail into each end and clip the nail-heads off at an angle; this gives you a sharp point to stick into the wood of a branch or trunk.

Notching

There's an awesome way to produce a flower bud or shoot growth. The hormones of a tree move around in such a way as to allow you to place a shoot or fruit bud exactly where you want one.

By scouring a notch above a dormant bud, you cut off the "don't sprout" hormone coming from the apical bud. Without this hormonal signal, your bud will sprout into a shoot.

The carbohydrates of a tree must be stored in a bud for it to form a flower. When carbohydrates are generated in a branch, they're often sent down the limb into the trunk and roots. Notching below the dormant bud stops the carbohydrates from traveling down any further and stores them in the dormant bud, causing it to form a flower bud.

Notching works best on shoots that are one or two years old, especially if you do it two to four weeks before full bloom. To notch, file across the branch with a 3/8-inch round-rat tail file as if you're playing a violin. Score above or below the bud just deeply enough to remove the green tissue under the bark. Be sure to score at least halfway around the shoot. So, with one twist of the wrist, you've got a new shoot or flower bud. Pretty cool, no?

 Bob sez: *It's almost magical; with a single stroke of a file you produce a flower or a shoot. Can't save much more time than with this technique.*

It's July, I'm off my tush and going outside to spread it...

Figure 63: After notching below a dormant bud you will have a fruiting bud that becomes a fruiting spur (below) or when notching above a dormant bud you get a young shoot (above). * = drawn by Ben Levitt.

Unlike apple and pear trees, there is a class of fruit trees that form fruit on the current season's "wood"—it's called apical bearing. Such trees start growing in the spring and then produce flowers. If you never prune them, they make plenty of fruit. And, more importantly, such trees will produce fruit if you prune them "hard" (back into older wood). Never prune or whack away—you always have a harvest. Examples include many tropical fruits and:

Avocado
Chestnut
Feijoa (Pineapple Guava)
Fig (and a crop on one-year-old wood)
Grape (some)
Lemons (citrus)
Loquat
Mulberry
Olive
Pecan
Persimmon (American & Asian)
Pomegranate
Quince
Strawberry Tree
Walnut

CHAPTER 11

Rainwater Catchment

Gather nourishing rain for decades of free irrigation.

In the 1986 French film *Jean de Florette*, a family in southern France is destroyed during a severe drought because their cistern was too small to store enough water for the driest years. (But it's a great film anyways.) While your water-supply situation may not be that critical, rainwater catchment seems to be the first or second hottest interest of many gardeners, especially those attempting to use permaculture techniques. Cisterns are also another fine example, if appropriate for your situation, of how time and money spent upfront can save both in the future.

 Bob sez: *Many people now use the phrase "rainwater catchment" for this phenomenon. I still prefer the old-fashioned "cistern," from the Latin word for "box." (Guess I'm an old-fashioned, classical kind of guy.) Some distinguish cisterns from rainwater catchment because the former is in the ground and the later is above ground.*

Cisterns have been around for centuries, and are used throughout the world to catch rainwater for drinking, washing, irrigation, and flushing toilets. In the 1800s and early 1900s (before municipal water systems were installed), water-storage tanks were common in America, even in cities. I'm happy to say that cisterns are experiencing a welcome and well-deserved revival,

due to dwindling sources of clean water, erratic supplies during droughts, and a renewed interest in water independence. And most gardeners will readily tell you their plants look and grow better with rainwater.

You also might want to take into consideration that ongoing use of municipal water in outdoor gardens and lawns, especially in arid climates and/or with alkaline soils, may have a mild adverse effect over time—browning of leaf edges and yellowing of foliage. Its use on indoor plants can have even more bad juju. The salts and minerals found in many water supplies, plus the chlorine buildup in the limited soil volume of the pot, will often form a white crust on top of the soil, and, over time, may even kill sensitive houseplants. For all kinds of gardeners, a cistern, even just a rain barrel under their home's downspout, is a must for watering indoor plants, and is a great way to harvest a consistent free supply of water for gardening. Cistern tanks now come in all shapes and sizes, ranging from the aforementioned rain barrels to round wooden tanks, stone wells, black plastic drums, or hulking gray concrete containers.

Cistern systems are remarkably simple, but it does take a bit of effort to install one. This is how they function in a gardening situation: the rain must be gathered, stored in a tank in or above the ground, and gravity-drained or pumped to the garden. In most cases, rainfall is collected from the roof of a building—home, garage, barn, etc. An ordinary roof gutter funnels the rain into a downspout, hose or pipe that leads to the cistern itself. A diverter valve is built into the downspout/pipe, so that the first rains after a dry spell can be diverted away from the cistern and flush accumulated filth off the roof. Usually, a simple device or grate screens out twig and leaf debris that may have accumulated.

Even for such a basic and age-old idea, there are a lot of parts to assemble (gutters, spouts, diverters, screening, etc.) in a modern cistern. Installing a catchment system may be a bit of a stretch for a languid gardener, but the assembly can be done by a well-directed college kid, or stretched

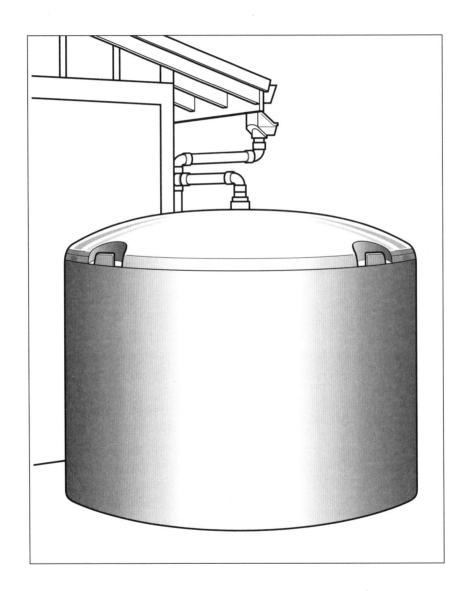

Figure 64: Here's a 3,000-gallon tank. It sits on a pad of tamped, crushed rock. In my area, if you have a tank over 5,000 gallons you need, in my county, an engineered concrete pad and a permit—a considerable extra cost.

in a relaxed way over two or three weekends. Once done, you'll have decades of easy, sustainable use, and the freshest possible water for plants, indoors and out.

The Cost of Storing "Free" Rainfall

The average roof can capture a phenomenal amount of water, even in fairly arid climates. The formula for deciding the size of your cistern more often involves determining how much storage you can afford than calculating how much rain can be captured. The most important part of designing a cistern is to research thoroughly the cost of different types of storage. Some types to consider include: traditional underground brick cisterns; coated metal tanks; plastic tanks, large expandable vinyl or nylon bags, large wooden barrels or cylinders; Ferrocement containers (wire mesh containers plastered with a concrete-like stucco); poured cement tanks; and plastic liners inside all manner of used /recycled drums, tanks and containers, including old wine tanks, used water heaters, and abandoned aboveground swimming pools.

Some of these (poured-concrete tanks, large wine tanks and brick cisterns) require the work of a hired contractor or craftsman. Others can be built or installed by the average homeowner. Homemade cistern systems usually link up a number of small recycled or salvaged tanks; this saves money, and small units are easiest to move into place before filling. Such systems can end up storing an impressive amount of water, but may wind up looking like Rube Goldberg contraptions. Owner-builders can also use various sizes of plastic tanks placed on compacted bare soil, a packed gravel base, or a poured concrete slab, depending upon the tank's size and the type of plastic. Be sure to ask your dealer for the specifics.

Prices for cistern materials vary across the country. The best way to compare expenses is to

 Bob sez: *Cisterns may be too complicated or expensive for a truly laid-back gardener. But, if well done, they provide a good level of independence (free water for gardening, drinking water during emergencies), control, and sustainability for many decades. (And your houseplants will love that chemical-free water). Don't be afraid to hire somebody to do the installation. (For one listing of installers, go to: The American Rainwater Catchment System Association website. See: http://www.arcsaresource.com/listing/arcsa-master,arcsa-ap) For more on cisterns, their costs, and concerns, see Appendix 2.*

convert all costs to the price per gallon of storage. For example, where I live, north of San Francisco, costs range from $.50 per gallon for ugly aboveground storage to $1.50 per gallon for contractor-installed tanks.

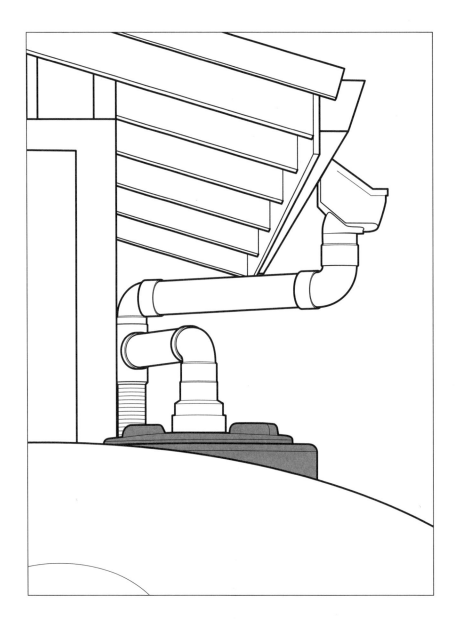

Figure 65: This shows the hardware needed to gather the rainwater from the roof and fill the tank. The part just below the gutter helps keep leaves from entering the tank. Here, the dark grey is the hatch to enter the tank and clean it. The downspout enters the tank just behind this hatch. The corrugated downspout pipe is part of the mechanism that allows the first rains to be flushed away fom the tank so it doesn't clog.

Figure 66: Here is an assembly of four 55-gallon tanks joined together to make one cistern. The downspout to the tanks has a part to screen leaves from entering the tank. This setup can cost more than a large, single tank, but fits in a narrow space a large tank wouldn't fit. Use food-grade used or new tanks.

CHAPTER 12

The Good, the Bad, and the Bugly

**Frustrate those weeds; tame those pesty bugs;
then lure the good bugs for a vital garden.**

NOTE: This chapter is riddled with scientific sources and quotes. That's because relying on gardening myths and anecdotes on these subjects can lead to a big waste of time and energy on your part. Every bit of science here contains a juicy nugget of information on dealing with pests in ways that have been proven to actually work. So, hang in there!

The Wicked Ways of (Some) Weeds

Weeds. Every gardener who hasn't gone hydroponic has to deal with them. They've been variously described as: 1) plants whose virtues have not yet been discovered; 2) the right plant in the wrong place; and 3) nature's way of colonizing bare ground.

There can be some interesting impacts when you allow unrestrained diversity in your garden or landscape. For instance, if you're growing lots of heirloom tomatoes, you may think twice about also nurturing the nutritious edible weed known as lambsquarters (*Chenopodium album*), because it harbors verticillium wilt—the Achilles heel of many non-hybrid heirloom tomato

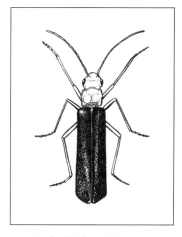

A Soldier Beetle

Figure 67: Larvae eat the eggs and larvae of beetles, grasshoppers, moths and other insects. Adults feed on aphids and other soft-bodied insects.

plants. Here's a rundown of the drawbacks and virtues of a number of common so-called weeds.

Lambsquarters

In the University of California's Agriculture and Natural Resources Publicaions, we read: "Common lambsquarter is also susceptible to many viruses that affect several crops and ornamentals. These include beet curly top; potato viruses X, M and S; ring spot viruses of tomato, pepper, potato, *Prunus* spp. (plums), and mulberry; and mosaic viruses of alfalfa, bean, beet, barley, lettuce, cucumber, squash, eggplant, hops, *Primula*, watermelon, and wisteria." Yikes.

Lambsquarters, along with another common weed species, *Malva* spp. (known colloquially as cheese-weed), can also host the tomato spotted wilt virus. These two weed species are also prone to a number of pox viruses, such as watermelon mosaic virus-2, spread by several species of aphids. Mosaic virus overwinters on perennial weeds and is spread by insects—like aphids, leafhoppers, whiteflies and cucumber beetles—that feed on them. Soil, seed, starter pots and containers can also be infected and pass the virus to the plant.

Here's some of that science: Elizabeth T. Maynard at the Department of Biological Sciences at Purdue University did an analysis of winter squash yield that showed that one lambsquarters plant in a 10-square-foot plot would be expected to reduce the yield of squash by ten to 15 percent. Along with redroot pigweed, London rocket, sow thistle, alkali mallow, Wright's ground cherry, and silver leaf nightshade, lambsquarters can spread cucurbit yellow stunting disorder virus. Double yikes!

The Flip Side of the Coin…

…is that lambsquarters are astonishingly nutritious. A 100g/3.5 ounce serving supplies an amazing 26% of calcium, 232 % of Vitamin A, and 133% of Vitamin C for the daily needs of the average person. Other nutrients include:

Element	Amount	Percent
Fiber	4g	16%
Iron	1mg	8%
Manganese	0.8m	27%
Potassium	452mg	13%
Protein	4.2g	8%
B1 Thiamin	.2mg	13%
B2 Riboflavin	.4mg	24%
B3 Niacin	1.2mg	6%
B6	1.2mg	17%
B9 Folate	30mcg	15%

Figure 68: A look at the nutrient levels in common lambsquarters may convince you to try to eat your weed problem.

Goosefoot

Nettleleaf goosefoot (*Chenopodium murale*, also known as wormseed) is used medicinally for everything from rheumatism to intestinal

Bob sez: *Tansy has long been touted as a beneficial insect repellent. One of the books I read in the mid-70s recommended it as a way to repel ants, flies, and mosquitoes, so I planted it beneath an apple tree with an ant problem. I was appalled when I saw how it spread, taking over big stretches of ground. Still, I believed in its ant-repelling properties until I bought a potted tansy plant that turned out to have ants living right in its soil! (See the discussion on P. 136-141 for a lot more on companion planting.) Tansy continues to show up in the literature and on the Internet as a companion plant; luckily, more and more references also mention its invasive nature.*

worms. It's also a host for viruses that affect several crops and ornamentals, and can spread cute-sounding but gnarly afflictions like cherry leafroll, beet curly top, and plum pox viruses; ringspot viruses of pepper, hibiscus, and tomato; and mosaic viruses of beet, lettuce, apple, cucumber, parsnip, radish, tomato, turnip, watermelon, hop vines, poplar trees and primroses.

Shepherd's Purse

Another example of a beneficial but disease-harboring weed is shepherd's purse (*Capsella bursa-pastoris*). It's used by herbalists as a tea for urinary and menstrual problems, but it may also be a host to clubroot disease that can decimate your cabbage-family crops.

Comfrey

Russian comfrey (*Symphytum officinale*) is a leafy perennial planted nd used by gardeners for many reasons: as a nourishing herb for tea, a healing poultice, chicken food, compost material, soil improver, and mulch. It's not a weed, says horticulturist and comfrey enthusiast Lawrence D. Hills, if segregated in a "Comfrey Corner." As I recommend, plant comfrey in a permanent place where there will be no till-age—ever. Better yet, plant it in your neighbor's yard. It will continue to spread with a vengeance when pulled or dug up, as each tiny piece of root left in the ground will sprout into a whole new plant.

And, for the same reason, be very careful when composting it. It takes a very hot compost pile to even have a chance of killing a piece of comfrey root. Since virtually no compost pile gets hot all over, rootlets can trigger an unrestrained invasion into other parts of your garden. I've seen abandoned gardens with their raised beds and pathways covered with a living mulch of comfrey.

Lemon Balm
Another potential "living mulch" is lemon balm (*Melissa officinalis*), often planted by the un-wary as a source of tasty and calming herbal tea. However, if the plant is untended and allowed to make seed, you'll be stuck with wall-to-wall lemon balm in no time. Yet another "right plant in the wrong place."

Here are even more weeds to be wary of: (by Trevor Hearn, University of Arizona, 2012.) Some of these plants, like the nutritious chick-weed, are valued as "wild" edible greens. But I'd think twice about leaving them to proliferate.

Eating Leafy Pests?
You could eat your way through certain weed patches and get some great nutrition. A few edible weeds include:
*   Dandelion (*Taraxacum officinale*), vitamins A, B, C and D
*   Purslane (*Portulaca oleracea*), vitamins A, C and E, best plant-based source of

omega-3 and omega-6 fatty acids
*   Red clover (*Trifolium pratense*), vitamin C
*   Lambsquarters (*Chenopodium album*), calcium, beta-carotene and phosphorus, potassium, 44% the daily value of Vitamin A, 35% vitamin C, 25% iron
*   Plantain (*Plantago major*), same amount of vitamin A as a large carrot
*   Chickweed (*Stellaria media*), vitamins A, D, C and some B
*   Mallow (*Malva* spp.), vitamins A and C
*   Wild amaranths (*Amaranthus* spp.), vitamins A, C, and folate
*   Sorrels (*Oxalis* spp.), vitamin C and also contains vitamin A
*   Stinging nettle (*Urtica dioica*) - YES, if blanched in hot water or steamed. Vitamins A, B2, C, D and K
*   Kudzu (*Pueraria montana*), leaves and stems are 16-18% protein (INVASIVE)

As for controlling other weeds, you'll find plenty of information salted throughout the book, especially in the chapter on tillage, "Tillage - From Some to None." (Bugs may be snug in rugs, but carpeting can also be used to deal with a weed problem. Check it out.)

Now on to bug info.

Bob sez: *For heaven's sake, don't plant kudzu! It's ten times more invasive than comfrey or lemon balm, and will eat your entire garden.*

Companion Planting: Gettin' Buggy With It

Companion planting in gardening and agriculture is the planting of different crops in proximity for any of a number of different reasons, including pest control, pollination, providing habitat for beneficial creatures, maximizing use of space, and to otherwise increase crop productivity.

Some bugs (known as "beneficial" insects) use the pollen and nectar of flowers to fuel their relentless pursuit of the kinds of creepy-crawlies we think of as pests (beneficial insects think of them as lunch). Bugologists (entomologists) over the years have discovered a number of plants that seem to attract beneficial bugs.

Growing plants to attract good bugs that terrorize and eat nasty bugs is another way to kick back, and perhaps to skip having to deal with tedious, time-consuming, and potentially carcinogenic bug sprays. Take some time to survey the insect activity in your garden before getting up to kill all the little buggers. If you're patient and observant, you may find that the good bugs do all the work of controlling the pests. Many of the helpful good-bug-attracting plants belong to the parsley and sunflower plant families.

The parsley or carrot family of plants (it used to be *Umbelliferae*; now it's *Apiaceae*—botanists seem to maintain job security by changing botanical names) is identifiable by large flat umbrella-like heads of tiny flowers, often white or yellow in color. The small size of the flowers allows teensy bugs to easily tank up on pollen and nectar. Many culinary herbs belong to this family—anise, dill, parsley itself, caraway, and fennel. Other parsley-family members that attract beneficial bugs when left to flower include: angelica (*Angelica* spp.) and carrots (*Daucus carota*).

The sunflower family (*Asteraceae* or *Compositae*—botanists again messing with our brains) also has tiny and readily accessible flower parts.

Bob sez: *Cilantro or coriander (Coriandrum sativum) is an herb often used in traditional Mexican cookery. I hate the stuff. I grew up in the Midwest, and didn't taste cilantro until I was 21 or so. It tastes like soap to me—and to many others, but its flowers are yummy to bugs. The small and accessible nectar-bearing cilantro flowers have been observed by entymologists to attract a large array and high number of "good bugs"—specifically the beneficial Tachinid fly, a hungry parasite of grasshoppers, beetles, sawflies and caterpillars. (See P 146-148 for a list of more bugs that prey on garden pests.)*

A tremendous number of our ornamental flower-garden plants are part of this large floriferous family. Examples include: marigold, dahlias, daisies, *Artemisia* spp. (wormwoods), chamomile, zinnia, asters, cosmos, ornamental thistles, camphorweed (*Heterotheca subaxillaris*), coyote bush (*Baccharis pilularis*), wild lettuce (*Lactuca canadensis*), and yarrows (*Achillea* spp.).

Composites with edible flowers include: dandelion (*Taraxacum officinale*), chicory (*Cichorium intybus*), calendula (*Calendula* spp.), endive (*Cichorium endivia*) and daisies, all members of the *Asteraceae* family.

Figure 69: A parasitic wasp. (From: *Erucarum Ortus*, by Maria Sibylla Merian, 1679.)

Bob sez: *Using edible flowers in your meals is great, but leaving plenty of them in your garden may be a natural form of pest control—another way to relax and let nature scramble to balance things out. Here's an example: each year in early spring I see lots of black aphids gathering on the new growth of my fava beans, at about the same time my calendulas are blooming. If I wait a bit, some very tiny aphid-killing wasps and ladybugs show up to appreciate the calendula flowers. In a short time there are no more aphids, and the plants produce plenty of beans.*

Myths and Realities

Uh-oh, here come the dreaded scientific citations. (The text here is numbered and the citations are listed in Appendix 6 in the back of the book for the benefit of skeptics and the curious.)
There is so much BS out there on this topic that I dove deep to find examples that are backed up by science. (The subject isn't new to me. In my 1986 book—*Designing and Maintaining Your Edible Landscape - Naturally*—I list, on pages 239-241, 23 studies where companion planting didn't work and 68 examples where it did, on pages 241-244.)

The main reason for including all this tediously important information is that companion planting, if done right, does have the potential to help your garden prosper with a lot less effort. You may be able to sit on your keister longer, or do other fun gardening stuff instead of battling bugs. This is another let-nature-do-the-work approach. OK, it's great in theory, but does it really work? In the '70s I really wanted to believe in the gospel of companion planting as presented by Rodale Press and others. And I did believe, until I looked for the science to back up what turned out to often be unproven anecdotal information. Luckily there's been some important research since then.

There are many definitions of companion planting. One is: "a specific type of polyculture (simultaneous cultivation of two or more plants) in which two plants are grown together because they're thought to have a beneficial, synergistic improvement on each other's growth." (This not to be confused with intercropping, which is the good use of space by planting vegetables close together, or in close sequence.) The definition I like best is "...*We define companion plants as interplantings* [italics mine] *of one crop (the companion) within another (the protection target), where the companion directly benefits the target through a specific known (or suspected) mechanism.*" According to Joyce Parker, William Snyder, George Hamilton and Cesar Rodrigues in *Companion Planting and Insect Pest Control*.

To this day my favorite example of the complexity of companion plants is Rodale Institute Farm's own study of intercropping bush beans with marigolds—one of the most common "guidelines" of companion-planting books.

It was believed that French marigolds (*Tagetes patula*) and African marigolds (*T. erecta*) would help keep Mexican bean beetles (*Epilachna varivestis*) away from green beans. Turned out that the control plot without the companion plants sustained more insect damage than the marigold rows, but the control plot produced more beans. It's now thought that the exudates produced by marigolds (thiopene and alpha-terthienyl) stunt the growth of plants nearby as a form of evolutionary competitiveness over other plants.

(French marigolds are, however, a proven controller of nematodes (worms of the large phylum *Nematoda* spp., such as roundworms or threadworms). Plants growing in nematode-infested soils are usually stunted, yellowish, and have galled and decayed roots. Some of the cultivars that work the best for controlling nematodes are 'Nemagold', 'Petite Blanc', 'Queen Sophia', 'Tangerine', 'Golden Guardian', 'Single Gold', and 'Nema Gone'. These are best planted as a green manure one or more seasons before planting the crop. Intercropping with them has little effect, as once the soil is planted to an additional crop the nematodes begin to reappear.

So let's look at the different ways companion planting is thought to work, and find out which plants actully can work. (And remember that the science of companion planting is still in its infancy, so be wary of any recommendation that doesn't have a citation to back it up.)

There are a number of very different ways in which a given companion plant might work (definitions follow):
• As a "trap crop"
• By actually repelling the pest
• By masking the target plant (the one you're trying to protect) or camouflaging the crop
• By physically blocking the pest
• As an attractant and harbor for beneficial insects.

Trap Crops
Trap plants are those that attract pests away from the target vegetable. With proper timing, having a lot of pests in one place on a trap plant can allow you to kill a good number of them with your hands, a water spray, or an organic pesticide. It's also possible that the pests will stay on the trap plant and away from your target veggies. As mentioned, I've seen this every spring with fava beans.

Here are some examples from scientific studies where this dynamic has been shown to be effective:
• Soybeans can be protected from Mexican bean beetles (*Epilachna varivestis*) with a trap planting of snap beans. (1)

• Even staggered plantings of the same plant can work; in one study, an early-planted potato crop was used to protect later plantings of potato. (2)

• Collards have been used to draw diamond-backed moths (*Plutellidae* family) away from cabbage.(3)

• Here are four examples from the Connecticut Cooperative Extension:

• Collards around the perimeter of the field reduced diamondback moths by 89%.

• To stop pepper maggots on bell peppers, cherry peppers were planted as a trap crop—producing 98% pest-free fruit.

• Blue Hubbard squash reduced the cucumber beetles on yellow summer squash by 95%.

• The same Blue Hubbard squash planting reduced squash vine borers by 88% by killing the squash vine borer populations in the perimeter trap crop. (4)

• Diversifying your trap crops can be done attractively. For example, in Finland, mixtures of Chinese cabbage, marigolds, rape (the mustard-family source of canola oil), and sunflower were used successfully as a diverse trap crop to manage the pollen beetle (*Brassicogethes aeneus*, formery *Meligethes aeneus*) in cauliflower. (5)

• Diverse trap crops consisting of three trap-crop species (Pacific gold mustard, bok choy and rape) provided the most effective trap-crop mixture. (6)

In the above examples, in which the trap is the same or in the same genus as the main crop, it's important to plant the trap crop before the main crop. This allows you to spray (toxic chemical or "organic" sprays) or otherwise deal with the trap-crop pests to keep them from migrating to your intended crop. For pests like aphids, you can place sticky yellow boards throughout the garden so the aphids are lured to the boards and trapped. (Yellow is the favorite color of common pests like: aphids, leaf miner, fungus gnats, thrips, whiteflies, black flies, fruit flies, and midges.) Be sure to control the pests in the trap crop so that they don't build up to become a "nursery" for pests that allows them to spread to the target crop. The area dedicated to the trap plant should be no more than 20% (some say 10%) of the entire planting.

Repelling Pests

• In one study, the companion plants that helped protect *Brassica* crops (broccoli, cabbage, mustard, etc.) included sage (*Salvia officinalis)*, rosemary (*Rosmarinus officinalis*), hyssop (*Hyssop officinalis*), thyme (*Thymus vulgaris*), dill (*Anethum graveolens*), southernwood (*Artemisia abrotanum)*, mints (*Mentha* spp.), tansy (*Tanacetum vulgare*), chamomile (several genera), and orange nasturtium (*Tropaeolum majus*). (7) Some of these, like tansy and mints, are invasive and need to be controlled by only planting in containers with the hole at the bottom blocked.

• In another study, intercropping of spring onions as a companion plant was found to protect broccoli (target crop) from pest attack. The onions acted as a repellent to "push" pest insects away from the broccoli. (8)

• Basil (*Ocimum basilicum*) planted along with tomatoes has been found to repel thrips (tiny insects that feed on plants by puncturing and sucking up the contents) and tomato hornworms. (9)

Perhaps now is a good time for you to stop reading, get a beer (or soda) and wander aimlessly around the house until your head clears!

Mask or Camouflage the Crop
OK, back to it: in a study dealing with pitted seeds in beans damaged by lygus bugs (*Lygus* spp.) various companion plants were tested: summer savory (*Satureja hortensis*), marjoram (*Origanum majorana*), sage (*Salvia officinalis*), big marigold (*Tagetes erecta*), red beet *(Beta*

vulgaris), onion (*Allium cepa*), dill (*Apium graveolens*). The lowest percentage of damaged seeds came from the samples obtained from plots cultivated in the close proximity of dill and marigold. [not the French marigold used in home gardens. Ed.] (10) In this study it was thought the dill and marigolds literally covered or camouflaged the intended crop.

Blocking Pests
There are situations where physical blocking works: tall plants can impede pest movement within a cropping system. For example, maize has been used to protect bean plants from pest attack, and dill has been used as a vegetative barrier to inhibit pest movement in organic farms (author's personal observation). (11)

Hedges and Flower Borders for Companion Pest Control
One of the most important crossovers from agricultural research to useful practice in large home gardens is information on how to enhance the habitat for beneficial insects. These are aspects that can truly be scaled down from an agricultural setting to the backyard.

There's been a lot of bug research at the University of California, Davis, using suburban backyards in a nearby development called Village Homes. One set of studies extrapolated from the use of borders (hedgerows) of farm fields as shelters for beneficial insects that help control pests in the field. The primary research on this was done by Robert Bugg (his real name—must be destiny), and Miguel Altieri. Altieri found that many beneficial insects could migrate 25 meters (82 feet) from one hedgerow into a neighboring field of corn (from my personal communication with him on 10/29/10). Since 82 feet covers most gardens and some landscapes, this was found to be a useful strategy in suburbia—a hedgerow can provide plenty of habitat for beneficial insects to pursue pests throughout the yard or garden.

• In another study, significantly more hoverfly eggs were found in fields surrounded with *Phacelia tanacetifolia* (known as lacy phacelia, blue tansy, or purple tansy) than in control fields. Hoverflies are syrphid flies that look a lot like bees but can, unlike bees, hover in place—thus the name. They belong to the insect Family *Syrphidae*. (See below for more on these useful predators) The biological control of aphids by syrphid larvae can reduce the use of nasty insecticides. (12)

• When predators of the Colorado potato beetle (*Leptinotarsa decemlineata*) in eggplant fields were studied it was found that the flowers of dill (*Anethum graveolens*) and coriander (*Coriandrum sativa*) were attractive to Colorado potato beetle predators. The number of predators were found to be significantly higher in fields interplanted with dill and coriander than in the control field without these plants. (If you try this, don't put each dill or coriander plant adjacent to each eggplant, but alternate strips of the herbs with continuous rows of eggplant) (13)

Figure 70: A tachinid fly that has hatched. (From: *Erucarum Ortus*, by Maria Sibylla Merian, 1679.)

• The effects of the flowers of sweet alyssum, (*Lobularia maritima*) were studied to assess their use in the suppression of aphids in California lettuce fields. The presence of alyssum resulted in more hoverfly larvae and fewer aphids (*Hemiptera Aphididae*). The results of this study showed that increasing the mass of the flowers can enhance aphid suppression and crop quality due to the resulting elevated levels of natural enemies. (14)

• In another study involving hoverflies, scientists studied plantings in broad- and narrow-sown flower strips, grassy strips and (as a control) in wheat fields. This included studies of landscape complexity within a .5-4.0 km radius around the strips. Syrphid density was higher in narrow- and broad-sown flower strips when compared to grassy strips and wheat. The syrphid flies were the most concentrated within the flower strips at a radius of .5-1.0 km. This means you would get some control in a yard as wide as 1.0 km (.62 miles)—much bigger than most gardens. It was also discovered that growing local flower strips near your target plants is more effective in simple landscapes, while in complex landscapes, keeping the overall diversity is more important. (15)

Here's another important study's conclusion (it was done on a hedgerow next to a farmer's field, but is also applicable to to home gardens): "...Many (beneficial) insects moved 250 feet [from the hedgerow] into adjacent field crops. Studies...showed that syrphid flies (70% of the introduced flies), parasitic wasps and lacewings fed on flowering cover crops in orchards and that some moved 6 feet high into the tree canopy and 100 feet away from the treated area (ed. where the beneficial insects were released). The use of nectar or pollen by beneficial insects helps them survive and reproduce. Therefore, planting flowering plants and perennial grasses *around* (my italics) farms may lead to better biological control of pests in nearby crops." (16)

"Marking studies demonstrated that ladybeetles, lacewings, syrphid flies and parasitic wasps fed on nectar or pollen provided by borders of flowering plants around farms; many insects moved 250 feet into adjacent field crops. Studies also showed that syrphid flies, parasitic wasps and lacewings fed on flowering cover crops in orchards and that some moved 6 feet high in the tree canopy and 100 feet away...."

Here's another tip: Plants such as borage, *Limnanthes* spp. (poached egg plant) *Echium* spp. and members of the *umbellifer* family (let several parsnips go to seed) attract predatory hoverflies, parasitic wasps and other beneficial insects. Companion planting and mixed cropping increases the biodiversity of plants and the insects it attracts.

The Good Guys
Ladybugs

The common name of this cute little beetle (even its Latin moniker is pretty— *Hippodamia convergens*) originated in North America, where the insects became known as "Our Lady's bird," the "Lady beetle," or "ladybirds." The Virgin Mary (known as "Our Lady" in a number of Christian faiths) was often depicted wearing a red cloak in early paintings, and the spots of the seven-spot ladybird (the most common in Europe) were said to symbolize her seven joys and seven sorrows.

Unfortunately, to purchase lady beetles for aphid control is, according to Dr. Ken Hagen of UC Berkeley, "simply throwing (one's) money away." The lady beetles sold by mailorder and through nurseries are captured from large winter congregations in the Sierra Mountains in Cali-

Figure 71: A ladybug larvae. (From: *Erucarum Ortus*, by Maria Sibylla Merian, 1679.)

fornia. Entomologists have discovered that these insects get together and party each fall with plenty of stored fat for both the winter and part of the spring. Unless the lady beetles are defatted before sale, the awakening bug you might purchase isn't even hungry. Also, since up to 10% of the overwintering lady beetles are infested with parasites, selling the beetles only speeds up the spread of these parasites. While parasitized beetles do eat, they can't reproduce.

Dr. Hagen says: "*Hippodamia* ... gathered from aggregations in the Sierras (are) ineffectual predators; green lacewings [*Chrysopidae*] are better." This ladybug is more inclined than some other species to leave your yard. Those that do hang around, however, eat up to 5000 aphids in their lifetimes. The young larvae eat up to 400 aphids before they form a pupae.

You can lure ladybugs to your garden with the same beneficial plants that attract most good bugs—especially members of the sunflower and parsley families. To keep these good bugs alive, however, you must stop spraying with anything. Yes, skip the "organic" sprays, as they're often too broad-based to avoid harming the ladybugs and their larvae.

The larvae look like small alligators and are often mistaken for a pest. Since they're soft-bodied, they're very susceptible to all kinds of pesticide sprays—both chemical and organic. Treasure those ladybugs that are black with one orange spot on each wing; they're the ones that don't fly away to congregate in the mountains each winter, but stay in your garden in ground litter to revive in the spring. They are called the twice-stabbed ladybug, *Chilocorus stigma*.

Syrphid flies

As mentioned above, the syrphid fly (of the family *Syrphidae*), also called a hoverfly, is often mistaken for a bee or wasp. This insect, however, lives up to its common name—it hovers in the air like a helicopter in front of flowers. (Bees can't do this.) If you've ever paused near a patch of cosmos on a sunny summer afternoon, you're certainly familiar with the unique flight of the hoverfly as it zigzags about the blossoms, occasionally stopping in mid-air, its shimmering wings barely visible. With their distinctive yellow-and-black striping, they're often mistaken for a "pest," but the truth is that the hoverfly is a much better predator of aphids than ladybugs, especially the syphid's larvae. A single hoverfly larva can eat much more than its body weight in aphids, while its mom and dad help pollinate the garden as they fly from flower to flower to gather the nectar and pollen to survive.

Because the larvae of hoverflies, like those of ladybugs, look like tiny slugs, they're also often mistaken for a pest and squished or sprayed. (The poor little guys get it on all fronts.) And don't forget that all sprays, organic or chemical, will kill not only the hoverfly's favorite food—aphids—but many insects, whether they're beneficial or not. When you spot aphids on a plant, look more closely; it may be harboring such a low level of the bugs that it's not a problem. In this case, you leave the plant alone while nature

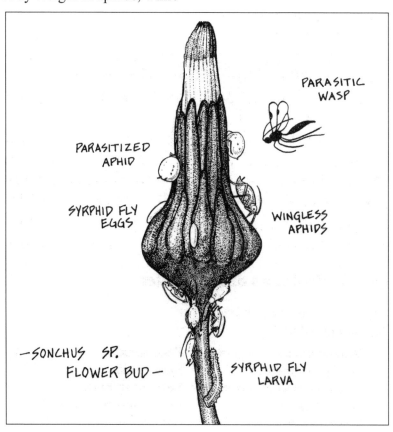

Figure 72: Many syrphid fly larvae are killed because their tan, almost slimy bodies look like a slug. Each larva can eat up to 400 aphids during their "lifetime"—before becoming a fly. Once an aphid has had an egg deposited inside by a parasitic wasp, it bloats up to a round, brown sphere. When the wasp hatches, it leaves behind a tiny open hatch door.

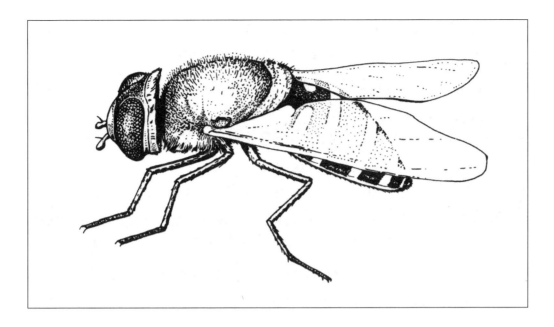

Figure 73: A syrphid fly, also called a hoverfly.

maintains its natural balance. The good guys can't survive without some of the bad guys. And there are plenty of syrphid flies—300 species of them, just on the American west coast.

A complex habitat and diversity of flowering plants found in most gardens creates an ideal environment for attracting hoverflies, which seek out pest colonies in which to lay their eggs. Because many species pupate and overwinter in leaf litter, a permanent mulch will encourage persistent populations. Hoverflies are also sensitive to wind, so provide some shelter near flowerbeds for windy days.

Their favorite flowers are the daisy (*Asteraceae*), buckwheat (*Polygonaceae*), and umbel (*Apiaceae*) families. They also feed on nectar and pollen in a wide range of other plant families, including rose (*Rosaceae*), buckthorn (*Rhamnaceae*), borage (*Boraginaceae*), and willow (*Salicaceae*).

A Companion-Plant Summary

Holy cow, you say, what does all this mean? It boils down to a very simple guideline. Research often shows that bugs can fly long distances—how do you think the pests found your garden?—and that many beneficial insects will fly a long stretch to pursue a pest. This means that to work, **most beneficial plants DO NOT have to be planted right next to the plant you want to protect from pesky insects.** That concept of companion planting is often irrelevant, and much of companion planting "literature" is either anecdotal, the result of faulty deduction, or just plain horse-pucky. Remember, if a beneficial insect can travel 82 feet and still terrorize a pest, you can plant the companions almost anywhere in the garden. It's a rare home garden that stretches 82 feet in two directions or 164 feet across.

"But Bob," you ask: "how do you plant a garden to attract good bugs"? I put all the plants that attract and feed beneficial insects in a flower border near, but not in the veggie beds. I may not even explain to a landscape client the complexities of companion planting, but just simply put the insect-attracting plants in what looks like a cut-flower garden. The client has ornamental flowers to enjoy, while other blossoms provide the food (nectar and pollen) and habitat for beneficial insects. So be lazy! Plant a cut-flower garden full of plants that attract the good guys. Then sit back and watch the mêlée.

Congratulations! You made it through the most tedious (but most important) section of the book. Go to P185, and fill out the awesome "Your Buggy Diploma."

Other Pest Strategies

Alas, companion planting or insect habitat doesn't always take care of an insect problem. We have to fall back to an arsenal of tools to nurture the situation into a resemblance of balance. Here are a few examples of difficult pests and how to deal with them:

Aphids

If need be, female aphids can give birth without the company of males. (I guess the guys stayed in their "man caves.") Nature so often gives creatures alternative ways to proliferate. Now you know why aphids can be so hard to manage or eradicate.

While aphids may be a total drag, they don't actually suck. They have a mouthpart (called a stylet) that opens and closes, but it's the fluid pressure of the plant that causes the sap to enter the aphid. This means that the way a plant is grown will affect its vulnerability to this frequent pest. Too much nitrogen, for instance, increases the sap pressure and supports more aphids. Be aware.

Patience is a virtue. All aphid populations do not necessarily require sprays. Observe and wait a bit to see if the tiny black parasitic wasps, as shown in Figure 69) arrive to terrorize the aphids. As I've already mentioned, each early spring my fava beans' foliage (I love fava beans) acquires a

"herd" of black aphids. Gaggle? Flock? Whatever. As the days warm, more and more parasitic wasps arrive. It doesn't take too many wasps to do a lot of damage to the aphids. (As I've said before, I often see ladybug larvae arrive shortly thereafter.) In most situations, the aphids don't become a problem to other plants and the favas grow well enough to set seed. The favas act as an early home to populations of beneficial insects that go on to prevent future aphid outbreaks.

A population of as few as two to five parasitic wasps per 100 square feet may be all that's needed. Technically speaking, 'parasitic wasps' are not really parasites—they are parasitoids. A true parasite is something that lives at the expense of its host but doesn't actually kill it, whereas parasitoids nearly always kill their host.

You can tell when the wasps are on the hunt, because you'll see aphids that have swollen into a round shape and turned bronze or brown. A closer look at these will show you a little hatch door on the back of the aphid where the adult wasp emerged after the larvae consumed its innards. Some of the beneficial wasps parasitize over 200 species of other pests, including mites, armyworms, cutworms, thrips, mealybugs, green stink-bugs and loopers. (Unfortunately they also prey on Lepidoptera [butterfly] eggs—nature ain't for sissies—but that category does include cabbage moths whose larvae are very destructive.)

If you've run out of patience, or the aphids continue to proliferate, it's time to attack. Many books and people say squirt them off with a blast of water. I consider this to be practical hogwash. The plants can take quite a beating when you use enough water pressure to be effective. Instead, I reach for neem—a byproduct of a tropical tree. Read the instructions and gently spray both sides of all leaves.

Tomato Hornworms

Tomato hornworms are hungry little devils. Overnight they can do a lot of damage to your tomato plant's foliage and fruits. Picking them off is the first strategy. As a kid my dad paid me a nickel for every hornworm I found (much more than the penny I got for pulling dandelions). If picking them grosses you out, you can use a special spray—*Bacillus thuringiensis*. This approved organic spray is a type of bacteria that only kills caterpillars after they have swallowed it. Be sure to spray both sides of the leaves,

 Bob sez: *Of course, you'll let insects do a lot of work so you don't have the extra hassle of stirring up chemicals and trying to keep the spray bottle from clogging. Beneficial insects are a real benefit to gardeners—they do a lot of damage while you rest, sleep, or troll Facebook.*

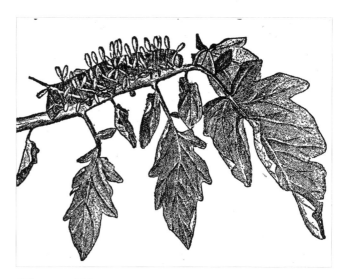

Figure 74: A tomato hornworm with the cocoons of a parasitic wasp. Don't kill hornworms with white cocoons, after the wasps "hatch" the hornworm will die.

Do not spray if you see a lot of tiny white lumps on the back of the hornworm. These are actually the cocoons of a parasitic wasp. Spraying the caterpillar will kill these beneficial wasps that would otherwise go on to kill more hornworms. The wasp inserts eggs into the caterpillar, and the resulting larvae devour the guts of the hornworm (it's a jungle out there), but they don't kill it outright. They let the hornworm limp along until they are ready to make cocoons, hatch, and fly away. Creepy, but true.

(I once tried to teach a hornworm to fly, but it appeared to be a slow learner.)

A Summary of the Top Eleven Beneficial Insects and Spiders

Reproduced with permission from *"Beneficial Insects and Spiders in Your Maine Backyard,"* bulletin #7150, University of Maine Cooperative Extension, 2004. https://extension.umaine.edu/publications/7150e/

SPIDERS
Description: Spiders have two body parts, no antennae and eight legs. There are about 3,000 species in North America.

Value in the garden: All spiders are predators, and most feed on insects caught in a web. Spiders are often the most abundant predators, They live on a wide range of plant material in the home landscape.

GREEN AND BROWN LACEWINGS
Description: Both green and brown lacewing larvae are alligator-like. Brown lacewing adults are half the size of green lacewing.

Importance in the garden: The larvae are called "aphid lions" because they consume large numbers of aphids, mites, lace bugs, and other small insects.

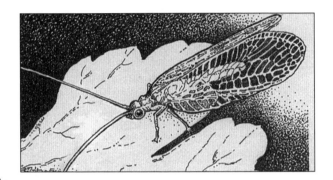

Figure 75: Lacewings *(Chrysoperla carnea)* eat a large number of aphids.

LADY BEETLES
Description: They range in size from one-sixteenth to three-eighths of an inch. And include orange, black, pink, or yellow on their backs. And may or may not have spots.
The adult female beetle lays 10–50, tiny orange, football-shaped eggs. The eggs produce spiny, alligator-like larvae. They feed on mealybugs and aphids. Then the larvae pupate and emerge as adult lady beetles.

Importance in the garden: The larvae and adults eat hundreds of aphids. Some species have favorite prey—mealybug and spider mites.

GROUND BEETLES
Description: They are shiny brown, black, or blue-black insects and are one-quarter to one inch long. They have long legs and long antennae and have prominent jaws used to kill caterpillars and small snails and slugs.

Importance in the garden: One larva can eat 50 gypsy moth caterpillars in two weeks and 300 gypsy moth caterpillars and pupae each year. Some adults can live for two to four years.

PRAYING MANTIDS
Description: These can be green, tan or gray and up to three inches long. They have a pair of enlarged front legs that look like they are praying. Females deposit tan, foamy egg masses at the end of summer. The egg mass can contain as many as 200 eggs.

Figure 76: **Praying Mantids** (*Stagmomantis californica)* eat almost anything including ladybugs.

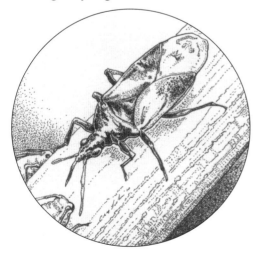

Figure 77: **Minute Pirate Bugs** (*Anthocoris* spp**.)** are predatory bugs.

The art on these two pages by Craig Latker©

Importance in the garden: They eat anything they can catch: pests, honey bees, each other, lady beetles, and other beneficial insects.

HOVER FLIES (SYRPHID FLIES OR FLOWER FLIES)
Description: These flies closely resemble wasps and bees because they have a yellow abdomen circumscribed by black and brown stripes. Adults are one-half to three-quarters of an inch long. The larvae are legless and are often mistaken as tiny slugs.

Importance in the garden: The larvae can eat over 400 aphids before pupation. Nectar- and pollen-feeding adults are supported by planting flowers.

PREDATORY BUGS
Description: Big-eyed bugs. This insect has large bulging eyes on the sides of the head. They are one-eighth inch long, with black and white silvery wings. They are predators of chinch bugs, small caterpillars, mites, and insect's eggs.

Importance in the garden: Predaceous stink bugs consume over 100 types of insects, including leaf beetle larvae and caterpillars.

Damsel bugs are about one- to three-eighths inch long; gray, brown or black. They eat aphids, small caterpillars, leafhoppers, plant bugs, and insect eggs.

PREDATORY WASPS
Description: The bald-faced hornet (*Dolichovespula maculata)* is five-eighths to three-quarters of an inch long, with black and white on the head, thorax, and abdomen. Yellow jackets (*Vespula* spp.), the most aggressive wasps, nest in the ground and produce large, enclosed paper nests. They have black and yellow stripes.
Importance in the garden: Yellow jackets, bald-faced hornets and paper wasps are important

predators of caterpillars and other soft-bodied insects. Because of this, only destroy nests (taking all safety precautions) where they pose a hazard to people or pets.

PARASITIC WASPS
Description: The parasitic wasps are tiny, black, and less than an eighth of an inch long, and hard to see. There are thousands of parasitic wasps species.

If you spot an aphid that has a swollen, puffed out body with a tan, the wasp has placed her egg inside the aphid. After the egg hatches, the larva eats the insides of the aphid, Then it pupates by cutting a round exit hole, often looking like a hatch.

Some parasitic wasps lay many eggs in a hornworm, with white, egg-like cocoons on its back. These are the pupae of parasitic wasps that soon hatch after the caterpillar has died.

Importance in the garden: Parasitic wasps attack aphids, many scale insects, caterpillars, cicadas, sawfly larvae, lace bugs, insect pupae, whiteflies, ants, leafminers. They also eat the eggs of codling moths, tomato hornworms, cabbage loopers, imported cabbageworms, and European corn borers.

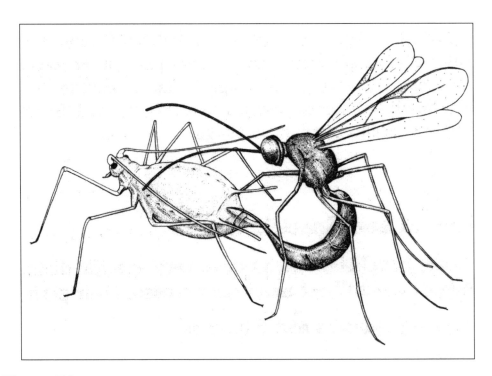

Figure 78: A parasitic wasp laying an egg inside a wingless aphid.

CHAPTER 13

The Knolls Know Interplanting

**The Knolls have got it together!
Here they show us how to blend many of the
techniques in this book to form a beautiful,
dynamic, and productive whole.**

The elusive Holy Grail of natural gardening is easy to define: the creation of a cultivated oasis of such extraordinary diversity that its fertility and resistance to pests and disease springs from a natural momentum. The perfect garden, so the dream goes, would be composed of an ecological web, a dynamic interweaving of carefully-chosen vegetables, perennial tree crops, habitat-sustaining ornamentals and domestic and wild animals)—all nurtured by perceptive gardeners or organic farmers.

(The goal is to let nature do a lot of the work for you so you can go to a movie or watch TV.)

The search for this perfect natural momentum has always involved, in part, a practice called intercropping The word intercropping has many names: companion planting, interplanting, crop rotation, polyculture, forest farming, agroecology or permaculture. For the vegetable garden, intercropping can be defined as a mixture of different crops or vegetables which are planted with and among ornamental plants to produce a healthier or more productive garden. For many, the intercropping dynamic happens not only all at once, in the current growing season, but also as a sequenced mixture of crops and beneficial plants over the seasons.

Some of the methods of intercropping vegetables include:

• layering sun- and shade-loving plants,
• combining non-competitive shapes and sizes (tall and narrow among short, round plants),
• cultivating a quick-maturing crop among slow-to-harvest vegetables,
• using soil-improving plants after harvesting a heavy-feeding vegetable,
• using plants which attract and feed helpful insects or obstruct and repel bad ones.

These techniques and others are used by Rick and Christie Knoll in their remarkable farm-as-garden. Carefully shaped and tended, this environmentally balanced labor of love comes pretty close to the Holy Grail. Any gardener could benefit from learning about the multitude of intercropping techniques which the Knolls use here to produce a naturally bountiful harvest.

Warning: What follows is straight-forward text. Nothing silly. It's important and it's the way Rick Knoll works. You'll probably save a lot of time if you incorporate some of his ideas and work into your garden. For example, "In the early fall, Knoll grows arugula among beans and black-eyed peas. He has found that 'a mixed late-summer seeding of arugula with beans helps keep the arugula leaves from being ravaged by flea beetles, because now they're hidden by the bean plants.' The arugula never competes with the stature of the beans." So, by the simple mixture of these two plants you may well skip the considerable hassle of spraying a pesticide. It's great to ignore the considerable aggravation of filling, and especially cleaning out the sprayer's tank. He's particularly good at exploring intercropping explanations and suggestions. Skip television, stay on your rear end and read. Carry on.

The Place

The Knoll Organic Farm lies along the western outskirts of California's Central Valley--the Detroit of American agriculture—and borders the Sacramento River delta some 70 miles northeast of the San Francisco Bay. Here oppressive summer heat and swirling dust-devils quarrel with tongues of cooler, moist bay breezes from the west. The Knoll Organic Farm is completely encircled by conventional farms where monocrops are rolled out like dirty, old 100-acre carpets. In spite of this the Knolls have cultivated, over the past 30-plus years on their diverse truck farm, a refuge for insects, spiders and birds threatened by chemical sprays. Rick Knoll, who has a PhD in Chemistry, offered an explanation other than the obvious for the "Knoll" in the farm's name; "the combination of the local farmers' constant discing and the wind deposits their topsoil inside our windbreak. Thus we've gotten higher every year and they've gotten lower—they're building us a knoll." It's evident that Knoll's finely-tuned observational skills make him as much of a naturalist as a farmer. (He's a serious guy, so I'll dispense with the frivolities for now.)

The Farm

This is not your usual truck farm. For instance, windbreaks surround it on all sides, providing shelter from the searing afternoon winds and from the neighbors' chemical spray-drift. Both the windbreaks and the tree crops shelter beneficial insects; in addition, the almond trees were intentionally underplanted with perennial bunch grasses which provide a stable, attractive habitat for insect-devouring spiders. A small army of geese graze beneath apricot trees, eliminating weeds while adding fertilizer. The geese are rotated through blocks of trees and sometimes followed by a fallow of rosemary and lavender planted as a floral crop.

Organic, you see, doesn't mean just food crops. In fact, floral crops are a increasingly important source of income for the Knolls. The rows of scented fig trees which are the backbone of the farm's economics are interplanted with artichokes sold for their spectacular blooms. Nuts and fruits are no longer harvested from certain rows of almond and apple trees; instead, stems cut for the February florists' market in New York City make far more money. Rows of black locust trees overgrow rows of cardoon, an artichoke relative which yields an edible celery-shaped leaf stem. In place of time-consuming wrapping, the cardoon stems are blanched by the shade of the locust trees. The cardoon's late-summer multiheaded purple flower stalk is yet another popular floral product.

The Vegetable Beds

Within this botanical cornucopia, the vegetable beds, each about 30 inches wide, play an important role. These strips are found in clusters between rows of tree crops such as figs or almonds, and there is also microcosmic diversity within the beds themselves. Rick acted as my patient guide as we toured the beds on a perfect autumn day. He began by emphasizing the importance of intercropping, "this farm is really a big garden, and we intercrop so the plants can be lost in space and time to confuse insects and to help maintain fertility."

Arugula and Associates

In college, Knoll researched the science of *allelopathy*—the study of the chemicals known as *secondary plant metabolites*, which plants produce to stunt the growth of other plants or suppress the germination of other types of seed. With arugula, that fashionable zesty-tasting salad green, as with all other members of the Brassica family, Rick points out an important intercropping dynamic: "Brassica roots exude a secondary metabolite (mustard gas) which inhibits grass seed germination; this slows down the grasses and lets the Brassica get a really strong start. It doesn't kill *all* the grasses; it's just a mechanism for competition."

For sequential intercropping, the black-eyed peas or beans are followed by an early-fall (early October) seeding of spinach, before which "the beans must be mowed off at the soil level so that both the rhizobial-produced bacterial nodules (which are full of nitrogen) and the entire root mass can rot in place." The spinach beds are weeded fairly thoroughly to expedite harvesting.

The spinach is often followed in the spring by cilantro, the tangy leaf of the coriander plant, because the bountiful cilantro foliage helps shade out weeds. Then, in early summer, tomato or eggplant seedlings are transplanted into the "trash" left from mowing the cilantro stems down to the ground. This brings the bed full circle; sequentially, the next crops in the cycle would be the arugula-and-bean combination, but the cycle is not repeated.

Instead, the next spatial rotation is a *fallow*, meaning the seeding of a soil-improving non-vegetable crop, or a "non-crop" plant such as bell beans, grasses or managed mixtures of so-called weeds. "The use of a fallow," according to Knoll, "is the only way to maintain fertility without too much manure or compost, which can force the plants into disease and pest-prone growth. All wise farmers in Europe have lengthy fallow periods with sophisticated cover-crop combina

tions built into their rotations." The fallow lets the garden replace subtle micronutrients which even compost can't adequately replace.

The Basil-Eggplant Connection

In another section of the farm, even though it's the third week of October, beds of basil alternate with eggplants. This was an attempt to protect the eggplant foliage from flea beetles. Knoll has found basil to be an insectary plant "which attracts syrphid flies, predatory wasps, spiders, a lot of parasitic flies and mantids." He recommends that everyone let basil go to seed because, "as with members of the Apiaceae, formerly the Umbelliferae (parsley) family, its flowers are so attractive to beneficial insects." Knoll hoped that using the basil (instead of expensive and labor-intensive row covers) would protect the eggplants by attracting enough predators of the flea beetle.

Alas, it didn't work too well, but this isn't upsetting to Knoll. This setback is, after all, part of the diversity of this farm. Next season, he'll experiment with more planting strategies to protect his eggplants. For Knoll, the excitement of playing with intercropping combinations is a lot more interesting (and less expensive and time-consuming) than row covers.

Artichokes and Tomatoes

As for mixing perennial and annual crops, consider cherry tomatoes and artichokes. "A late indeterminate tomato, like 'Early Girl', can use an artichoke plant like a trellis," says Knoll, "to keep the fruit off the ground so it's clean and undamaged, especially after the rains begin." The large foliage of the artichoke is frost-tolerant and helps protect the tomatoes hiding underneath from early frost damage--stretching the season just that little bit more.

Beeting the Heat

Beets can also take advantage of the artichoke's leaves. The heat of summer makes it difficult to grow beets during the entire season, unless, like Knoll's, your mind works a bit differently. Interplanting beets among the shady artichoke leaves allows the beet to "oversummer"—it actually loses its foliage, but in spite of this starts growing again in the early fall and tastes good and sweet.

According to Knoll, "the artichoke leaves which lay down on the ground are actually herbicidal and inhibit weeds among the beets." The mulch of the artichoke leaves suppresses most weeds, yet the beets can grow up through the mulch.

Salad Days for Almond Trees

On the western edge of the farm, almond trees are planted in rows with 50- to 60-foot wide-open areas between rows. A gaggle of geese are penned in one section where they graze and transform all weeds into rich avian fertilizer. When the gaggle is moved to a new section, the area is either put into a fallow of rosemary and lavender for the floral market, or into a mixture of salad, green-stem garlic and soil-improving plants. During my visit, the warm autumnal light lights up the young growth of bell beans, salad greens and grasses like a stained-glass window. The mixed salad greens include: broccoli raab, cilantro, peas, red mustard, regular green mustards and arugula. In this area, a load of strawy horse manure has generated a few too many grasses to suit Knoll and will require a cleanup hand weeding, all part of life in an organic garden.

Close inspection will reveal, at a time when most people are just planting their garlic cloves, a crop of oddly out-of-season garlic leaves, as much as 14 inches tall. Green-stem garlic is one of Knoll's specialties; he has selected a strain of *rocambole* which is planted in May and yields a very succulent garlic stem by fall, "not at all the woody stems most chefs are used to buying." While the garlic will rotate in time, for now it remains a well-weeded single-crop bed. A double row of bell beans a few feet out from the almond-tree trunks will feed the trees when disced in next spring. Eventually, the area along the line of the trunks will be planted in native bunch grasses, which attract and harbor beneficial spiders.

The Importance of Perennials

Knoll sees all things within a web of context. While vegetables are important to him, he's quick to add that "my goal is to nurture my soil to that magic threshold of 5% organic matter, and I think that's almost impossible using vegetable crops only." He is not a proponent of using too much manure. In his experience, "foliar tests show my plants are happiest with 12% leaf nitrogen, but manure ups that to 30-40% nitrogen which just makes the plant food for insects." "I have a carbon-based farm here," Knoll explains, "we're trying to favor all the free-living nitrogen-fixers in the soil, which work to balance the carbon-to-nitrogen ratio." To stimulate the nitrogen fixers, (carbon)—fiber or organic matter—must be added. When carbon is provided, the nitrogen-fixing critters try to balance the nitrogen-to-carbon ratio by making nitrogen from free nitrogen gas. As Knoll sees it, his work is to stimulate the rhizobium, azotobacter, algae, mosses, various bacteria and other nitrogen-fixing soil life to produce "time-released" nitrogen which is "available in little packets in the soil for plants to use as they need."

The Limits of Diversity

Fortunately, Knoll doesn't treat diversity as a panacea. Far too many organic gardeners think of garden diversity as simply throwing together as many plants as possible. In fact, as discussed in the more recent scientific literature on ecology, it's a limited, select diversity, rather than an arbitrary hodge-podge, which propels natural dynamics. Knoll's number-one rule is "leave the garden alone; messing with it may disrupt the renewal of nature, the revival." He has a unique and valuable view about cultivating an ecosystem which stresses, in his words, that "the quality of the habitat is much more important than the diversity."

CHAPTER 14
Eccentric Gardens

**Some gardeners like to cultivate eccentricity.
(It may even be art.)**

Foolin' Around

Why be serious at all in the garden? Why not really frolic around?

Cleveland Turner, after 17 years as an alcoholic, made a covenant with his Creator. If God would help him stay sober, Turner would devote his life to the cultivation of beauty. Known to fellow residents of his quiet Houston, Texas neighborhood as "The Flower Man," Cleveland Turner filled his entire yard with an exuberant living tapestry—colorful roses, canna lilies, zinnias, periwinkles and a myriad of other ornamentals rioting brilliantly amid watermelons, cotton, corn, squash, papayas, and peaches.

Turner's "living covenant" (he died in 2013) is a classic example of what's known as folk, native, outsider, visionary or naive art.

Many folk-art gardens actually rely on lots of curious "things"—windmills, bottles, hubcaps, beer cans and bottles, labyrinths, or miniature gnome-cities—for their display. Others rely primarily on plants, or on unique themes, for the substance of their art. Other names for this approach are "folly" or "eccentric garden."

A Carnival of Trees

Some horticulturists exhibit superior technical skill. Others possess monumental drive. And a very few manifest pure art. Axel Erlandson, a 20th-century visionary who sculpted trees into never-before-seen shapes, combined all of these traits. This retired surveyor and nurseryman literally bent nature to his will, creating a body of work unrivaled in the history of horticulture. Over a 20-year period, Erlandson grafted, shaped, and pruned 70 trees on a quarter-acre lot in Scotts Valley, California, into the most amazing shapes. In time, this fantastic collection came to be known simply as "The Tree Circus." Legacy or lunacy? Serious horticulture or pure theater? It's all in the eye of the beholder.

You may never try to mimic Erlandson's work. It's hard to describe what Erlandson actually did with trees. But what he did is unusual, fascinating and thought provoking. And I have an endless interest in his work—so more details. Or, skip to page 159 for the 10 steps to cultivate an eccentric garden.

Although he used grafting on occasion, his Felliniesque forms also required careful bending, shaping and tying to armatures. He used pleaching (plaiting or interlacing limbs, usually to form arbors) to join together many parts of each living sculpture into a single fabulously patterned tree. The word topiary applies to clipped and shaped foliage, but here the foliage grows mostly above the main "composition" of limb and trunk. His techniques defy neat classification.

Born in Sweden in 1884, Axel Erlandson's family moved to Minnesota when he was a year old. He left school after the third grade, though copies of a journal he kept as a 12-year-old reveal a keen eye for the details of nature. When he was 20, his family moved to a Turlock, California, farm that they bought sight unseen; it turned out to consist of poor soil over shallow hardpan that killed orchard plantings. Erlandson eventually taught himself surveying. Though he failed at making money with a windbreak nursery, it was there, according to Mark Primack, Santa Cruz, CA, architect, self-described "Tree-Circus" historian (the collection was dubbed the "Tree Circus" by Erlandson's daughter Wilma, after listening to the comments of guests), and author of a manuscript on Erlandson, that he first noticed "inosculation," the self-grafting properties of sycamore trees.

In his early 40s, Erlandson began his hobby of sculpting living trees. In 1946, with the idea of developing a roadside attraction and living in a more hospitable climate along the coast, he and his wife Leona moved 75 miles west. Erlandson bare-rooted and transplanted nine of his "living sculptures," the results of 20 years' work in Turlock, to new land in Scotts Valley. A year later, he put up a sign inviting visitors to "See the World's Strangest Trees Here." However, according to Primack, "from 1947 through 1963 only about 1500 visitors came through in a good year."

Erlandson devoted himself full-time to his trees, and never put off a visitor He draped sheets to isolate each tree for photographs, and often sent photos to Robert Ripley's Believe It Or Not newspaper feature, which featured them in 10 separate panels.

Erlandson named almost every specimen, including the Basket Tree (on page C15), and the Needle-and-Thread (on page C16). The symmetrical sycamore arch on page C16 spanned the entryway near Erlandson's castle-like house. He shaped many varieties of trees, including sycamores (*Platanus acerifoli*a), willows (*Salix* spp.), birch (*Betula* spp.), Bailey's acacia (*Acacia baileyana*), persimmon (*Diospyros kaki*), alder (*Alnus* spp.),

box elder (*Acer negundo*), and loquat (*Eriobotrya japonica)*, all of which have natural-grafting properties. One of his few notable failures was a redwood tree he attempted to train into a "living ladder" in Turlock.

How Erlandson trained the trees is mostly based upon the recollections of a few contemporaries and upon horticultural deduction, as he jealously guarded his "trade secrets." In Scotts Valley he started many specimens behind a privacy fence, and each grafted or pleached union was wrapped in cloth bandages, not only to protect the healing wound from the sun, but also to conceal his technique.

No one has studied Erlandson's trees more than Mark Primack, whose thesis for the School of the Architecture Association of London was on botanic architecture. According to Primack, there are three important principles to Erlandson's work: (1) Sap will always take the path of least resistance, so, asymmetrically-shaped limbs will grow unevenly, favoring the shortest or most direct path. (2) Symmetry encourages equal flow of carbohydrates to the roots and water and minerals to the limbs, producing balanced sap-flow and even growth. And (3), it's necessary to retain enough foliage to feed and direct the flow of the sap, at least while shaping the growth of the tree.

Primack is most impressed by the scope and refinement of Erlandson's methods. "The Lorette system of pruning (the difficult French technique for training espalier fruit trees—ed.) is child's play compared to what Erlandson grew." Primack asserts, "He wasn't just an eccentric; he was taking horticulture to the next step."

Erlandson died virtually broke in 1964. Though he tried to sell his land and trees in his last few years, he never trained anyone in his methods. The Circus languished, going through several Disneyland-like phases—including the humiliating addition of large fiberglass dinosaurs for a "Lost World" attraction.

Hearing that a developer planned to clear the trees, nurseryman Michael Bonfante purchased them in 1985, and 30 of the healthiest specimens were boxed up and transported to Bonfante's Tree Haven Nursery. Bonfante replanted these rarest of trees in the Gilroy Gardens Family Theme Park in Gilroy, California, hopefully the final home for the last living "performers" in Axel Erlandson's Tree Circus.

Cultivating a Folly Garden

Everyone has the seed of a folly deep inside waiting to bloom. Here are ten ways to cultivate your own eccentric garden:

10. **Think differently.** Disregard all gardening magazines, books, catalogs, and newspaper columns, and create a unique, personal style. Think about what moves you.

9. **Get to know your yard.** Take time to sit and walk in the space where the garden will grow; even wait through a year to gather seasonal inspiration .

8. **Embellish personal eccentricities.** Take pride in what makes you a bit odd. So-called peculiar traits or thoughts can be the springboard for creative thinking. If you *hate* pruning, for example, consider growing a "wilderness," with hidden pathways and artistically tangled mixtures of foliage and blossom.

7. **Go all out.** If you enjoy a certain kind of plant or object, then go whole hog. Plant every possible variety of rose or grow hundreds of varieties of flowering plants with just shades of yellow. Collect not dozens of colorful bottles, but thousands. Display your entire collection of lobster traps among the perennials.

6. **Combine unrelated thoughts to form a new idea.** One eclectic gardener mixed an old toi-

let, potting soil, and sweet peas to create his own private horticultural joke.

5. **Get inspired by "unrelated" things to synthesize new garden ideas.** A childhood love of glassy-black Indian bird points (tiny arrowheads) led me to incorporate visible and hidden chunks of raw obsidian (each waiting to reveal the arrowhead inside) into my own garden.

4. **Put aside normal social guidelines.** Vegetables and perennials planted in the soil between a curb and a sidewalk violates the norm in many neighborhoods, but makes for a festive, unique patch you—and the neighbors—will enjoy.

3. **Follow your passion.** Inspired by Axel Erlandson, Richard Reames, of Aborsmith Studios in Williams , Oregon, has begun to grow a living house. About two years old, the walls are being formed by 77 Red Alder trees planted 11 inches apart in a 22 foot diameter circle—the trunks are expected to fuse together into one tree. Reames is planning to install windows and a door. Such commitment over time is best driven by resolute devotion.

2. **Collect what you love, the garden will follow.** Sculptor Marcia Donahue of Berkeley, California loves to collect old bowling balls. She's massed dozens of them in her garden, tucking curious plants in and around them for a unique and striking effect.

1. **Ignore all rules** (even the previous nine).

Folly gardens open the eyes to unique vistas, free the spirit to soar to new places, and "grow" original thoughts. Nurture the soul as well as the soil with your own eccentric garden.

APPENDIX (ODD FACTS, ELABORATIONS, AND DETAILS)

Normally there is a set of appendices at the end of a book. Well this is a bit different. Much of what follows is stuff that didn't fit nicely into the main text. Some stuff is here because it's a notch above being a total slaggard. If you have a bit more energy and initiative, then some of these activities are for you. If not, skip them and go back to searching You Tube or eating an ice-cream cone. I had a good time using my computer to find a lot of this info. (Saved you *mucho, mucho* hours.) Enjoy.

Green Manures 1

Green Manure? How Gross! (But not really.)

This is in the back because it is not for a true lazy-ass. It requires once-a-year digging or roto-tilling, but is a great way to improve soil without having to schlep manure or buy fertilizers.

You say you want to garden all-naturally, but the closest source of animal manure is many miles away? Then green manuring might be for you. Green manuring is the process of tilling fresh green plants into the soil to help make it drain better and allow it to hold onto more moisture, with an added bonus—the plants, as they decay, act as a readily available fertilizer. Green manuring is also pretty darn close to free

fertilizer—discounting the cost of a few seeds and plenty of elbow grease (the truly indolent can always hire some elbows; or, you can simply cut the foliage off and take it to a compost heap and let the remaining roots do all the work—this is technically called "cover cropping." Cover cropping takes longer than green manuring to improve the soil, but is much less work.)

So why does green manuring appear in a book for lazy gardeners? It's a valid way to care for the soil for a few years before jump-starting its improvement on the path to a no-till garden. Any old plant material, dead or alive, can help improve your soil. Eventually, any kind of organic matter will be fully decomposed and converted into humus— that most wonderful, stable, moisture-holding, nutrient-rich constituent of the soil. Humus plays a essential role in nutrient exchange, especially in an organic garden that's untouched by chemically reduced fertilizers.

Learning how the natural cycle of decomposition works means you'll know exactly what part of the cycle to influence, how to speed up the natural processes, and how to improve the soil in either the short or the long term.

Dry or Juicy?

If your plant refuse is dead, dry, and straw-brown when it's turned under, it will improve soil structure—but only over a long period of time. The soil bacteria that digest it need moisture, warmth, and nitrogen to increase their populations to levels high enough to decompose the raw material. If that raw material is dry and crusty, that means it's also low in nitrogen and high in carbon, so it'll take the bacteria a longer period of time to convert the higher percentage of carbon to a more decomposed, partially decayed form known generally as "organic matter."

Because it takes many weeks, or even months, for the high carbon content of the dry organic matter to be converted into available nutrients, the nutrients won't be of any value to a recently planted crop. In fact, incorporated dry material will probably rob nitrogen from the surrounding soil for a while.

Common theory has it that the loss of soil nitrogen that occurs with the drier stuff helps to build up the bacterial populations needed to decompose the more carbonaceous material. (One interesting theory, as discussed in the book *Mineral Nutrition of Plants* by J. B. Page and G. B. Bodman [the Wisconsin Press] postulates "that the commonly observed depression in plant growth immediately after adding large amounts of green manure...may be due to competition between the higher plants and microorganisms for the limited supply of oxygen than any other single factor.") Either mechanism will often cause new crops to appear stunted,

produce yellow leaves, and grow poorly. Using dead, dry and crusty plant matter to improve soil is like putting money into a long-term bank note; there are few immediate benefits but the long-term payback is good.

If the plant matter is turned into the soil when it's fresh, green and, therefore higher in nitrogen, than the soil bacteria can easily and readily decompose its tissues. The premier virtues of green manure are that the plant matter is decomposed quickly, and that you can plant relatively soon after tilling it in. As a rule, the prudent gardener need only wait two to four weeks after tilling a green manure into the ground before transplanting or seeding. Green manure is more like playing the fast-moving stock market—the gains can be immediate and significant. To put the largest amount of green-manure fertilizer into your portfolio, however you'll need to know how to leverage all aspects of the green-manure cycle. (If you're using taller and bulkier green-manure plants like fava beans and vetches, the foliage can be cut and hauled away to a compost heap to rot over time—very much less work than tilling.)

Green Manure—The High Fiber Diet

Because of its rapid decomposition, green manure is also a good way to add fiber to the soil. As the fiber decomposes into organic matter, it will help loosen heavy clay soils and assist sandy soils in retaining moisture. Since the plants are turned under when they're fresh and green, the next crop planted there will also get a healthy boost of nitrogen.

The best green-manure plants for sheer bulk of fiber are the grasses and cereals. While these plants are growing, their very extensive and massively fibrous root systems help loosen clay soil by actual penetration and ramification of it.

"Free" Nitrogen with Good Timing

The optimal time to till under a green manure crop to provide maximum nitrogen for a subsequent crop is just as it begins to bloom. Yes, the conscientious green manurer must ruthlessly "sacrifice" beautiful blossoms for the optimal amount of nitrogen.

A Balanced Regimen for Green Manuring

There's really no reason why you can't have the best of both green-manuring worlds, using materials both dry and juicy. Like any good investment plan, a diversified portfolio is the wisest and safest strategy. While too much of a good thing can work against you, "moderation in all things" is a more beneficial approach with green manures. With grasses, cereals, non-leguminous plants, and legumes all blended together into one seeding, you'll get a broader range of nutrients, root zones, and secondary benefits (such as weed suppression).

Perhaps one of the most classic green manure blends is a combination of oats (or ryegrass), vetch, bell beans and Austrian peas. This combo has a history that goes back hundreds of years in Europe. Some version of this blend of grasses and legumes has been the nutrient backbone for many a farm, and for much longer than chemical fertilizers have been around.

The percentages of each component vary from supplier to supplier. Peaceful Valley Farm Supply's mix (see their website address on P 188) is composed of 40% bell beans, 20% Austrian field peas, 20% purple vetch, and 20% Oregon annual ryegrass. Gardeners steeped in the history of European gardening methods often add some oats to this mix to add the fibrous bulk of a cereal grass. Other gardeners figure their soil already has so much existing wild grass seed (mostly forms of ryegrass) that just adding a blend of legumes produces the same effect as the traditional European mix. Don't forget, roots are working 24 hours a day, "cultivating" soils far deeper than even the most compulsive,

maniacal gardener could till.

Planting Your Green Manure

All green manures should get off to a good start with the same careful soil preparation that you would use for direct-seeded crops such as beans, corn and carrots. (Tossing green manure seeds out into rough or untilled soil is like throwing some of your valuable stock certificates into the wind.) As a general rule, seeds should be covered with a layer of soil equal to three times their diameter. Big seeds, such as bell beans, need only a rough seedbed, but finer seed, like ryegrass, does much better if the soil preparation more closely resembles that used to prepare for a bed of carrots or radishes.

Green Manures in the Grand Scheme of Things

Green manures, coupled with fallow periods and cover crops, are an integral part of crop rotations that range from four- to 27-year cycles. (Yes, 27 years, measured by observation of traditional

 Bob sez: *I was visiting edible-landscaping guru Rosalind Creasy one year when almost a third of her front yard was covered in crimson clover in full, glorious bloom. I timidly mentioned that the best effect for nitrogen occurs prior to bloom, or perhaps when only up to 20 percent of the plants are blooming. "Yes," she replied, "I won't get as much nitrogen, but look how absolutely gorgeous the bloom is! I don't mind giving up some nitrogen for the floral display. Besides, crimson clover has a decent amount of nitrogen to spare and my soil isn't in horrible shape." Yep.*

farmers sharing fields in Europe.) With a rotation of sufficient length to allow the soil to "rest" and accumulate nutrients, you can grow all your own fertilizer in place, without having to leave your yard to haul in smelly manure.

Nitrogen Gathered by Legumes

(depending upon the type of legumes and the study)

**Common Name
(Botanical Name)**

Common Name (Botanical Name)	Pounds per acre
Hairy vetch (*Vicia villosa*)	80
Dutch white clover (*Trifolium repens*)	100
Alsike clover (*Trifolium hybridum*)	140
Red clover (*Trifolium pratense*)	140
White sweet clover (*Melilotus albus*)	160
Alfalfa (*Medicago sativa*)	250

Bob sez: *My favorite personal story about green manuring stems from the drought of 1975 to 1977 in Northern California. Since my clients couldn't afford enough rationed water to keep all their landscapes alive, I reasoned that an annual green manure would help the soil. I planted a number of flowerbeds with a fall crop of vetch each year. The grasses and vetch that sprouted in the fall rains grew fine throughout the periodic winter rains. As the soil began to dry out in the spring, I turned under the crop as a green manure and mulched the beds for the summer. After three winters, the soil had noticeably improved. One former client, whose soil was a black clay gumbo, even called a year after the drought to thank me for the fantastic improvement in her soil. I was touched by her gratitude, but I knew that Mother (or Father—equal-opportunity household) Nature had done most of the work.*

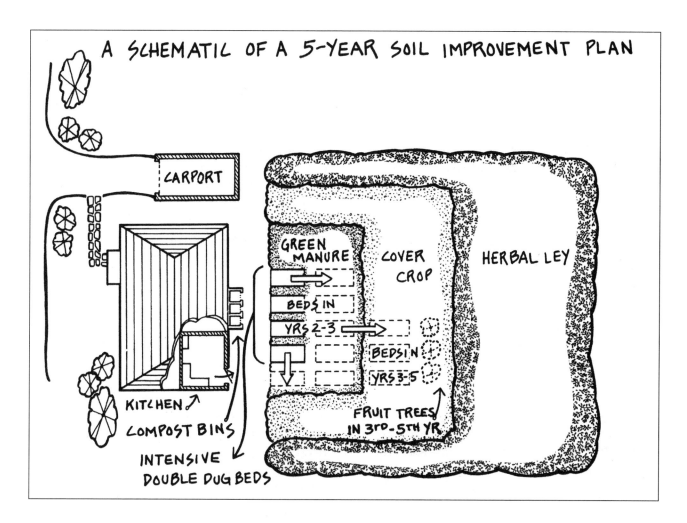

Figure 79: Before you plant your vegetable beds, there are things you can do to improve your soil and eliminate or reduce the need for purchased fertilizers. If you maintain hot-compost bins, you can speed up the soil-enriching process with the rapid generation of fertile compost. If you're opting for a "cold" compost pile, place the heap out of view in an "herbal ley." In England, an "herbal ley" is another term for a type of cover crop. Usually it applies to the addition of nitrogen-fixing plants to grass pastures, but here it refers to a ley that contains at least 30% legumes, thus eliminating the need for artificial nitrogen fertilizer.)

Begin your soil-improvement plan with raised beds fertilized with compost. At the same time, plant: 1) a green manure crop in any raised beds in which you plan to plant regular crops in a year or two; 2) a cover crop with an emphasis on grasses;
3) an herbal ley with more legumes.

You should start your green manure planting three to five years before planting vegetables, and it's a good plan for trees as well. You can choose not to plant vegetables in the cover crop and herbal ley areas and use the cut herbal ley plants as cut greens for a hot or cold compost pile.

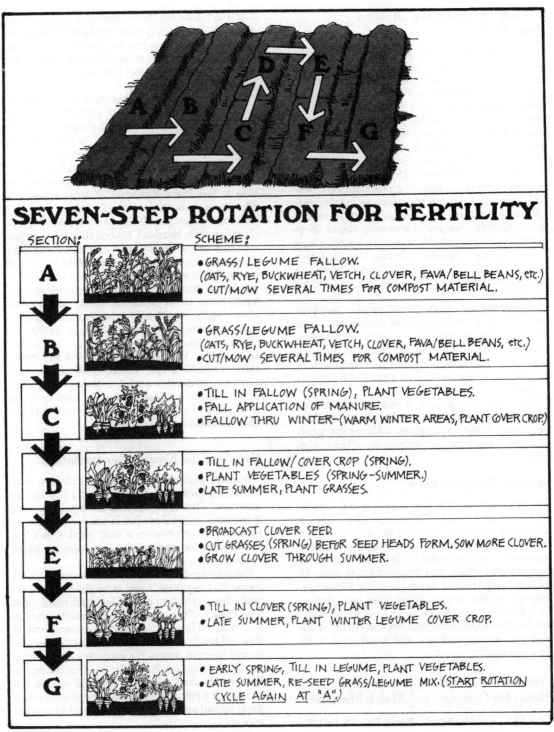

SEVEN-STEP ROTATION FOR FERTILITY

SECTION:		SCHEME:
A		• GRASS / LEGUME FALLOW. (OATS, RYE, BUCKWHEAT, VETCH, CLOVER, FAVA/BELL BEANS, etc.) • CUT/MOW SEVERAL TIMES FOR COMPOST MATERIAL.
B		• GRASS/LEGUME FALLOW. (OATS, RYE, BUCKWHEAT, VETCH, CLOVER, FAVA/BELL BEANS, etc.) • CUT/MOW SEVERAL TIMES FOR COMPOST MATERIAL.
C		• TILL IN FALLOW (SPRING), PLANT VEGETABLES. • FALL APPLICATION OF MANURE. • FALLOW THRU WINTER—(WARM WINTER AREAS, PLANT COVER CROP.)
D		• TILL IN FALLOW/ COVER CROP (SPRING). • PLANT VEGETABLES (SPRING–SUMMER.) • LATE SUMMER, PLANT GRASSES.
E		• BROADCAST CLOVER SEED. • CUT GRASSES (SPRING) BEFOR SEED HEADS FORM, SOW MORE CLOVER. • GROW CLOVER THROUGH SUMMER.
F		• TILL IN CLOVER (SPRING), PLANT VEGETABLES. • LATE SUMMER, PLANT WINTER LEGUME COVER CROP.
G		• EARLY SPRING, TILL IN LEGUME, PLANT VEGETABLES. • LATE SUMMER, RE-SEED GRASS/LEGUME MIX. (START ROTATION CYCLE AGAIN AT "A".)

Figure 80: How's this for complicated? If you don't have room for seven raised or soil-based vegetable beds, skip this drawing and save your brain. These seven steps involve a progression of cover crops for two years (A and B); followed by vegetables (C); then another cover crop (i.e. fallow-D) after tilling in the fallow; followed by a clover cover crop (E); then more vegetables, and finally, in year seven (G), plant late-season vegetables after tilling in the legumes. By using a lot of cover crops for parts of all years, you can avoid adding fertilizers altogether.

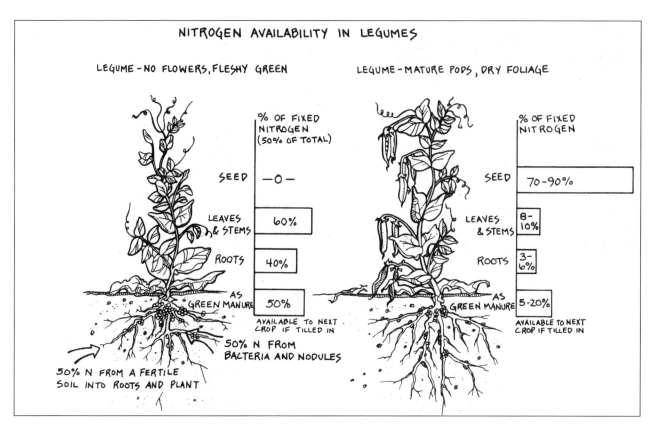

Figure 81: This drawing may look scary, but relax and read on. Basically, it's a way to demonstrate a simple fact: to get the most nitrogen out of a legume you need to till in or harvest the plant before it blooms. On the left we see that 60 percent of the nitrogen is tied up in the foliage and stems of a plant, so that the nitrogen can easily "dump" into the seeds when they start forming (The seeds can contain up to 90 percent of the plant's nitrogen, which is needed to form the protein in them.) When you till in or harvest a legume before it blooms, up to 50 percent of the fixed nitrogen is available to the next planting. If you wait until seeds form, only 5-20 percent of the nitrogen produced is available to the following planting.

Cisterns for Rainwater Catchment, cont. 2

The Cost of Storing "Free" Rainfall
Prices for cistern materials vary across the country. The best way to compare expenses is to convert all costs to the price per gallon of storage. For example, where I live, north of San Francisco, costs range from $.50 per gallon for ugly aboveground storage to $1.50 per gallon for contractor-installed tanks. Here are some sample costs for the north San Francisco Bay Area:

Type of Cistern

These prices do not include fittings, valves, pipe or plumber's bills. In some cases, the base or pad is an additional cost (where I live, it's much more than the cost of the tank). Basically, the larger the tank, the lower the cost per gallon. Smaller tanks are easier for the do-it-yourselfer to work with, but this convenience will cost a bit more because of the economies of scale that favor bigger tanks.

Cistern Type	Size In Gallons	Cost Per Gallon
Liquid storage bags (bladders, mail-order)	300	$1.00
Plastic liner (provide your own box)	Varies	$.11-.30/ sq. ft.
Plastic downspout barrel	42-55	$2.00+
Polyethylene tanks	5000	$.50
Poured-in-place, aboveground concrete	5000	$1.50

Innovations in plastic tanks have made them competitive with concrete tanks, which can settle and crack or be damaged by earthquakes. In my area, you need a permit and a costly engineering plan to install a concrete base for any tank over 5000 gallons. If you spend a little more money for a plastic tank that holds less than 5000 gallons, you'll quickly be compensated for that extra expense by the savings on the installation costs. This is because the plastic tank can be set on compacted level ground or gravel without the expense of a reinforced concrete slab and engineering.

The location of the cistern is usually determined by three factors: convenient proximity to the collecting surface, aesthetics, and cost. Naturally, the closer a cistern is to the roof, the more convenient it is. Systems that rely on gravity to disperse the water to the garden are usually constructed with an aboveground tank, so that some gravitational pressure is built up by the difference in levels.

Pumped cisterns can be aboveground or underground, although because most storage tanks are so bulky and ugly looking, many people would rather bury them. The cost of an underground tank can be quite high, however, because it must be engineered to withstand compression of soil around its walls. Plastic tanks that can be buried can wind up costing $1.50 per gallon or more.

When considering a large tank, by the way, make sure it has a lid or hatch large enough to allow you to climb inside to clean or repair it. (Be sure to lock it so you don't find some curious creature floating inside it some day.) Aboveground tanks should also have screen-covered air holes to help keep the water fresh but bug-free. Every kind of tank needs a large-diameter pipe for a bottom drain to flush out any accumulated sediment.

Choosing the Size of Your Cistern

With a mere 12 inches of rain, a 2500-square-foot roof will generate about 18,000 gallons of runoff water. A simple way to determine how much rain you have to work with is to multiply the square footage of the roof by 0.6; this will give you the number of gallons of water your roof will collect. (The more accurate number is .62, but leaving off the .02 takes into consideration factors such as evaporation, leaks, splattering and absorption by roofing materials made of composites, wood, ceramic, or concrete.)

Rather than building a cistern to accommodate the maximum rainfall your roof can capture, there are two more practical approaches to determining size. First, you can simply store all the water you'll need to get through each dry spell, diverting the rest. If you want to use this method and you live in an arid area where the seasonal

Bob sez: *Like a cash-for-grass lawn-reduction program, some cities are once-again encouraging cisterns. They help with paying for one. In my town (Santa Rosa, CA, 60 miles north of San Francisco) you can get a rebate of $0.25 per gallon of storage (they pay for the tank only, none of the plumbing). That covers up to 50 percent of the cost of a typical tank! But, maximum gallons eligible for rebate are calculated by being based on square footage of irrigated landscape, the plant types, and the peak month (July) water requirement for planted areas. (100 gallon minimum.)*

drought always lasts five to six months, money had better not be a limiting factor—you'll need a big tank.

Typically, you'll need to know the average length of the dry spells in your area. Talk to the weather reporter for the local newspaper, radio station, or television station; consult the weather records at the closest fire or forestry station; or contact the Master Gardener program through your Cooperative Extension.

The other way of determining cistern size is to bend your mind around a bit of math and estimate your landscape's irrigation needs. Look at past water bills and calculate your total water usage for the irrigation season. Many bills present water use in Hundred Cubic Feet—HCFs. Each HCF equals 748 gallons. Now estimate how much of your total water use goes to the garden (check with your local water department for the average percentage for your climate). In temperate climates with summer humidity, exterior plant use may account for only 30% to 50% of total water use. In areas with dry hot summers, your garden or landscape may soak up 50% to 70% of the total.

Delivery

With a simple gravity system, all you need is a hose long enough to reach the plants downhill from the tank. To protect the hose from sucking too much grunge off the bottom of the tank, make sure the discharge pipe is placed at least six inches above the bottom. This pipe should come through the side of the tank and be fitted with a standard hose-bib.

Pumped systems require an electric centrifugal pump or a sump pump. A $200 to $400 sump pump may not develop more than 15 pounds of pressure per square inch (psi), which is enough to power a limited drip-irrigation system. Be sure to check the specifications on the box or in the owner's manual to make sure your purchase has enough gumption to lift the water out of the

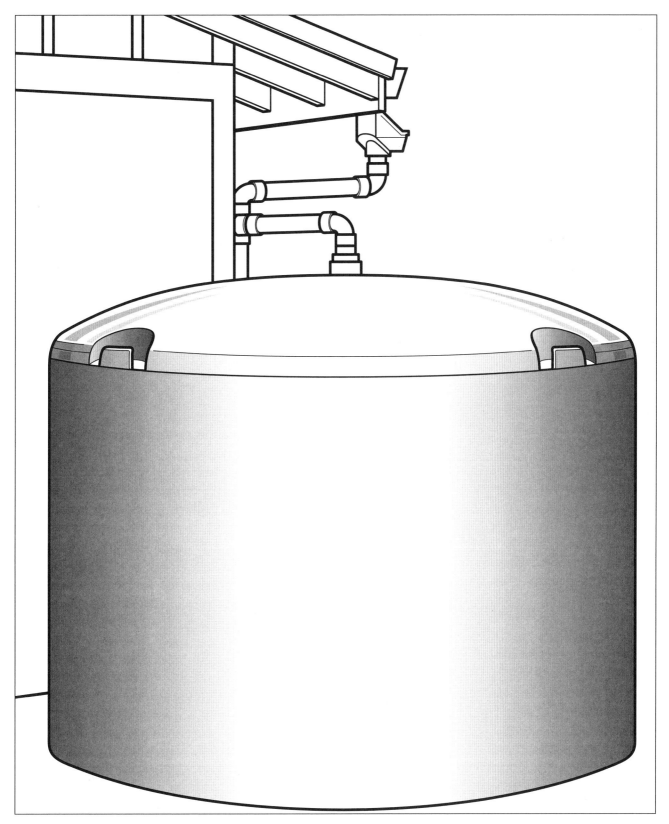

Figure 82: Here's a 3000-gallon tank. It's placed on a crushed rock base with packed sand to keep the rocks from puncturing the floor. In my county, you need an expensive permit for tanks over 5000 gallons.

tank and pump it high enough uphill to meet your gravitational needs. This lifting capacity is called the "head," and is measured as the vertical height, in feet.

Pressure tanks fitted with electric centrifugal pumps are more expensive—well over $1200—than sump pumps, but can pump more water with plenty of pressure. A self-priming pump will be much easier to operate. As with sump pumps, remove the water from a slightly elevated discharge pipe so dirt can settle out.

Oh Deer, Native Deer Diets 3

Bambi may be adorable in the movies, but in your garden it's a very different story. As houses move into the forest and deer penetrate into the suburbs—even into some urban neighborhoods—more plants are at risk. There actually more deer in the country now than there were in the 17th century when Europeans showed up.

There are many exceptions to all generalized guidelines for deer resistance. Most are composed of well-meaning but totally bogus "rules." Here are some of them (with a token sample of one exception to each):

• **Deer don't eat thorny plants.** (As mentioned, they'll decimate roses).
• **They avoid plants with strong odors such as herbs.** (Not always—skip the basil; deer love it.)
• ***They won't touch native plants.*** Wow, is this ever wrong! Deer have co-evolved with the native plants around my house in Sonoma County, California, and will happily gobble many of them. The ubiquitous ungulates can tolerate a wide range of toxins—like the alkaloids, tannins, glycosides, terpenoids, phenolics, and certain amino acids that are often found in native plants. When you see a healthy native plant, you have no idea as to how many specimens of it died from grazing before the one you see survived. I call it the "silent screams of the forest."
• They avoid dry foliage. (And *Cotoneaster* spp. is just one exception.)
• **They won't eat silver foliage.** (Yeah, yeah, just don't try to grow snow-in-summer (*Cerastium tomentosum*) or *Artemisia* spp.)
• **They dislike fuzzy-textured plants.** (Rose Campion (*Lychnis* spp.) is just one of the many exceptions to this.)

Some books have the audacity to propose there are plants you can grow that keep deer away, obviously written by someone who's never gardened around the dear creatures. Deer can and will squeeze through dense hedges of so-called deer-resistant shrubs to munch on your favorite petunias. Please note that there are five species of deer in North America. To think that all species avoid the same plants is ridiculous. So, I consider books about deer-resistant plants useless. Get real.

In summary, the only accurate guideline is: "There are no deer-proof plants, only some resistant ones." Native plants? I tried planting many native plants over three decades of gardening, but the deer ate most of them.

And I know from experience that over time some currently deer-resistant plants may become the next ungulate salad. Deer evolve, and can "learn" to eat plants after years of exposure and sampling. Maybe ten to twenty percent of the plants that were deer-resistant when I planted them in my garden became Bambi fodder five to ten years later.

So, if you happen to live near me (Sonoma County, CA, 60 miles north of San Francisco), learn from my experience to cut your losses. Read the following lists to save plenty of time and cash. Read first: buy plants second. If you don't live near me, find an experienced local gardener and coax the info from him or her before you plant.

Remember, deer are very different from region to region. What works for me may not work in your yard. Check with the Master Gardeners and local gardeners in your area.

The deer didn't eat about half of the exotic plants I've tried. So here's a list of what's worked with the black-tailed deer around my house. I've tried

83 of the 244 plants listed on the University of California Cooperative Extension deer-resistant plant list. Forty of the plants I've tried were not eaten and forty-three were gobbled up in my small low-budget garden. Check with local experts and experiment.

Plants Deer Seem to Avoid in My Garden

Agave spp. Agaves
Amaryllis belladonna Naked ladies
Artemisia 'Powis Castle'
Asarum caudatum – (Eaten each late summer) Wild ginger
Baccharis pilularis Coyote brush
Brodiaea spp. Triplet lily
Carex spp. Sedges
Ceanothus spp. California lilac, tick brush. Most eaten. Shrub varieties torn apart when used by deer to rub the velvet off their horns.
Corylus cornuta var. California hazelnut
Cyperus spp. Cypress
Digitalis purpurea Foxglove
Echium fastuosum Pride-of-Maderia
Euphorbia spp. Spurge
Euryops pectinatus Euryops
Ferns, most species except *Pellaea*
Festuca ovina glauca Blue fescue
Grevillea spp. Grevilleas
Ilex spp. Hollies, except thornless
Iris spp. Irises
Juniperus spp. Junipers
Lavandula spp. Lavenders
Leonotis leonurus Lion's tail
Leptospermum spp. Tea trees
Mentha spp. Mints
Myosotis spp. Forget-me-nots
Narcissus spp. Daffodils
Nerium oleander Oleander
Nepeta spp. Catnips
Phlomis fruticosa Jerusaleum sage
Rhododendron spp. Rhododendrons and azaleas
Rhus ovata Sugar bush
Ribes spp. Currants
Rosmarinus officinalis Rosemary
Santolina spp. Lavender cotton
Trillium spp. Trilliums

Reasonably Safe Bets

Clarkia spp. Clarkias
Dietes vegeta Fortnight lily
Erigeron karvinskianus Santa Barbara Daisy
Hedera helix Ivy
Myrica californica Pacific wax myrtle
Oxalis spp. Sorrels
Tulipa spp. Tulips
Vaccinium ovatum Huckleberry
Viola odorata Violet
Wisteria spp. Wisterias

Plants that have worked for me that are not on some of the lists.
Echium pininana Tree Echium
Echium wildpretii Tower of Jewels
Brugmansia x candida Angel's trumpet
Cortaderia selloana 'Sun Strip' pampas grass that makes no fertile seed. NOT the invasive pampas species.
Ozothamnus rosmarinifolius Sea Rosemary
Ruta graveolens Rue- the worst-smelling plant I know of. Yuck.
Salvia apianna Silver sage, native California
Salvia clevelandii California blue sage
Stipa gigantea Giant feather grass
Symphytum officinale Comfrey (Remember, it spreads easily from root pieces and is then very difficult to eradicate or control.)
Thymus spp. Thyme, every species I've tried.

De"fence"ive Maneuvers

Deer, unfortunately, don't know from lazy-ass. It can be hard work and expensive to keep them out of your edibles, so the relaxed ethos of this book is suspended for the section below, simply because there's no point in gardening just to feed deer.

The type of fence that will reliably exclude Bambi and friends depends very much on local deer-population density and habitat. Simple fences work quite well when populations are low and there's plenty of alternative forage. Under these conditions, a relatively inexpensive one-wire electrical fence with a high-voltage (4000-5000 volts), low-amperage charger has worked quite well in parts of the East and Midwest. It's actually a dirty trick; 12.5- or 17-gauge wire is placed 30 inches aboveground, and small foil tents dabbed with peanut butter are draped over the wire. Any deer attempting to taste the peanut butter gets a mouthful of electricity—not enough to cause injury, but enough to make a very big impression.

In places where deer populations are higher and/or hungrier, a one-wire electric fence might as well be made of tissue paper. A more secure option is the three-wire "New Hampshire" or "Figure-four" fence with two wires running 28 inches apart on a vertical plane (the lower wire is strung 10 to 15 inches above the soil), with an additional wire installed 30 inches above the ground on a separate line of posts inside the first set of two.

Another popular agricultural fence is composed of five strands of "hot" wire, with the first wire strung six inches from the ground and the rest above it at 12-inch intervals. In some studies these fences, especially the five-strand type, have resulted in 100% success, or nearly complete effectiveness. The bad news is that all electrical fences can become ineffective when short-circuited by accumulated snow or heavy vegetation.

Where I live (Sonoma County, north of San Francisco), much of the deer forage dries up in California's arid summers. In the 1980s, orchardists who tried 12-inch spacing of electric wires still found plenty of apple-loving ungulates browsing happily on their trees. Experience has since shown that a deer-proof electric fence requires high-tension wire (the so-called New Zealand 200,000 psi, 12.5-gauge wire); a high-voltage, low-impedance "energizer;" a weed-free zone below the first wire; and sturdy corner construction for all the tensioned wires. The first wire must be within four inches of the soil, and there should be no more than six inches between all wires up to six feet (12-inch gaps are OK upwards from the six- to eight-foot level). Deer fencing around here is serious business.

California farmers and homeowners also eventually learned that electricity isn't required if a deer fence is made of heavy 2-by-4-inch mesh fencing that's at least six feet tall (where the deer density is very light) or up to eight feet (the usual minimum height for most garden or orchard settings). On sloped land, fences ten feet or higher are required so a deer can't jump from an uphill "runway."

An In of "fence" ive Deer Fence

The above examples of fencing styles may work well, but boy, are they ugly. Six-to-eight-feet-tall deer fences with lots of posts and plenty of stretched wire or mesh are great for protecting crops, but the aesthetic is pure prison-perimeter. The fencing that provides the single best combination of low visual profile, convenient construction, easily integrated gates, and low maintenance is the "double-four-foot" deer fence, actually two parallel four-foot-high fences, separated by a five-foot-wide area of open ground. This works like a charm, because the hooved raiders would have no place to land if they try to clear the first fence, and somehow they're smart enough to figure this out.

I built a version of this double fence in 1988 for

Myra Portwood of Sonoma County, and it still works. Myra wanted to face the most visible fence with rustic wooden strips (around here they call them "pallens") that look like split grape stakes. By staggering the tops of alternate pallens and leaving a two-inch gap between each one, we created a light, airy, rustic feeling. The inner fence is the tried-and-true four-foot tall, 2-by-4-inch wire mesh, planted with ornamental vines.

It's necessary to keep the space between the fences fairly clear so deer get the idea, but the fences themselves can be planted with vines. In Myra's yard, honeysuckle (*Lonicera japonica*) was planted on the inside fence to disguise the wire and a deer-proof hedge of English lavender (*Lavandula angustifolia*) was planted along the outside of the outer fence for good looks. (See page C2 in the color section.)

It would seem that this structure could be adapted into any well-designed landscape, and anywhere that has no deep winter snow—I think the deer might just walk on deep snow and discover your tasty trees and perennials. And there's a good chance they will remember the garden for summer grazing of everything—vegetables included.

Figure 83: The dark grey shading on this map shows the territory of the pocket gopher (*Thomomys bottae*) in the United States. The common name is from the large fur-lined external cheek pouches it uses for gathering food. There are several genuses of gophers. If you live elsewhere count your blessings.

Gophers—The Bane of Western, Southwestern Gardens

Those of us who live west of Texas and south of Oregon face a formidable foe. It's estimated that California alone is home to at least a billion rodents, of which the most abundant is a critter known as the pocket gopher (*Thomomys bottae*). This animal gets its common name from the large fur-lined external cheek pouches it uses for gathering food. When the Russians attempted to settle and farm on the Sonoma County coast (80 miles north of San Francisco) in 1809, they gave up after 30 years of trying. One Russian settler's diary, found on his ill-fated farm, lamented: "We could have made a go of it here, if it were not for the ground rats."

Amazing Gopher Facts; Impress Your Friends

They may be a pain in the butt, but gophers are

actually pretty amazing. From *Conversations With A Pocket Gopher* (Jack Schaefer, Capra Press, 1992):

• Gophers' lips are behind their incisors to keep their mouths clean.
• Their upper incisors can grow 14 inches per year. Thus their relentless burrowing activity (especially in gravelly soil) to keep their teeth from growing toward and impaling their devious little brains!
• An average gopher tunnel remains two and seven-eighths inches round. The gopher is as wide as the tunnel, yet the gopher can easily turn around. Go figure.
• A gopher can tunnel up to 150 feet every day.
• Pocket gophers may turn over three to seven tons of soil per acre every year.
• Plant-species diversity is five to 48 percent higher where gophers are present—the mounds of soil they leave behind are favored places for prairie wildflowers to germinate and flourish. After the 1980 volcanic eruption of Mt. St. Helens in Washington State, it was the activity of gophers, specifically their defecation, that brought in mutually symbiotic fungi (mycorrhizae) to inoculate other plants for a better and healthier life and restoration of the disturbed soil.
• Also, gophers turn over the soil more effectively than earthworms. And the mounds are actually good for the soil; one report states: "… Total above-ground plant production [would be] increased by roughly 5.5% by the presence of the mounds," according to one study. So, as much as you want to get rid of them, they aren't completely malicious critters with no worth whatsoever.

But in spite of their virtues, these voracious herbivores will tunnel both shallow and deep in order to feast on the roots of your plants. An average of 22 gophers per acre translates to four pounds of fresh vegetation consumed per day. Many poor gardeners have watched helplessly as a young garlic top or tender bunch of lettuce suddenly begins to wiggle and disappears beneath the ground.

Gophers are territorial and mostly nocturnal creatures that travel and skirmish across open land at night, looking for likely new places to burrow. In the spring, young gophers stage their own version of "March Madness" as they leave home and frantically try to acquire their own territories. Once a gopher has established a territory, it maintains it for life, but male gophers are polygamous, which means that their territories overlap, or that they wander at night to court their next "babe."

In spite of its name, the common gopher snake gets only 6.4% of its nourishment from gopher meat. (They're also quite territorial, so don't try to import one into your garden, as it will just set off looking for home.) Rattlesnakes acquire only 2.5% of their protein from gophers, as the rodents' tunnel system makes l it hard for the snakes to recoil and strike (and who wants a rattlesnake in the garden?). The most significant gopher predator is the barn owl, which will eat an average of 155 gophers a year (53 pounds), or 71.4% of its diet. Alas, any great horned owl within four miles will scare off or eat barn owls.

Gopher Solutions

Raised bed boxes with bottoms made of chew-resistant hardware cloth are a good solution (Instructions for building one are on on P. 169). Another great option is a raised-bed box constructed of cinder blocks. Here's how you construct a gopher-proof raised bed that will foil the ground rats and last your lifetime:

 Bob sez: *A friend of mine noticed a gopher "throw" (the mound they make when surfacing) piled up against the wood of one of his foot-tall boxes, and watched as a gopher used it as a ramp to hop into the box. He now builds 24-inch-tall boxes, which also have the added benefit of lessening back strain, and capturing all of the roots—see Figure 1 on page 15.*

- Lay down one quarter- or one-half-inch hardware cloth to cover an area slightly larger than the planned outside dimensions of your box. There should be several inches protruding on the ground outside of the cinder blocks when you build the box.

- Set the blocks with their holes facing up. For the second row, stagger the blocks by one-half. Higher is better; to protect your plants from relentless gophers, two to three "courses" of cinder block are ideal.

- Fill the bed and the top holes of the cinder blocks with composted soil mix to kick-start your garden.

- Install half-inch in-line drip-irrigation tubing down the length of the bed. Use two lines if the bed is three feet wide, and three or four lines in four-foot-wide beds.

- Install quarter-inch tubing along the top of the blocks to irrigate the soil pockets, which are a good place for useful herbs, or leave the top un-irrigated to use as a sitting bench.

Use no-till methods in your new box by layering compost and compostable materials as needed. Be sure to include a layer of black-and-white newspaper on top to thwart stray seeds in the compost or soil mix. Add a weed-free mulch to hold down and hide the newspaper.

Here's a recipe for creating proper balance between nitrogen and woody (carbon) sources when layering raw materials: one part fresh greens (lawn and garden clippings, fresh hay, etc.) to three or four parts of brown material such as dried leaves or straw.
In gopher-occupied territories, wire baskets are required planting additions for perennial flowers, shrubs and trees, and usually work if you keep as much of the wire barrier above the surface mulch as possible—they usually don't

like to climb over the prickly edges of the wire. Once, however, a wire basket protruding four inches above the mulch around one of my apple trees didn't stop a gopher from climbing over for a meal. The tree leaned over and simply died. I later found a research paper in which the observed gophers scaled a 10-inch-tall wire barrier. Diabolical.

Flower Power
For you in the West who are avidly reading this, here's the Holy Grail of Gopher Management—a

 Bob sez: *If you have gophers, move. You'll never get rid of all of them. Exclude the little "ground rats" with wire under a raised bed or in the form of planting baskets.*

list of California native plants that they don't like to eat! Use caution as gophers have never read this list. I don't know how accurate this list is; but it was put together by the reputable Walter Earle and Margaret Graham, former owners for 40 years of Mostly Natives Nursery in Tomales, CA.

(All single genus names have multiple species—spp.)
Achillea (Yarrows)
Anemopsis californica (Yerba mansa)
Aquilegia (Columbines)
Arbutus menziesii (Pacific madrone)
Arctostaphylos (Manzanitas)
Armeria californica (California sea pink/thrift)
Artemisia (Wormwoods, sagebrushes)
Baccharis pilularis (Coyotebrush)
Carpenteria (Bush anemone)
Ceanothus (California lilacs)
Chlorogalum (Soap plants)
Dicentra formosa (Western bleeding heart)
Erigeron glaucous (Seaside daisy)
Fragaria (Wild strawberries)
Frangula californica (California coffeeberry)

Heteromeles (Toyons)
Heuchera maxima (Island alum root)
Iris - (Native irises)
Mimulus (Monkeyflowers)
Oxalis oregana (Redwood sorrel)
Penstemon heterophyllus (Foothill penstemon)
Polystichum (Swordferns)
Potentilla gracilis (Slender cinquefoil)
Ribes (Wild currants)
Rubus parviflorus (Thimbleberry)
Salvia (Native sages)
Sidalcea (Checkerblooms)
Sisyrinchium bellum (Western blue-eyed grass)
Vitis californica (California wild grape)

For a longer list, go to the Mostly Natives web site: www.mostlynatives.com/plant-characteristics/gopher-resistant.

The following non-natives also seem to be un-grazed by gophers in my garden:

Echiums (*Echium* spp.)
Euphorbias (*Euphorbia* spp.)
Fortnight lily (*Dietis iriodes*)
Foxglove, Purple (*Digitalis purpurea*)
Grevilleas (*Grevillea* spp.)
Junipers (*Juniperus* spp.)
Jerusalem sage (*Phlomis fruticosa*)
Lavenders (*Lavandula* spp.)
Common mullein (*Verbascum thapsus*)
Naked ladies (*Amarillis belladonna*)
'Powis Castle' artemisia (*Artemisia* 'Powis Castle')
Rosemary (*Rosmarinus officinalis*)
Rue (*Ruta* spp.)
Santolina (green and lavender cotton) (*Santolina* spp.)
Strawberry tree (*Arbutus unedo*)
Thymes (*Thymus* spp.)

Mammals

As if all those gophers and deer weren't enough, members of the warm-blooded animal kingdom lust after your garden/landscape as well. Some tunnel and attack from the bottom; others munch on tender top leaves. Killing them is, for moral, logistical, or health reasons, not a desirable option for many gardeners. So here's a rundown of some of the easiest ways to deal with mammalian pests other than gophers and deer.

Voles

Voles (originally vole-mouse, from Norwegian vollmus, meaning "field mouse") are burrowing mouse-like rodents with rounded muzzles, and are found in both wet and well-drained soils. They construct runways near the surface and far-reaching burrows underground, and may even "borrow" gopher tunnels. These hungry little rodents feed mainly on the leafy parts of sedges, as well as a wide range of grasses and herbs, and tend to store seeds and other plant materials in underground chambers for snacks. On the surface, they can do a lot of damage to garden plants and lawn grasses; underground, they feed on the roots of trees, shrubs, herbaceous plants, and bulbs.

If you see the bark of a tree gnawed a few inches above and below the ground in the fall and winter, yep, you've got voles. The pine vole doesn't use surface runways, but can go aboveground to find new food sources and new areas to prowl.

To keep voles out of your vegetable garden, surround its perimeter with 24"-wide metal flashing or ¼ inch hardware cloth. Bury it 12" to 14" in the ground and leave the rest exposed {voles don't like to burrow very deeply). You can also use a raised bed with a wire bottom as described above. Trapping them is very problematic, as they wander around, and you can't find a regularly used tunnel. Figuring out where they are going to go is like the old joke: I'm on a bus and I want to get off at Pine Street. So I ask another traveler - "Can you tell me where to get off? And they reply: "Sure. Watch me and get off one stop before I do."

A Cornucopia of Pests: More Marauding Mammals and Feathered Foragers

OK, I have to state that living where I do and growing mostly ornamentals, I've had limited experience with the following critters (but, boy howdy, can I go on about deer, moles, and voles). The information below was gained by talking to local folks with actual experience of battling these pests, with a few forays onto the Internet. You can also Google "How do I keep _____ out of my garden?" for all kinds of creative solutions that don't involve shotguns or poisons.

Hare Today, Gone Tomorrow

Rabbits. You just want to cuddle them. That is, until they strip the bark from a fruit tree or pillage your vegetables. Many of us have had pet bunnies that were easy to supervise and corral, but what about Snowball's evil cousin, the wild rabbit—gray/brown, clever, taut with exercise, and ready and willing to dig under fences in pursuit of yummy forage? Here are some tips for protecting your crops from the long-eared munchers:

• Rabbits need the protection of cover from predatory birds. Keep your yard or garden clean, with no brushy piles.

• Add barrier fencing at the border of your vegetable patch. Sink one edge of a two-foot-high strip of one-inch wire mesh into the soil. Bend a 12" portion of the exposed wire and lay down an "L"-shaped fence facing away from the garden with the bottom of the "L" on the ground. A four-foot-wide roll of wire (with holes no larger than one inch across) makes it quite easy to construct a useful barrier.

• Contact Elmer Fudd, who has a lot of experience with "Wascally Wabbits."

• Keep a dog. All dogs were originally bred to hunt specific animals (or herd them, like Border Collies). For rabbit comtrol, consider getting one of the following breeds:
1. Mini Beagle
2. Basset Hound
3. Dachshund
4. Jack Russell Terrier (good for rats as well)
5. Redbone Coonhound
6. Weimaraner

Don't mess with ultrasonic devices, unless you find a neighbor who can show you clear evidence of one that works. (The sonic repellents for gophers never did for me.)

Spraying with repellents may be the last resort and may have to be done after every rain. What a drag; off your couch and away from a Game of Thrones marathon you go, to spray for... bunnies?

A site advertising Tomcat™ pest repellents offers these additional suggestions (besides, of course, encouraging you to buy their rabbit repellent):

• Pick your plants wisely. Rabbits favor young, tender plants. Consider planting things they have a natural distaste for, including strong-scented plants like garlic, onion, rhubarb, oregano, basil, and geranium.

• Scare them away. Lights, shiny aluminum pie tins, and motion scare devices can be enough to ward off rabbits, at least for a time. Dogs and cats running free in the yard are a great deterrent, too.

• Put up barriers. In addition to big appetites and even bigger families, rabbits are big into digging, too. Keep them from getting to your plants with chicken-wire fencing, hardware cloth, or plant cages made of livestock wire. Just be sure barriers are at least two feet high and buried at least six inches deep (though higher and deeper is better). Monitor barriers for holes, making sure to quickly repair tears and other critter-created openings.

• Skip the live traps. While it may be tempting to try the catch-and-release method, it's best to leave that kind of animal control to the experts. Live trapping can lead to injury to the trapper.

A Little Squirrely

Watching squirrels is kind of like watching cartoons, but they're not so funny when they're stealing your edibles. Frankly, I don't know of any non-lethal way to control these frenzied mammals. To shape a tree high enough to keep them from jumping onto it would mean limbs four feet off the ground, with at least nine feet of spacing between the edges of each tree's foliage canopy. I sent my Dad 12 or more fruit trees over the years—and he never got to pick a ripe fruit, even when he used live traps to relocate the fluffy-tailed thieves. Don't consider netting, they'll eat right through it. The Tomcat™ folks suggest mulching, dogs, motion-detecting lights, noisemakers, and, of course, their squirrel repellent. Again I say: good luck with all that.

Meandering Moles

Another way to lose your hair (and I can't afford to) is to attempt to trap moles. The little critters make random tunnels that mound up and they eat worms and other useful soil citizens in the process. (Gophers are vegetarians, moles are carnivores.) Unlike with gophers, it's very hard to predict where a mole will head. And they don't necessarily use the same tunnel more than once. For the truly desperate, there's a guillotine-like device that spears them (if you can predict what direction they're going). Gassing is another messy and dangerous option.

The thing most landowners have against moles is the damage they do to lawns. One tactic is to get them to tunnel more deeply, thus fostering peaceful co-existence while avoiding those unsightly and potentially ankle-spraining lumps and dips in your turf. Avoid over-watering your lawn, because that attracts grubs and worms (mole food) to the surface.

Another strategy is to keep stomping down the surface tunnels, or flattening them with a shovel (Whack-A-Mole, anyone?), and eventually they may start to tunnel more deeply.

Birds

I live near the place where Alfred Hitchcock filmed his unforgettable movie, The Birds. Luckily, no residual hostile ravens and crows haunt this area, which is lucky, because these Corvidae are among the birds that can be the most destructive to a garden.

So what to do when birds dig up your newly planted seeds, or become veggie-scavenging pests?

With the patience of a saint or nun and the resolve of an Army commander, you can keep them away from the fruit with netting, available at garden-supply stores. Put it on early in the season so the birds don't eat the green fruit, and be sure to secure the perimeter of the netting cloth to the trunk. Training your apple tree to dwarf sizes of five, eight, and 12 feet makes it much easier to net (and harvest) vulnerable crops. My editor says her dad used to drape their cherry tree in an Army-surplus parachute—and it worked.

The folks at the Farm and Dairy magazine website have the following suggestions:

Aluminum screening. Michigan State University Extension explains how bending a roll of narrow aluminum screening into a U-shape and placing it over a row of seeds or seedlings will provide protection from birds. The screening can be held down by pushing slim sticks or heavy wire through the screening and into the dirt.

Hardware screening or cloth. Hardware screening can be cut and bent into hoops for your seeds or seedlings. Michigan State University Extension warns that the screening should have openings small enough to keep birds out, such as one-half inch or smaller.

Rutgers Cooperative Research & Extension offers the following ideas for keeping birds out of your fruits and vegetables:
Reusable plastic netting. Reusable plastic netting or even cheesecloth or wire mesh can be placed over plants or seed rows. The netting must be secured close to the crops so that birds don't find a way through.

Paper bags. If you're growing sweet corn, you can place paper bags over ears once pollen shed is complete, or after silks have turned brown.
Stakes and flags. Attaching pieces of cloth to the tops of stakes and placing them every 15 to 20 feet in your garden may work to ward off birds.

Stakes and string. Attaching string to stakes and running the string across your garden will help to keep birds out for a week or two. Attach

streamers or cloth to the string every 5 feet or so, too.

The Humane Society offers a few more ideas, specifically for controlling crows:
Mylar streamers. Shiny Mylar streamers can work to scare off birds.

Fishing line. Fishing line, or even cord or fine wire, can be stretched across a garden in a grid pattern. Consider tying reflective tape or some other visible material to the fishing line so that you can avoid it.

Plastic owls and snakes usually don't work to scare crows. However, effigies of dead crows, items like CDs or balloons with reflective surfaces, and garden hoses with motion sensors typically work to frighten crows, especially if they're used consistently and are moved around the garden area.

Like I said, a cornucopia of pests. I pass along these strategies in the hope that they work for you.

On to the yucky pests.

Slimy and Sneaky— Snails and Slugs
OK, using beer to trap and kill slugs has three big drawbacks:

1. It uses up your beer.
2. Baiting saucers with beer takes you away from YouTube.
3. You realize that you're bending over yet again to do a garden task. Bummer.

Copper strips will also stop snails (and perhaps slugs) in their tracks; the copper sets up a very mild electrical field, and snails don't cross it. This works great on trees; I once saw a copper strip around the trunk of an avocado tree holding back a traffic jam of snails (but most trees don't have much of a snail problem). Copper strips are also very useful on the sides of wooden containers, although it's almost impossible to keep a three-inch wide strip of copper continuously flush with the boards of a wooden raised bed.

Here's a really laid-back approach: make fewer trips to your city's green-waste bin; instead, save your branch clippings and make a heap in the backyard. Don't get too carried away; a few feet high and five or six feet wide may do the trick. Brush piles plus little mounds of rocks are great habitat for all kinds of critters—including lizards that eat slugs as part of their diet! Yummy.

Brush piles, however, are also a possible habitat for roof rats. If you do get rats, give up on the lizards and dispense with the pile (or introduce an anaconda). Brush piles are also a "habitat" for ugliness; if your yard is too small it's out of the question.

But wait! There is a way to terrorize slugs 24 hours a day—carabid beetles, an insect group containing ground beetles and tiger beetles And these bugs just love slugs (for fine dining, that is).

So how do you make the garden a habitat for ground beetles? They like a permanent piece of vegetated land, so create a "beetle bank" by providing a two-to-five-foot-wide bed of native perennial grasses. Carabid beetles are twice as plentiful in uncultivated habitat than in gardens. (Yo! yet another reason for no-till methods.) Stands of diverse perennial plants also support diverse carabid beetles. Also refrain from blitzing your land with broad-

spectrum insecticides, as they have ruinous effects on the beetles' health (and possibly your own). Besides, spraying means getting up off your fanny.

When it comes to snails, you can also turn them into food—for chickens, if your zoning allows. Although taking care of the chickens can be a real chore, you'd be transforming snails into eggs for breakfast.

It's also worth considering paying kids a bounty of one cent per slug or snail—it might put them through a state university!

So that's the pest roundup. However, if your garden is afflicted with buzzards, moose, prairie dogs, racoons, or woodchucks, you're on your own.

Trees & Hardscapes 5

Trees Incompatible With Paved Areas

Common Name, Latin Name, Cultivar, followed by comments, Zones and Height x Width. (This information provided for placement in woodland plantings or in large lawns. All trees are deciduous unless noted.)

'Superform' Norway Maple, *Acer platanoides* 'Superform'. Tolerates dry summer soils. Yellow fall color. Considered to be an invasive tree in Virginia. Ask your local Cooperative Extension person about how it performs in your climate. Zones 3-7, 50'x 40'.

Silver maple, *Acer saccharinum*, The fastest-growing of all the maples. But easily damaged in rain and ice storms Well known for ability to buckle concrete. The roots are also invasive and clog drainpipes. Yellow to rich red in the fall. Zones 3-9, 60'x 40'.

Sugar Maple *Acer saccharum*. Fall color reveals brilliant shades of yellows, oranges and reds. Leaves are medium to dark green and follow the greenish-yellow flowers of spring. Needs lots of room to grow. Zones 3-8, 70'x 45'.

European Beech, *Fagus sylvatica*. A large tree with large roots. Often planted as a large shade tree in a lawn. An attractive smooth, gray bark revealed after the golden-brown leaves of fall. Zones (4)5-7, 55' x 40'.

White Ash, *Fraxinus americana*. Grows best in deep, moist soils. Needs a lot of room for its roots. Fall color changes from reddish purple at the outer, upper portion of the canopy to almost yellow down low toward the middle of the canopy. Zones 3-9, 60'x 60'.

Tuliptree, *Liriodendron tulipifera*. A handsome specimen tree with stature and good yellow fall color. Is susceptible to drought. Due to its size, not a practical tree near walkways, patios or house foundations. Zones 4-9, 80'x40'.

Sweetgum, *Liquidambar styraciflua*. Nice fall color—the color depends upon the cultivar. (The cultivar 'Rotundiloba' is fruitless, thus avoiding the obnoxious prickly "sweetgum balls.") Well known as having invasive roots. Prefers moist soils. Zones 5-9, 70'x 45'.

Southern Magnolia, *Magnolia grandiflora* and magnolia 'Little Gem'. Evergreen. The species Magnolia is a native tree with gorgeous waxy-white flowers up to 15" wide. Blooms late spring and sometimes off-and-on during the summer. ('Little Gem' is a compact tree, 20'x8' with three-to four-inch flowers, and grows well in narrow places or by patios, has shallow roots.) Both Zones 6-9, *M. grandiflora* 60'x 50'.

London Planetree, *Platanus* x *acerifolia*, syn. *P.* x *hispanica, P. hybrida*. Fascinating mottled brown, tan and pale-green bark. Has been listed as an approved street tree in some communities. If planted in a narrow space between two paved areas, it will often heave concrete walkways and curbs. Zones 4-8(9), 80'x 70'.

American Sycamore, *Platanus occidentalis*. A native tree throughout the Eastern and Midwestern parts of this country. Evolved as a riparian tree. Needs at least eight feet between hardscape surfaces or away from a single hardscape like a patio. (Although it drops tons of large leaves, a drag with a patio below.) Best planted in deep, moist soil or in a well-watered lawn with deep soil. Zones 4-9, 80'x 80'.

Lombardy Poplar, *Populus nigra*. Used to a riparian habitat, the roots of this tree are near the surface. More of a problem with lawnmowers scalping the surface roots. But still keep it away from patios or other paved surfaces. Famous in allées where trees line both sides of the driveway—with plenty of room for the roots. Zones 3-9, 80'x 12'.

Weeping Willow, *Salix babylonica*. Not used as a street tree as its limbs cascade down to the ground. Prefers to be by a water feature—and looks better, more in its element. In a lawn, the shallow roots will "surface" and be easily scalped by the lawnmower, but probably won't crack the pavement. Zones 6-8, 30'x 40'.

Hardscape-Friendly Trees

The following are some recommendations for street trees with minimum planter width in Chico, CA. Other tree lists for acceptable street trees from the lists of St. Helena, CA; St. Louis, MO; Iowa, and Seattle, WA, These trees will cause problems if they are planted too close to paved surfaces like patios. In some cases I've found the specific minimum distance from the hardscape. The trees allowed in street-side plantings may be very different—check with your local planning department. Be certain of the mature height, spread and cold- and heat -tolerance, for your garden before planting. Check to make sure the mature tree won't interfere with phone and power lines. Ask your neighbors what hasn't worked. Talk to Cooperative Extension people. Visit old cemeteries to see how big some trees get.

Trees for Near the Hardscape, taken from various city street tree approval lists

Common Name, Latin Name, Cultivar

(if any) followed by comments, Zones (using the USDA Hardiness Zone Map) and H x W.
(All trees are deciduous unless noted.)

European Hornbeam, *Carpinus betulus*. 'Fastigiata'. Usually 'Fastigiata' stands for a columnar shape. However, this tree matures to have an oval-vase shape. Deep green leaves and smooth silver-gray bark. Sturdy tree with strong branch attachment. Prefers a seven-foot area between hardscapes. Can get scales. Zones 4-7(8), 50'x 40'.

Cornelian Cherry, *Cornus mas*. Oval rounded canopy of dark-green leaves that turn a slight purple-red in the fall. One of the first trees or shrubs to bloom in early spring—as early as March. Red fruit are eaten by the birds in midsummer. No serious pests. Tolerates alkaline soil. Zones 4-8, 25'x 20'.

Green Ash, *Fraxinus pennsylvanica*. Tolerates high pH, wet soils, dry soils and hot, arid winds. Used as a windbreak. Very common as a large street tree. Yellow fall color. Needs a minimum of seven feet for a healthy root system. Do not plant both male and female trees as the seed pods will be abundant and cause quite a bit of litter. Zones 3-9, 55'x 40'.

Ginkgo, *Ginkgo biloba* 'Fastigiata' and 'Autumn Gold'. An ancient tree, with "roots" back some 150-200 million years. A living fossil. Each fall there's a glorious display of hot yellow fan-shaped leaves. Be sure to by a male tree such as 'Fastigiata' to avoid the female tree's smelly fruit. 'Autumn Gold' is a male tree with spreading canopy. Ginkgos are pest and disease resistant. It's a good city tree as it tolerates ozone and sulfur dioxide pollutants. Resistant to oak root fungus, but medium salt tolerance. Prefers at least seven feet for its roots. Zones 4-9, 60' x 40'.

'Shademaster' Thornless Common Honey Locust, *Gleditsia triacanthos* 'Shademaster'. A popular street tree with bright green foliage. Prefers at least seven feet of root space. After leaf fall, there are many long, twisted fruit pods that can be messy. Good yellow fall color. Medium sensitivity to salt from winter deicing. Bark on new trees is tender and will probably get sunburn on the southwest side unless it's painted. Zones 4-9, 25'x 16'.

'Skyrocket' Rocky Mountain Juniper, *Juniperus scopulorum* 'Skyrocket'. Evergreen with blue-gray foliage. The species is pyramidal but rather wide. 'Skyrocket' is the most narrow of all the columnar junipers. Can be used in a classic landscape design with parallel rows along a driveway, walkway (called an allée), or around a pool. Zone 3-7(9), 15'x 2'.

Eastern Red Cedar, *Juniperus virginiana*. Evergreen. Grows well under many conditions where other trees fade. Can be pruned to form a great hedge. Female trees produce berries the birds love to eat. Zones 2-9, 50'x 20'.

Goldenrain Tree, *Koelreuteria paniculata*. A wonderful tree that blooms from June through late July with bright-yellow flowers. Makes interesting pale-green seed pods that turn brown and look a bit frayed. Blooms three- to four years after planting. Makes a great tree for the patio or street (low to medium salt tolerance). Zones 5-9, 35'x 35'.

Crabapples, *Malus* spp. Many sizes, colors and shapes to choose from. Birds eat the fruit. Some are disease resistant, with yellow-red fall color. Medium to high tolerance to salt. Many need five feet for a planter area. Zones 4-8, Many choices, consult with your local nursery.

American Hop Hornbeam, *Ostrya virginiana*. When first planted the shape of the canopy is pyramidal, as it grows older it becomes more rounded. Good tree for smaller spaces. Needs only four feet as a minimum planting area. The bark has an interesting shaggy look. Sensitive to salt. Zones 4-9, 35'x 35'.

Persian Ironwood, *Parrotia persica*. One of the top ten trees for fall color—yellows, orange

and scarlet reds. The new leaves even have nice shades of red-purple and then turn to a glossy green. Also has a fascinating brown shaggy bark. With a well-drained soil and a bit of moisture the tree is virtually free of pest and diseases. Prefers slightly acidic soil, but will tolerate some alkalinity. Zones 4-8, 30'x 20'.

Chinese Pistache, *Pistacia chinensis*. Not the tree the nuts come from. A popular ornamental street tree in the west. Fantastic fall colors of a mix of hot oranges and reds. Be sure to buy a male tree if you don't want red berries to drop onto your patio. Takes drought and is relatively free of pests. Resistant to oak root fungus. If overwatered in a lawn area, it may get verticillium wilt. Zones , 9-10, 40'x 40'.

Willow Oak, *Quercus phellos*. Needs at least six feet between two hardscapes to grow well. Considered to have the most graceful foliage of all the oaks. Leaves may hang on the tree though the winter. Established trees are drought resistant. Zones 5-9. 50'x 35'.

Scarlet Oak, *Quercus coccinea. Q. palustris, and Q. rubra* are often confused as being this tree. But this species has a more glorious red fall color than other oaks that may last up to one month. Most large oaks need at least a 7' wide distance from hardscape. Hard to transplant. Transplant large-sized trees (B&B or 24" x 36" box) and give it plenty of room. Zones 4-8(9), 70'x 45'.

Pin Oak, Swamp Oak, *Quercus palustris*. A very popular street tree. Has gold red fall leaves. But in milder climates they turn brown and hang onto the tree for most of the winter. On of the better oaks for growing in a lawn. Zones 4-7, 50'x 30'.

'Fastigata' English Oak, *Quercus robur* 'Fastigiata'. Said by many that this oak is one of the best-looking oaks if you want a more columnar tree. The species form is a grand sight—very noble looking—up to 60' tall and 35' wide. High resistance to salt. Most large oaks need at least a 7' wide distance from hardscape. This cultivar and the species are prone to mildew. The cultivars 'Asjes' (Rosehill®, and 'Skyrocket' are more resistant to mildew. 'Fastigiata' is 60'x15'. Both Zones 3-7.

American Arborvitae, *Thuja occidentalis*. Evergreen. Common tree in home landscapes. Due to its "well-behaved roots" it is often planted near the house. A very sturdy tree that is often sheared to make a low hedge or low windbreak. Crisp, rich green in the spring and summer fading to a brownish-green color in the winter. Hardy to –40° F. Takes all kinds of soils. Zones 2-7, 50'x15'.

Littleleaf Linden, *Tilia cordata*. Can't take heat, prefers a cool climate. Common street tree where it thrives. Prone to pests and diseases: Japanese beetles, aphids and their subsequent sooty mold. Zones 3-7, 60'x45'.

Buggy Citations and Bugology Certificate 6

Citations for Companion Planting
I've listed every citation to prove my point and allow you to investigate further if you like. The sad news is this might be too complicated to do in a recliner or hammock. A comfortable desk may be the best setting. (I sure wasn't a lazy-tush to do all this, but I enjoyed it.)

1) Rust R. W. 1977. Evaluation of trap crop procedures for control of Mexican bean beetle in soybeans and lima beans. *Journal of Economic Entomology*; 70: 630-632.

2) Dorozhkin N. A., S. I. Bel'skaya, and A. Meleshkevich. 1975. For 50 years in the Republic of Belarus, (an Eastern Europe country bordered by Russia to the northeast, Ukraine to the south, Poland to the west, and Lithuania and Latvia to the northwest),. Zaschita Rastenii. 7: 6-8.

3) Kuepper, George and Mardi Dodson, *Traditional Companion Planting*, ATTRA, a project of the National Center for Appropriate Technology. July 2001.

4) T. Jude Boucher, Agricultural Educator-Commercial Vegetable Crops, Robert Durgy, Research Assistant, *Integrated Pest Management & Nutrient Management*, UConn Cooperative Extension, Vernon, CT, April 2003, Reviewed 2012.

5) Hokkanen, H. M. 1989. Biological and agrotechnical control of the rape blossom beetle *Meligethes aeneus* (Coleoptera, Nitidulidae). *Acta Entomologica Fennica*. #53:25-29.

6) Arker, J. E. 2012. Diversity by design. Exploring trap crops and companion plants to control *Phyllotreta cruciferae*, the crucifer flea beetle, in broccoli. Washington State University (Doctoral Dissertation). Experiments were done exploring the use of simple and diverse trap crops to control the crucifer flea beetle (*Phyllotreta cruciferae*) in broccoli (*Brassica oleracea* var. *italica*). The trap crops included monocultures and polycultures of two or three species of Pacific gold mustard (*Brassica juncea*), pac choi (*Brassica rapa* subsp. *pekinensis*) and rape (*Brassica napus*). Results indicated that broccoli planted adjacent to diverse trap crops containing all three trap crop species attained the greatest dry weight suggesting that the trap crops species were not particularly effective when planted alone, however, provided substantial plant protection when planted in multispecies polycultures.

7) Isman B., Botanical insecticides, deterrents, and repellents in modern agriculture and an increasingly regulated world. Annual Review of Entomology, 51: 45-66.

8) Little, B. 1989. *Companion Planting in Australia*. Frenchs Forest, New South Wales: Reed Books Pty Ltd.

9) Anon. 2004. *Organic Vegetable IPM Guide*.

10) Szafirowska, A., Kolosowski, S. The effect of companion plants on *Lygus* feeding damage to bean. (The number of pitted seeds depended on the date of seeds sowing and the year of experiment.) Research Institute of Vegetable Crops, ul. Konstytucji 3 Maja 1/3, 96-100 Skierniewice, Poland.

11) Altieri, M. A. and J. D. Doll. Some limitations of weed biocontrol in tropical ecosystems in Colombia. In: T.E. Freeman (ed.), *Proceedings IV International Symposium on Biological Control of*

Weeds. University of Florida, Gainesville, pp. 74-82; 1978. (Note – Columbia.) (author's personal observation)

12) Hickman, J. M., S. D. Wratten. 1996. Use of *Phacelia tanacetifolia* strips to enhance biological control of aphids by hoverfly larvae in cereal fields. *Journal of Economic Entomology* 89(4):832-840.

13) Patt, J. M., G. C. Hamilton, J. H. Lashomb. 1997. Impact of strip-insectary intercropping with flowers on conservation biological control of the Colorado potato beetle. *Advances in Horticultural Science* 11(4):175-181.

14) Haenke, S., B. Scheid, M. Schaefer, T. Tscharntke, C. Thies. 2009. Increasing syrphid fly diversity and density in sown flower strips within simple vs. complex landscapes. *Journal of Applied Ecology* 46(5):1106-1114.

15) Drabble, E. and H. 1917!. The syrphid visitors to certain flowers. *New Phytologist* Vol. XVI, Nos. 5 & 6.

16) *California Agriculture* 52(5):23-26. September-October 1998.

17) Bender, D. A., W. P. Morrison, R. E. Frisbie. 1999. Intercropping cabbage and Indian mustard for potential control of lepidopterous and other insects. *HortScience* 34:275-279.

Note: The source of much of the above information is from: *Companion Planting and Insect Control*, by Joyce E. Parker, William E. Snyder, George C. Hamilton, and Cesar Rodriguez-Saona. 2013. *InTechOpen*.

cut here ·····→

Your Buggy Diploma

o' Master of the Garden,
Master of its Complete Domain,
Listen as I Praise Your Wisdom of Bugs.
verify, It is Known Throughout the Land that

_____

is the Wisest Smasher of Bugs of Pestilence.

My Favorite Useful Websites

Annie's Annuals

www.anniesannuals.com
Annie's started out as a retail nursery in Richmond, CA. It has since branched out to include a wonderful website and mail order business. They specialize in rare and unusual annuals *and* perennials now. *Lots* of information on hundreds of plants, including photos and even videos. A great resource.

Baker Creek Heirloom Seeds

www.rareseeds.com
In the Whole Seed Catalog, Baker Creek offers over 2,000 seed varieties—all heirlooms, many quite rare (though not necessarily organically grown). Dubbed the "The World's Fair of Pure Food," their annual National Heirloom Expo every September in Santa Rosa, CA features over 20,000 farmers and gardeners and more than 300 vendors (I'm there every year), showcasing thousands of heirloom varieties from across America. (www.theheirloomexpo.com)

Brad Lancaster's Rainwater Harvesting

www.harvestingrainwater.com
This is the best site on the Internet on this topic, with a huge range of data. Includes videos, articles, books, and more for both farm and residential settings.

CAL/IPC, Plants A-Z

www.cal-ipc.org/plants/profiles/
This is an excellent California-focused site for studying invasive plants. Browse it to see all plants on the Cal-IPC Inventory, including both invasive plants and "Watch" species—plants that may "escape" to become invasive. Clicking on the scientific name will take you to the Plant Profile, where you'll find links to more information on a given species.

Cooperative Extension

For the best local and microclimate information, be sure to look up your Cooperative Extension website.

Dave's Garden

www.davesgarden.com
With 86,188 entries, 58,365 images and 33,503 comments, this is a fantastic resource. Search by name or plant characteristics or just browse through the pictures. Check out this online directory that ranks more than 7,000 gardening mail-order companies based on the feedback from customers—sort of like a Yelp for the gardening world.

Dave Wilson Nursery

www.davewilson.com
Visit this must-see site for a fantastic look at all aspects of home fruit-tree culture, with an amazing number of YouTube videos. You can learn how to plant a tree and prune it to keep it below six feet for an easy harvest, and so much more. It's also a great place to read about their annual fruit tastings and to get a fantastic evaluation of flavors and a ranking of the best-tasting fruits. They also share information on finding your local retail outlets (by zip code) for their extensive variety of fruiting trees, vines and shrubs. davewilson.com/sites/default/files/assets/Fruit_Tasting_Report_2014_pp_1-5.pdf

DripWorks

www.dripworks.com
This is the best place to buy everything you need to drip-irrigate your garden or containers. DripWorks carries hard-to-find in-line emitter tubing on nine-inch centers (good for sandy soils), as

well as some good kits to take a load off your mind.

Gardening Products Review
www.gardeningproductsreview.com
Read this for an amazingly thorough analysis of gardening tools, generically and by brand name.

The Garden Professors
www.gardenprofessors.com
This is a great site for learning about gardening myths—organic or conventional. The website features Linda Chalker-Scott Ph.D (Associate Professor and Extension Urban Horticulturist at [Where?]), sharing her amazing, thoughtful insights into the facts and science of gardening. Her comments are always based on peer-reviewed, scientific papers. You must check out all that she does.
Other sites for Linda:
"The Informed Gardener" webpage:
www.theinformedgardener.com
"The Garden Professors" Facebook page:
www.facebook.com/TheGardenProfessors
"The Garden Professors" Facebook group:
www.facebook.com/groups/GardenProfessors
"Gardening in Washington State" fact sheets:
http://gardening.wsu.edu/

Grow Organic (the online presence for Peaceful Valley Farm Supply)
www.groworganic.com
Peaceful Valley's presence on the Internet has been changed to Grow Organic. For decades, this has been the single best place to mail-order organic garden supplies and plants. GO offers fertilizers, fruit trees, vegetable starts and seed, harvest equipment, irrigation supplies, weed and pest control, mushrooms, kitchenware, and much more.

MOBOT (short for Missouri Botanical Garden)
www.missouribotanicalgarden.org/plantfinder/plantfindersearch.aspx
Although biased toward the Midwest, this is per-

haps the best site to search for and read about ornamental plants.. From the site: "Look up, view a photo and read about the over 7,500 plants that are growing or have been grown in the Kemper Center display gardens (plus selected additions) by scientific name, common name and/or selected plant characteristics."

Netafim
www.netafimusa.com/landscape/products/drip-lines/techline-cv/
Manufacturer of Techline™ This is the landscape site for the manufacturer of the best drip-irrigation tubing.. There's lots of information about the tubing and how to design for its use. Offers manuals, product information and other literature for immediate download.

Oasis Design
A detailed site with lots of information—pages of text and lots of PDFs. . Has the thorough book: *Water Storage, Tanks, Cisterns, Aquifers, and Ponds For Domestic Supply, Fire and Emergency Use*. Also, from the graywater guru Art Ludwig, the best book on graywater management. The book *Create an Oasis with Greywater* covers everything you need to know on designing, installing, and managing a home graywater system.

Permaculture
www.permies.com
If you're into permaculture, this immense exchange for communicating with thousands of other like-minded people is the site for you.

A Permaculture Design Course Handbook
www.treeyopermacultureedu.wordpress.com/
For those interested in learning more about permaculture, this is a great (and very accessible) site for an overview of the principles, with lots of details of the methods (although a little too much info on tropical ecosystems for my taste).

Plants for a Future

www.pfaf.org/user/plantsearch.aspx
This database of 7,500 edible and medicinal plants is easily searched.

Raintree Nursery

www.raintreenursery.com
A listing of conventional, heirloom, unusual and rare fruits, from trees to vines to shrubs and ground covers, this is my favorite source of special edible trees and perennials. It's also a good source of rootstocks for home gardeners who want to graft their own trees.

Rant

www.gardenrant.com
As summed up by the site: "A great site looking at the myths of gardening. GardenRant has been online since June 2006 and quickly developed a following among garden bloggers, garden writers and editors and landscape nursery business professionals. Barbara Damrosch of the Washington Post enthused: 'Garden Rant gives good information, hosts lively and knowledgeable guest ranters, and is anchored by four outstandingly uppity women, excellent writers all.'"

Renee's Seeds

www.reneesgarden.com
This is a great place to get a wide range of seeds (some certified organic) for edibles, herbs and flowers. Renee features a lot of heirloom varieties. Be sure to subscribe to the monthly newsletter.

Rosalind Creasy (the grande dame of edible landscaping)

www.rosalindcreasy.com
Roz wrote the forward to my edible landscaping book (Designing and Maintaining Your Edible Landscape - Naturally—blatant plug) so I'm prejudiced. This is an amazing site with lots of her stunning photos. It features her front yard demonstration plot—the best edible landscape I've ever seen. Lengthy text provides a wealth of helpful information. The best Internet site on the topic of edible landscaping.

Royal Horticultural Society

www.rhs.org.uk
It may be based in England, but much of the information applies to a lot of the world. It features an interesting detail that I've not seen anywhere else: "Time to ultimate height." Extensive database of plants at: http://apps.rhs.org.uk/horticulturaldatabase/.

Soil and Health Library

www. http://soilandhealth.org/library-rules-and-copyright-notice-ag/
The Soil and Health Library is an amazing website. With hundreds of public-domain books on soils (of course), gardening, and farming in the agricultural library section, it has a strong bias (actually complete bias) for organic techniques. For any gardening topic, go here first to see what books cover your interest.

Spaces

http://www.spacesarchives.org/
"A nonprofit public-benefit organization created with an international focus on the study, documentation, and archive of art environments and self-taught artistic activity." Features over 35,000 photos (!) of American eccentric gardens with descriptions and maps to guide you there—"844 art environments."

Summer-Dry

www.summer-dry.com/drought-tolerant-is-irrelevant/
Saxon Holt's water-wise site showcases the best garden photographer in America and his special and informative take on drought-tolerant landscapes and plants. "Summer-dry gardens can be beautiful. The art and science of gardening is learning which plants prosper in garden settings. Many plants are meant for summer-dry climates and don't need lots of water, though careful irrigation improves their beauty. We don't need plants

that are simply tolerant of no summer water; we need plants that expect no summer water. That's not drought-tolerant, that's normal."

Toby Hemenway
http://tobyhemenway.com
The author of Gaia's Garden passed away in 2016, but his website is still alive and maintained. You can access his videos, audio commentary, newsletter, and articles.

WUCOLS, Water Use Classification of Landscape Species
ucanr.edu/sites/WUCOLS/Plant_Search/
This is a free database of 3,546 species of plants ranked by four levels of water needs in six climate zones in California. It's based on the observations and extensive field experience of thirty-six landscape horticulturists. This is a required resource for Californians who want to design the best drought-resistant landscapes.

Urban Gardening, Hydroponics and Aquaponics
www.epicgardening.com
Appearing in many top-50-garden-websites lists (and some top-fives) this one covers a wide range of topics, including hydroponics. (Be sure to check out Kevin's blog.) Also, go to www.epicgardening.com/best-gardening-blogs-and-web-sites/ for a great list of 59 interesting and informative blogs.

and finally...
Monty Python's Flying Circus
www.montypython.com
These are my favorite comedians of all time. After all, more and more these days we need to laugh out loud. Every lazy-ass gardener should watch these guys. Don't miss the sketches: "I'm a Lumberjack" and "The Spanish Inquisition." And their best film: Life of Brian.

Index

Note: Page numbers in *italics* refer to illustrations or photographs or information in captions

root hairs, 88, *89*
sinker roots, *95*
soil aerated by, 54, 78
See also nitrogen-fixing bacteria
Plants for Future, website, 203
plant toxins, in mulch materials, 40
playgrounds for kids, 12
plums, 44, 45, 46
poached egg plant (*Limnanthes*), 141
podocarpus, *24*
pollination of fruit trees, 44, *45*
polyculture, defined, 137
pomegranates, 125
ponds and pools, 12
poplar, Lombardy (*Populus nigra*), 192
poppy, California (*Eschscholzia californica*), C9
pore spaces, soil, 87–89, *88*
Portwood, Myra, 177–178, *C2*
potatoes, 41, 138
praying mantids, 146, *147*, 153
predatory insects. *See* beneficial insects
Preston Vineyards and Winery, *C1, C6, C7*
pride-of-Madeira (*Echium candicans*), 18, 85
Primack, Mark, 158
propane torches, for weed control, 60–61, *61*
prunes, pollination, 44
The Pruning Book, L.H. Bailey, 118
pruning plants, 115–125, *C11*
    apical-bearing fruit trees, 125
    basic tree growth, 116–117
    branch bark ridges/branch collars, 117, *117*, 119–120
    for espaliers, 122, 157–159, *C6, C16*
    fruit trees, 43
    modern cuts, 119
    to remove dead, diseased, dysfunctional wood, 117–118, 119
    for shape and bloom, 120
    in summer, 27–28, 118–121
    thinning and heading cuts, 119, *120*
    See also shaping plants
pruning tools, 103–106
    Felco shears, 103–104, *104*
    loppers, 105, *105*
    pruning saws, 105, *105*
    pruning "stick," 106, *106*

rose-pruning guards, 112, *112*
    sharpening tools, 106, *106*
Pseudotsuga menziesii (Douglas fir), 32
purple loosestrife, 7
purslane (*Portulaca oleracea*), 135

Q

Quercus. See oak
quince, 125

R

rabbits, 185–186
radish, 38, 39
rainfall statistics, 6, 83
rain gauges, 111, *111*
Raintree Nursery, website, 203
rainwater catchment (cisterns), 127–131, 169–172
    cistern size, 170
    cistern types, 169–170, *171*
    cost of, 129
    gravity systems, 170
    installing, 127–128
    pressure tanks, 172
    pumped systems, 170, 172
    rebates for, 170
    rooftop-water systems, 127–128, *130*
    tanks and barrels, *128*, 129, 131, *C12*
    websites, 201, 202
raised beds, 15–17
    benefits of, 16, *C7*
    cinder blocks, 17
    construction basics, 15–16
    galvanized metal tub, 15, *C6*
    for gopher control, 182–183
    irrigation, 16, 183, *C6, C10*
    old boat, *C6*
    plastic "wood," 17
    recycled lumber, 17
    shipping pallets for, 110
    used bricks, 16
red cedar, Eastern (*Juniperus virginiana*), 193
redwood (*Sequoia sempervirens*), 40
Renee's Seeds, website, 203
Rhododendron (azalea), *24*
rhubarb, 38

rock rose, alpine (*Helianthemum alpestre*), 23
rockrose (*Cistus*), 23, 85
Rodale Institute Farm, 137
root and crown rot (*Phytophthora*), 31, 56, 83
rosemary (*Rosmarinus*)
    'Arp' (*R. officinalis*), 23, 35
    drought tolerance, 83
    as fallow crop, 152
    as herb, 35–36
    as insect repellant, 139
    for patio plantings, 18
    water requirements, 24
rose (*Rosa*), *24*, 39, 143
Royal Horticultural Society, website, 203
rue (*Ruta*), 23
Russian olive (*Elaeagnus angustifolia*), 32
rutabaga, shade tolerance, 38
rye, in green-manure blends, 163

S

sage, Jerusalem (*Phlomis fruticosa*), 22, 85
sage, Russian (*Perovskia atriplicifolia*), 23
sage (*Salvia*)
    hummingbird (*S. spathacea*), *C4*
    as insect repellant, 139
    masking crops, 139
salad greens, 36–37
Salix (willow)
    plant toxins, 40
    for pollinators, 143
    weeping (*S. babylonica*), 192
sandy soil
    drainage, 84
    drip irrigation, 91
    no-till gardening and, 68
    soil amendments, 53
    tree root structure and, *58*
santolina or lavender cotton (*Santolina*)
    drought tolerance, 83
    green (*S.* 'Morning Mist'), 23
Sapium sebiferum (Chinese tallow tree), *30*
sassafras (*Sassafras albidum*), *30*
scions (grafting), *48*
sculpture, design role, *C1, C14*

X

Y

Z

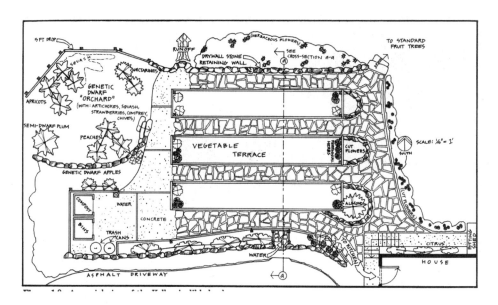

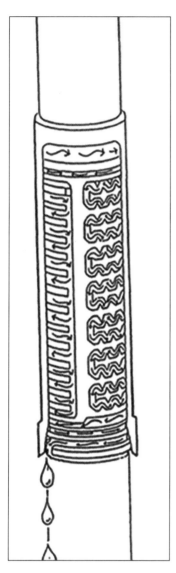

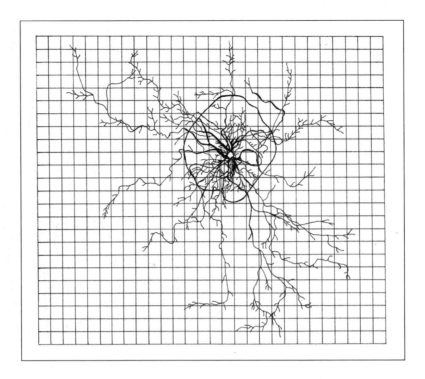

Understanding Roots...

discover how to make your garden flourish

232 fact-filled pages, with 141 detailed root drawings, including:

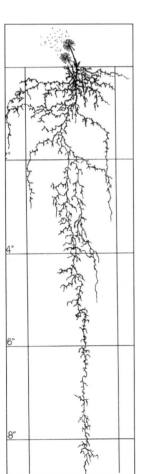

A dandelion.

- Root drawings of 13 ornamental and native trees, as well as dozens of drawings of herbs, weeds, and vegetables.
- Thirteen drawings of standard and dwarf fruit-tree root systems from a rare book published in Hungary.
- A living diagram of the roots of a 58-meter-tall redwood tree. (Spoiler alert—no taproot.)
- Diagrams comparing the root growth of apple trees in sandy versus loamy soils.
- A scientific paper illustrating 63 root drawings of dwarf apple tree growth with four types of mulch.
- An explanation about why deep roots aren't that important.

Plus:
- A list of citations for every scientific paper referred to in each chapter.

Just $20 includes -shipping, tax, and an autograph. **(list price is $24.95)**

Order at: www.robertkourik.com

Garden Myths: The Good, The Bad & The Unbelievable.

Guess what, much of gardening is not what it seems. There is a flip side to every coin. Same's true with gardening. Garden myths are the flip side of the gardening coin. Wanna know what organic fertilizer's production produces slightly radioactive tailings? Wanna know why those forged short-handled shovels promoted by Myth & Hawkin' are the worst digging tools? Wanna know why the word "kills" shows up in three of the titles of entries? Wanna know why gophers have to tunnel? Don't myth this eBook. Get to readin' the 111 pages (including the index—useful, but boring to read). Nearly 100 photographs. You'll dig it. (And learn why digging wet clay soil destroys it.)

Mustard Cover Crop

Famous for:
Appearing each spring in Sonoma County vineyards. Thought to improve soil.

Flip Side:
When I see gorgeously vibrant yellow mustard flowers, I see an indication of poor soil management. Mustard is one of those plants that prefers a heavy, clayey, or compacted soil. In consequence, only vineyards with heavy soils (or those that were tilled when the soil was too wet) will sprout mustard as a nearly continuous cover crop. Bright-yellow mustard-fields are actually an indicator of poor drainage, improper tillage, and a special influence known as allelopathy. Doctor of Chemistry Rick Knoll has researched the science of allelopathy—the study of toxic or antagonistic chemicals (aka secondary metabolites) that some plants produce. These compounds act, in Knoll's words, "as ecological chemicals to gain an advantage over other plants and act like an 'immune system' for the plant." Such chemicals have multiple impacts, such as stunting the growth of other plants or suppressing their germination of seed. For example, Knoll points out, "All *Brassica* roots exude a secondary metabolite (glucosinolates —related to mustard gas) which inhibits grass-seed germination; this slows down the grasses and lets the *Brassica* get a really strong start. It doesn't kill the grasses; it's just a mechanism for competition."

This chart provides guidelines to the blooming cycles of various insect-attracting plants—often referred to as "insectary" plants. (The term "insectary," which previously only meant a laboratory for the study of live insects, has been adopted among horticulturists as an adjective to describe plants that attract beneficial insects.)

The bloom cycle of 191 plants is presented.
13 beneficial insects are listed.
117 plants have notations of which of the 13 beneficial insects the flower attracts.
There are 30 full citations for further reading.

It will also inform you on how to choose the best plants to lure beneficial insects outside of the window of midsummer bloom. Because so many beneficial plants bloom in midsummer, that time of year is a banquet of blossom for helpful bugs. Since pests don't magically disappear in the spring and fall, this chart will help you choose the plants that will bloom in your garden during the "in-between" seasons.

Most of the bloom periods came from www.Calflora.org which is, as would be expected, Californiacentric. Some are from the Missouri Botanic Garden database. With careful observation, you will see how your garden blooms react to the seasons and "slide" the bloom-period bar on the chart toward Spring or Fall.

You will receive via email:
• A PDF document of the guidelines and citations and
• An Excel spreadsheet of the 191 plants and beneficial-insect visitations. (Use Excel version 14.7.1 or newer)
(Note: This is the product of 200-400 hours of work over three years by myself and Damien McAnany. This final set represents a tremendous amount of condensed information. The Excel spreadsheet is deemed to be the best way to present it for you.)

$9.95 for both, To Order: See www.robertkourik.com

The Biggest and Best Insectary Plant List in North America

Bloom Period of Insectary Plants

Common Name	Botanical Name	Jan.	Feb.	Mar.	Apr.	May	June	July	Aug.	Sept.	Oct.	Nov.	Dec.
Agastache[24,28]	Agastache foeniculum							■	■	■			
Alfalfa[1,7,9]	Medicago sativa								■	■	■	■	
Alpine Cinquefoil[1]	Potentilla concinna				■	■	■						
Alyssum, Sweet[1,3,7,9,13,14,16,21a,2]	Lobularia maritima				■	■	■	■	■	■	■	■	■
Angelica[1,3,5,9,22,26,30]	Angelica spp.						■	■	■				
Anise Hyssop[1,9,10,22,30]	Agastache foeniculum							■	■	■			
Columbine. Aquelegia[21a]	Aquelegia x hybrida 'Blue Bird'				■	■							

GREATER GARDEN YIELDS WITH DRIP IRRIGATION

Most people think of drip irrigation as primarily useful in times of drought and for saving money on the water bill. However, as the following examples will demonstrate, drip irrigation can also be used in any garden to increase vegetable and plant yields-even in climates that get periodic summer rain or are very humid.

Many studies reveal the overall horticultural efficacy of the slow dripping of water. The examples and research found in the next chapter illustrate the increasingly undeniable fact that drip-irrigated plants grow and produce more prolifically while actually using *less* water for irrigation.

Please note that (in my experience) the same effect is found when drip irrigation is used for the purpose of increasing ornamental growth and bloom, but this aspect hasn't been widely explored, as the focus of most studies is on economic food crops and results that farmers can actually use to maximize their yields.

I'll also present here a detailed review of how it's possible to simultaneously reduce water use *and* increase yields. This apparent contradiction is due to the intimate relationship of properly applied water and the health of the irrigated soil.

The following chapters will concentrate specifically on how to apply water to gardens for maximum growth and yields. Information on all other aspects of choosing, installing and using drip irrigation, down to the last drop and widget, can be found in the latest edition of my book *Drip Irrigation for Every Landscape and All Climates*, Metamorphic Press, Santa Rosa, CA, 2009. (see www.robertkourik.com)

And finally, this may well be the only drip-irrigation book in history that comes complete with recipes and dishes made from vegetables and fruits that naturally need less water.

$10 for 78 page eBook (PDFs). Order at robertkourik.com

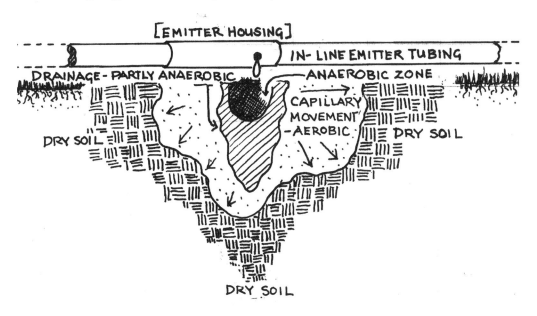

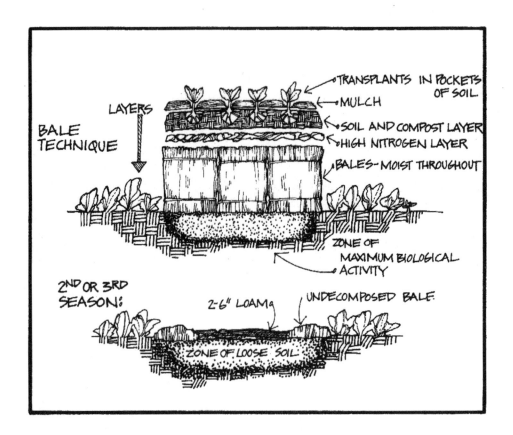

The image shows the "Bale Technique" with labels: LAYERS; TRANSPLANTS IN POCKETS OF SOIL; MULCH; SOIL AND COMPOST LAYER; HIGH NITROGEN LAYER; BALES - MOIST THROUGHOUT; ZONE OF MAXIMUM BIOLOGICAL ACTIVITY; 2ND OR 3RD SEASON; 2-6" LOAM; UNDECOMPOSED BALE; ZONE OF LOOSE SOIL.

No Digging - For a Healthier Soil and a Sustainable Garden

Mother Nature didn't bend over much to make soil. Nature slowly builds soil from the top down—it takes 1000 years to make an inch of topsoil. She (or he?) doesn't dig and invert soil. This handbook is an important introduction to No-Dig gardening. If you care about global climate change, (and it's not cool to deny it), you'll be amazed to learn that tillage releases a large amount of the carbon dioxide and methane. Tillage kills off many soil critters. Each one either coughs out or farts carbon dioxide and methane as they "expire". The handbook (how long does a handbook have to be before it morphs into a book?) also includes a word about surface cultivation when the top two-three inches of soil is skimmed (not inverted)—no shovels are used. This is a great stepping off handbook to an increasingly exciting way to garden. It can be easier on the backs of aging baby boomers. If nature doesn't bend over, why should you? Includes a description of permanent raised garden beds that thwart pesky gophers. (East of the Mississippi river you don't have these dreadful creatures. Lucky you.) Also includes a page of references.

Now only $3.00 for the 10-page eBook (PDF) version. See: robertkourik.com to order.